A PLACE IN TIME

Praise for

A Place in Time: Youth Community & Baseball

"It's often been said that all politics are local. Mark Lefebvre may just have proved that applies to sports as well in A Place in Time. Lefebvre does a masterful job of chronicling how a group of young men rallied around some legendary baseball coaching and united to achieve three seasons that will long shine in local baseball lore. Beyond the epic talent and the momentous wins, Lefebvre has captured how the bond between these players changed lives, bettered a community and still echoes today. A Place Time is a great read for anyone who appreciates the true value of sports beyond just the triumphs alone."

- Mark Bodanza, author of *Hostage Terror, Risk Takers & History Markers: The Story of Leominster, She Took a Stand, A Game That Forged Rivals,* and others.

"Never had I been able to read a more thorough historical account of the game of baseball played in Leominster, Massachusetts, my hometown. I always wondered about the baseball teams, players, and their stories told prior to 1963 when my own participation started in Little League, but also historical accounts until 52 years later when I retired from coaching baseball at Leominster High School. When I played semi-pro baseball for the highly successful Acton A's in the Stan Musial League, year after year, my manager, Bob Kramer, always hounded me about recruiting more baseball players from Leominster. Mark Lefebvre intimately helps to explain why, during his account of three consecutive Babe Ruth State Championship Teams from Leominster. I personally hope to see more books like this that highlight the superior traditional success of all levels on the baseball diamonds in my city, from the very beginning."

- Don Freda, Retired Educator, Former Leominster Baseball Player, and Leominster High School Baseball Coach

A PLACE IN TIME

YOUTH, COMMUNITY & BASEBALL

Mark Lefebvre

Copyright © 2022 by Mark Lefebvre
All rights reserved

No part of this book may be reproduced, stored or transmitted in any form or by any means, electronic or mechanical, including photocopying, recording, or by any information storage and retrieval system, without the written permission of the author, except in case of brief quotation embodied in critical articles and reviews.

Cover design by Steve Martin

ISBN: 9798352537343

Lefebvre, Mark
A Place in Time: Youth, Community & Baseball

Published by Mark Lefebvre

Front cover photos: the author; 1972 Leominster Babe Ruth All-Stars
Back cover photos: 1971 and 1973 Leominster Babe Ruth All-Stars

In loving memory of Brian McNally,
the best of us all.

We can be heroes just for one day.
- David Bowie

Table of Contents

Table of Contents ix
Dedication xi
Foreword xiii
Prologue xvii
Section 1: It Takes A Village 1
    Chapter One: Lightning in a Bottle 3
    Chapter Two: Growing Up In Leominster 6
    Chapter Three: Leominster is (Also) a Baseball Town 19
    Chapter Four: Leominster Little Leagues 28
    Chapter Five: A Brief History of Babe Ruth Baseball 39
    Chapter Six: Babe Ruth Baseball in Leominster 41
Section 2: Insane Talent - 1971 Babe Ruth All-Stars 51
    Chapter Seven: The Team 53
    Chapter Eight: The Games 70
    Chapter Nine: 1971 Leominster Post 151 Legion Team 106
Section 3: Home Cooking –1972 Babe Ruth All-Stars 107
    Chapter Ten – The Tournament 109
    Chapter Eleven: The Team 113
    Chapter Twelve - The Games 133
Section 4: True Grit - 1973 Babe Ruth All-Stars 161
    Chapter Thirteen: The Team 164
    Chapter Fourteen: The Games 186
    Chapter Fifteen: Not So Sour Grapes 236
    Chapter Sixteen: So Agonizingly Close - 1974 All-Stars 238
Section 5: Changes in the Game 241

Chapter Seventeen: Leominster Babe Ruth's Success 242
Chapter Eighteen: Leominster Babe Ruth Baseball Today 248
Chapter Nineteen: Changes Reflected in the Community 253
Conclusion: A Place in Time 257

In Memoriam 265

Acknowledgments 267

About the Author 271

Notes 273

Dedication

This book is dedicated to Brian McNally who was one of the greatest athletes to ever come from the Tri-City region of Leominster, Fitchburg and Lunenburg. Brian, who left us way too soon at the age of 23, was my friend, my teammate, and my hero.

Brian was dominant in all three of his chosen sports of hockey, football, and baseball, perhaps due to his years of playing with older brothers Terry and Kevin, and their friends. Or maybe Brian was really that gifted athletically. Based on my personal experiences playing with Brian as a teammate or against him as an opponent, it was likely a combination of the two. Sure, he had raw talent as evident by his physical gifts including size, speed and athleticism. However, I believe all those years of playing with and against older kids most certainly benefited Brian, who was so dominant and so fearless at every level he played.

During his final year playing for Werner's Sporting Goods in the Leominster Babe Ruth League, Brian was the ace for the Leominster all-star team that was eliminated in the 1974 Massachusetts State Championship final in Falmouth, MA. During the double-elimination qualifying round leading up to the state tournament, Brian was a perfect 3-0, all shut-out victories, including a no-hitter. He batted .566 during that stretch, just for good measure.

While at Lunenburg High School, Brian was the first player in school history to be elected as captain of three sports. He was a Wachusett League all-star in hockey, football and baseball. One of my favorite stories was how the Blue Knights were trailing 7-4 in the last inning against Tahanto in a game which had the league title and a playoff berth on the line. Brian came up to the plate with two runners on base and blasted a game tying home run which at the time was deemed one of the longest ever hit out of Marshall Park in Lunenburg - *as a sophomore.* Lunenburg went on to win the game and moved on to the districts.

As a pitcher, Brian was even more dominant, posting a high school career record of 22-6, four no-hitters, two one-hitters, and nearly 300 strikeouts. After graduating from Lunenburg High, Brian played a year of baseball at Wilbraham Monson Academy in Springfield, MA, and was named the school's Scholar-Athlete award. He pitched a no-hitter in his very first start at WMA.

On the advice of a Milwaukee Brewers scout, Brian enrolled at Miami Dade South Junior College which had a reputation of producing several major league baseball players. There Brian pitched and played infield for two years before enrolling at the University of Massachusetts in Amherst. It was during his freshman year at UMass that Brian became sick.

Despite all of those athletic achievements, the one thing that stays with me after all of these years was Brian's character. During the summer of 1979 when my younger brother Billy was in the final weeks of his own battle with cancer at the age of 18, Brian would come to our home in Leominster and visit with Billy. Brian was only a couple of years older than Billy and they had much in common. Looking back, the irony of Brian being there for Billy just a few short years before he too would be stricken with cancer is not lost on me.

Both excelled on the baseball diamond and the gridiron. Both loved fishing and the outdoors. And yet Brian's visits were about none of those things. During these visits he would sit and just listen to Billy. And to just be there to provide companionship. I'll never forget that about Brian McNally, my friend, teammate, and hero.

Foreword

Mark Lefebvre and I have been friends for about half a century. In the enlightened early 1970's, educators thought it would be a good idea to group students by their perceived intelligence levels. While that philosophy has gone in and out of popularity since then (go into any high school and see course designations and you will see something along the lines of College Prep, College, Honors and AP), at May A. Gallagher Junior High this meant Mark and I had every class together from grade 7 through grade 9. Our poor teachers! That is where our friendship began. I still have the MAG Yearbook from our 9th grade year, and our French teacher referred to me as one of the "unholy quintuplets". Included in that crew was Mark, Charlie Kirouac and Kenny Newcomb. As you might imagine, he was not the only teacher who felt that way. We had our own secret language, nicknames for staff and classmates and basically ran amok for three years, while somehow managing to get good grades and mostly keep out of trouble. Mostly.

The community of Leominster described in this book no longer exists. Back then, we drank Kool-Aid with sugar in it, bought albums and 45's and unlike so many of today's youth, found exercise for more than our thumbs through video games and texting. We couldn't 'post' anything and nothing went 'viral.' Like I said, it was a different era. Our town had traffic in only one spot — the Monument Square rotary at five o'clock. The Nashua River turned a different color daily, thanks to paper mills upstream, and because this was pre- high-tech boom, no one had yet decided an hour-or-so commute was a good trade-off for housing prices along the I-95 corridor. Therefore, developers had no reason yet to carve farmlands and woods into third of an acre lots. Or condominiums. It was a far simpler time and place. And quite simply, Leominster had a long tradition with sports excellence, and the teams

Mark celebrate embodied that.

In the Leominster I grew up in, youth sports were yet to be diluted by (in no particular order) family dysfunction, socioeconomics, so-called elite teams like AAU, school choice and a multitude of other entertainment options. On most days, you were outside. I can remember the start of summer vacation and my father asking me what I was going to do today. When I replied nothing, he said do it outside. And that was a large part of the reason why Leominster had multiple Little League and Babe Ruth Leagues with multiple divisions. If you made an All-Star team back then, it was from a pool of about 150-200 kids. And Leominster had a lot of kids who could really play! So the All-Star was just that – the best of the best.

In those days before school choice, the trajectory was linear. You went from Little League to Babe Ruth to Leominster High and then to Legion ball. You played where you lived – no one would dream of going to Nashoba or Wachusett or (Hell to the NO) Fitchburg if you grew up in Leominster. There were parochial school options of course, but nothing like it is today – be true to your school, is just a lyric from an oldies song now.

Unlike Mark, I was not a good baseball player. If any of the players he discusses in this tome were to throw one high and inside while I was at the plate, I would have had one foot in the dugout during their windup. But, like everyone else in the city, I was captivated by these teams. Many of the players were my friends and I rooted for them like crazy!

But like Mark, I owe much of my success in life to the lessons I learned on the fields of play. Like Mark, I have irreplaceable memories of youth sports: the smell of fresh cut grass on football fields, the packed courts at Bennett School, and the cinder track at Doyle Field. I too remember trying out for teams, the excitement and competitive drive. And humility.

Baseball likewise has changed. The best gift you could get back then was a new glove or bat from Werner's Sporting Goods. We played in sandlots, parking lots, backyards – anywhere there was an expanse of land. We played catch and pickle. Fantasy baseball was adopting the left-handed stance of Yaz when you were playing, or the funky jerking motion of Luis Tiant from the stretch. If you didn't have enough players, you just made right field foul. There was always a mechanism to play a game.

Our major league heroes whom we replicated pitched complete games in the 70's, not four innings then call it a day, as is the state of 'starting' pitching in the majors now. Players who could hit, hit for power and run were much more common than they are now. There was no inter-league play, so the MLB All-Star Game was something special. Baseball was still giving pro football a run for its money in popularity, and basketball players were a distant third. Now, the NFL Draft draws more viewers than most MLB games, and basketball players' popularity and outside endorsements dwarf those of baseball players. In the 70's you couldn't walk anywhere in the summer without hearing a Sox game on TV or on the radio. Today, baseball is largely viewed as a slow game that only old people watch.

Mark and I diverged a bit in High School, no longer in every class together. I played football and ran track, while he, like most of the players he mentions in this book, stayed true to baseball. Leominster High, as you could have probably guessed, had some great teams while we were in school, and I still watched and cheered as often as I could. Mark and I were still friends, still had our own secret language and we still often rode around doing the goofy things you did when you were in high school back then, when you were young and thought you were invincible.

When I look back, I realize I was blessed. My closest friends were kids I played sports with at one time or another. Some of the most influential people in my life were not only coaches and teachers, but the fathers and mothers of those friends. Like I said, it was a different time.

And so, this book is about much more than baseball, much more than the teams who galvanized a community, though it certainly is about those things. It is about a way of life that sadly is disappearing if not already gone. But no one around here will forget those long-ago days, when we had our own Boys of Summer to root for.

Fran Thomas
LHS Class of 1976, school administrator, author, parent
May 2022

Prologue

Longmeadow, Massachusetts - Saturday, July 28, 1973

"Please God, let him hit it to me," I thought as I bent over to pick up a pinch of left field grass and to check the wind for the third time in as many minutes. The timeout called by coach Jim Marrone and the trip to the mound to talk with Mike Leclair seemed interminable. Catcher Pete Gamache stood by Leclair's side with his catcher's mask in his mitt. Sweat was beading from Gamache's chin in the late afternoon humidity of the day. Gamache and Leclair listened intently as Marrone gave the Leominster battery a chance to catch their breaths. My heart was pounding as I internalized the enormity of the moment.

There were two outs in the seventh inning, and we were leading 2-1 over Burncoat of Worcester with the potential tying run on first-base. Another out and we'd be Massachusetts Babe Ruth State Champions, a feat achieved by Leominster in each of the prior two seasons. I did not know it at the time, but until then, no other Massachusetts town had ever won three consecutive state championships.

It wasn't that I felt that I was the only player on the field capable of making that third put-out. I wanted to be the hero. I wanted to fulfill every kid's dream of either knocking in the winning run in a walk-off, or making the final put-out on the field. Ted Rockwell was to my left in center field. Dave Arsenault in right. Dave Bergeron, who made a dazzling play to his left earlier in the inning to rob a Burncoat batter of a potential extra base hit was at third-base. Mike Gasbarro at short. Bob Angelini at second and Mike Catalfamo at first.

My mind drifted to the journey we took to get to this moment. In some regards it started in the summer of 1970 when I and several of my current teammates, were eliminated in the Massachusetts Little League State Championship tournament just three years prior while playing for the Leominster American Little League all-stars. And here we were again with a chance for redemption.

Back to the moment. We were sharp. We were focused. And we were very talented. Yet we were mentally and physically exhausted. We had needed to win five games just to advance to this tournament. And since we lost our tournament opener to Longmeadow, we were dropped to the losers' bracket which in turn required us to crawl back to play this, our fifth game in the last three days.

The stands at Strople Field were packed with fans, players from the other teams, and league officials. The lights were turned on to neutralize the late afternoon shadows. I could see my parents on the first-base side of the grandstands. They and the rest of the Leominster following were standing and clapping.

As coach Marrone jogged back to the dugout, I surveyed the situation. Two outs with a man on first. Joe McLean, Burncoat's right-hand-hitting first-baseman, stepped into the box. Leclair, pitching from the stretch, peered in for the sign from Gamache. I crouched into a ready stance on the balls of my feet, waiting for the pitch. From the set, Leclair fired a fastball to the mitt. I pivoted as I heard the crack of the bat....

Section 1: It Takes A Village

Chapter One: Lightning in a Bottle

Truth be told, none of us on that 1973 all-star team remembers the final out of the game. I've interviewed most of my surviving teammates, including those of us who were on the field for that last out. Not one of us can recall who made the final put-out. And none of the *Leominster Enterprise, Fitchburg Sentinel,* or *Worcester Telegram* articles state how the final out was made. Which perhaps is the point. We didn't care who made the final put-out. The point is we won, and we won as a team not as individuals. The final out didn't matter then. And it doesn't matter now. We were Massachusetts Babe Ruth All-Star State Champions. There is beauty in the ambiguity of that outcome.

This is a story about a place in time. The place was Leominster, Massachusetts. The time was the early 1970's. 1971-1973 to be precise. This is a story about baseball. Pick-up baseball. Little League baseball. Babe Ruth baseball. And eventually high school and American Legion baseball. But most importantly, this story is about community.

The original intent for this book was simply to celebrate the 50th anniversary of a spectacular three-year run of Leominster Babe Ruth All-Star Massachusetts state championships. However, the research and the interviews led me to a conclusion that this story is about so much more. This story is indeed about the players and coaches. But it is perhaps most importantly a story about the role of the Leominster community, its neighborhoods and schoolyards where kids had safe places and opportunities to thrive. It is about sports and other recreational activities that provided kids with the opportunity to develop the necessary skills to cope and succeed as adults. But sadly, this story is also about the erosion of those very things at a time when we as a society perhaps need them most.

Merriam Webster defines the word "place" as a particular position or point in space such as a setting. It defines "time" as the measured or measurable period during which an action, process, or condition exists or continues. The time and place to be was in Leominster during the early 1970's when the region was riveted by the drama and heroics of a group of 14- and 15-year-olds.

The Leominster Babe Ruth All-Stars from 1971, 1972 and 1973 won an unprecedented three consecutive Massachusetts State Championships. The 1971 team was eliminated in the New England Regional Championship game by the eventual 1971 Babe Ruth World Series champions from Puerto Nuevo, Puerto Rico. The 1972 Leominster team won the state title as the *host* team, which is unthinkable. Host teams are not meant to win state tournaments. They are traditionally granted an entry in exchange for hosting the tournament, and they gain a seat in the tournament without the need to play the typical 4-5 games just to qualify. And the 1973 team, on which I was privileged to play, came back from a stunning opening game loss to the host team from Longmeadow, to claw back with *five wins in three days,* and to beat undefeated Burncoat of Worcester *twice on the same day* to win the championship.

One could argue that the Leominster community caught lightning in a bottle those three thrilling summers. However, as one of the 45 players in aggregate who participated, I can speak for my teammates and those who played before me that it was not luck that earned those championships. You can't be *that* good at something over a sustained time period and simply chalk it up to luck.

Luck did not clear the bases with a double in the gap. Good fortune did not strike out the side with runners on second and third and a one-run lead. We players still needed to make the plays when opportunity and preparation created a game situation that required flawless execution. And my experience was that the 45 members of those three All-Star teams from 1971, 1972, and 1973 were the most talented, best coached, and most prepared teams on the fields of those Massachusetts state championship tournaments. And I believe there was a direct correlation between the success of those championship teams and the community environments on which we players developed our skills.

To me, our success was a perfect storm of opportunity, preparation, and execution. The community of Leominster provided us with the opportunity. On countless playgrounds, sandlots, parking lots, school athletic fields and neighborhoods, hundreds of us Leominster kids developed an interest in, developed the skills for, and sustained a passion for the game of baseball. Volunteers groomed the fields, sold the concessions, raised the money and coached the teams. Parents, relatives, neighbors and complete strangers showed to watch us play. Newspapers sent reporters to cover our games. Local community radio stations covered our games with live broadcasts.

The coaches prepared us by organizing leagues, running tryouts, and leading practices on weeknights and weekends. They drew up the game plans and ran the drills. They scouted the players. Those that did not coach were perhaps umpires instead.

All that said, it was still up to us players to execute. I remain in awe of the 1971 and 1972 teams that I followed during the two years prior to my 1973 squad. During those summers I combed the daily papers for game summaries and box scores. I listened to the games live on local radio. I could recite the lineups. And I did not miss an inning of the tournament games. I managed to hitch a ride with a family friend or convince my grandparents to make the trip to Lynn, to Nashua, and to Newport. Funny thing, I was among hundreds of others who did the same. Everybody talked baseball those magnificent summers.

So yes, Leominster did create lightning in a bottle. The community; however, delivered the goods. Leominster was a magnificent place to grow up as a kid. And the late 1960's and early 1970's were a magical time to do so. A place in time indeed.

Chapter Two: Growing Up In Leominster

Being a kid in Leominster in the 1960's and 1970's was a magical amalgamation of all of the senses, particularly in summer, when one could close one's eyes and listen to the purring of a lawnmower from a nearby neighbor, sample the sweet earthy smell of the freshly cut grass, or take in the savory aroma of charcoal smoldering from an upwind backyard. One thing that was certain during those idyllic summers, was the clamor and chatter of kids playing with friends on neighborhood playgrounds - both formal and ad hoc in nature.

Most of our daily lives in the late 1960's and early 1970's centered on family events that typically included grandparents, aunts, uncles and especially cousins. We piled into cars, all of them second-hand, and headed to holiday gatherings and cookouts that usually offered more food than could possibly be consumed. The grown-ups played card games such as Michigan Rummy, Buttons or Cribbage.

Summer gatherings gave us a chance to meet and make friends with the neighbors of our cousins. We swam in above-ground pools until the fireflies glowed like embers at dusk. We played whiffle ball and lawn darts, flashlight tag and hide-and-seek. As we got older, we stole kisses from our new-found girlfriends or boyfriends when our parents weren't looking. We were not yet exposed to the crises of the times, or at least we were blissfully unencumbered with the weighty issues of day.

The times were certainly different at the turn of the 1970's in that video games, cable TV, smart phones and other indoor distractions had yet to emerge as alternatives to outdoor neighborhood gatherings for kids. Our idea of indoor distractions usually involved playing Coleco table-hockey, or one of a myriad of board games such as Risk, Stratego or Battleship.

Whatever we were doing, we kids made all of the decisions regarding the event, structure, rules, and outcomes. Adult supervision was really nowhere to be found, nor was it required. The need for social interaction and competition was ingrained in all of us, and older siblings and friends who grew up ahead of us set that example. Our heroes were not only professional athletes. Our older brothers, sisters, friends and neighbors who went on to play organized leagues and high school sports captivated those of us growing in their shadows. Most of us grew up wanting to be that athlete. I know I did.

During this period, Leominster offered a plethora of restaurants and cafes with a wide variety of cuisines. We ate Chinese-American food at The Singapore, Dan Chan's or Double Dragon. For Italian it was the Lazy A which became the Gondola, Monty's Garden or El Camino. We ate fried smelts at the Boston Fish Market next door to Monty's or ventured across the street to the Little Kitchen for 2-in-a-bowl (meatballs and Italian bread). Tim's Diner, still in operation at the time of this writing, was a multi-generational stainless-steel diner tucked away on the corner of Mechanic and Water Streets, and which was known for its breakfast menu and world class chowder. After school or on Saturday afternoon's we'd venture to C&M Pizza. During our paper routes, we'd stop at Claire's Luncheonette on Lancaster Street for a box a French fries or a bag of M&M's. We were devastated when Claire's was destroyed by fire circa 1968. Newton's Dairy Farm on Manchester Street was always one of our favorite Sunday treats as a family before it too was destroyed by fire.

Biking on our newspaper routes, we could revel in the contemporary music that played from open windows and backyard stoops. The first time I heard Cream's, "Sunshine of Your Love" was while tucking the collection envelope inside a screen door on Wheeler Street. While our moms had the AM radios dialed in to WRKO, WMEX, or WROR in the kitchen, our older siblings had all the best counter-culture music playing behind closed bedroom doors. I "discovered" *Led Zeppelin II* in Bob and Gary Salvatore's bedroom on Florence Street. I first heard the newly released Beatles' *Abbey Road* from my cousin Grace's Latorre's room while visiting my great-grandmother at her three-story tenement on Lancaster Street. My cousin Nancy Arel was always up for a trip to Bradlees to buy 45 RPM records. Joe Charielle had the largest collection of 45 RPM records I had ever seen. Zager and Evan's "In the Year 2525" was always on the stack.

After school we watched *Batman* reruns. On weeknights it was *Room 222*, *Adam-12*, *Laugh-In*, *The Andy Williams Show* and *Mod Squad*.

Our older brothers went off to Viet Nam; our older sisters went off to nursing school or one of the local university/colleges to become teachers. Younger siblings typically joined whatever neighborhood activity or schoolyard scrum was in progress.

At the time, our city was dotted with elementary schools. Lancaster Street, Priest Street, Lincoln School, Bennett School, George Street, Pierce School, and Spruce Street School all seemed to each be built from the same architectural plan that typically included two levels of classrooms and a basement that doubled as a cafeteria and nuclear fallout shelter. K-6 occupied the same building - having lunch together, sharing playgrounds during recess and hopping on exhaust belching school buses from F&L Street Railway Company. There were very few if any parents dropping their kids off at school. We socialized at bus stops with kids of all ages. None of us froze to death while waiting for the bus on the coldest of winter days. Those of us close enough to school would often walk to and from school if the weather allowed.

My family lived on Elm Hill Avenue just off Lancaster Street opposite the Lazy A. My brothers and I would descend the terraced backyard of our home to the bottom of Litchfield Street, stop at the Charielle's at the top of Litchfield Street to meet Tony Charielle, and then walk past the upper Lancaster Street neighborhoods on Crescent Knoll, Florence Street, Wheeler and Johnson Streets, and up at the street level steps of the schoolyard and into the playground to await the school bell.

After school we'd reverse the trek, often stopping at Claire's for a snack. Along the way we'd see Tony Raffaele, Chris Marrone, Rusty Tata or Lenny Mallard. Sometimes Christina Marrama would allow me to walk her home from school and yes, I'd carry her books. Chivalry was alive and well in the 1960's and 70's.

We read Matt Christopher novels to fuel our imagination. Titles such as *Touchdown for Tommy, Tall Man in the Pivot, Catcher with a Glass Arm, Crackerjack Halfback*, and *Wingman on Ice* projected our fantasized athletic heroics. We scoured every issue of *Sports Illustrated* imagining we could be that Face in the Crowd. Our shoeboxes were overflowing with Topps baseball cards, and we memorized the statistics of each player.

The National Football League, with a hefty sponsorship from Ford Motor Company, held an annual Punt Pass and Kick competition for boys 9-15 (girls' competition was added in 1995). My dad took me to the local Ford dealership to register for the event late summer of 1968, as did the dads of most of my friends. The competition involved making one pass, one punt and one place kick from a tee with points awarded for distance and accuracy. I practiced in the vacant Borden Chemical parking lot across from our Elm Hill Avenue home in the weeks leading up to the competition. On the day of the competition I joined dozens of other boys in who were arranged by age, just above the football scoreboard on the upper Doyle Field grounds. I did well enough to win the silver trophy for second place and I could not have been happier. My future LHS classmates John Regan and Ted Fiffy won the gold and bronze trophies, respectively. We and the other winners were feted at an LHS football game later that Fall.

We looked forward to trips to Searstown Mall (presently the Mall at Whitney Field) for back-to-school shopping, buying our clothes and school supplies at R.H. White, Sears and Bradlees. Rockdale at the bottom of Whitney Street and Mills Ave was a Leominster landmark and is remembered for the wooden floors, low ceilings and of course, the low prices. In town we'd shop at Metro Music, Rubins, and Fini Shoe Store. One of my favorite places to visit in town was Electronic Werld, a combination record store and stereo equipment retailer. I'd browse records for hours and talk music with the staff. I can recall buying a pair of Koss headphones and a JVC car stereo system there.

On special occasions we'd spend an afternoon at the venerated Whalom Park. Walking from the parking lot across the street you could hear the shrieks and the wooden frame groan as the roller coast cart roared by. The sweet smell of cotton candy competed with the buttery aroma of popcorns as we'd approach the gate. As children we'd opt for the Scrambler, Octopus, Tilt-A-Whirl, Tumble Bug, and of course the Fun House. For many of us, the Flyer Comet was our first roller coaster experience. And Saturday night roller skating parties were always a hit in junior high school.

Playgrounds took the form of school yards, sandlots, recreation facilities, city parks and in the case of the Lancaster Street gang, St. Leo's Cemetery. In the late 1960's and early 1970's, kids from Lancaster Street School, heading south through Derwin Street, Johnson Street, Wheeler Street, Florence Street, Litchfield Street, Elm Hill Avenue, Dudley Street, Viscoloid Avenue, and all points in between, would be found playing baseball or tackle football at the undeveloped lot at the back end of St. Leo's Cemetery on Lancaster Street. Schwinn Stingray bicycles with banana seats would be strewn across the access road, many with baseball gloves hung like trophies on the ape-arm handlebars. The field had bases carefully paced to form a perfect diamond. On most days, there would be enough players to field nine players per side. We used baseballs that were donated by coaches that were left over from the prior Little League baseball season. Aluminum bats were not yet introduced. There were no "automatic" rules since all positions on the field were filled. Similar sandlots dotted the city and some of these fields were in the most unusual of places around town such as behind Solar Chemical off Marguerite Ave near the railroad tracks, and behind Ash Street.

Lineups would include future Babe Ruth All-Stars John Cantatore, and Doug Girouard. Many other families would be proudly represented. Joe and Tony Charielle, Ross Amico, Ted Fiffy, Peter Andries, Joe and Ritchie Decarolis, Chris Marrone, Rusty Tata, Lenny Mallard, Dave Mercik and others were regulars. My younger brothers Mike and Billy would always participate. One notable participant was future best-selling author, Bob (R.A.) Salvatore who always seemed to have the diplomatic skills to ensure the sides were even. Often times the ice-cream truck would make a stop at the bottom of that cemetery hill, a testament to the regularity of that gathering.

Other neighborhoods across Leominster would have their playgrounds, including Fall Brook School, George Street School, Lincoln Street School, the fields up at 12th Street, (site of the American Little League), Bernice Avenue (home of North Leominster Little League), Northwest School (home of the National Little League), and many others.

As the summer evenings grew shorter and the upcoming school year beckoned, interest and activities would naturally turn to football. It was a tradition in our Lancaster Street neighborhood to play tackle football on Sundays. Many Saturdays would find us at Doyle Field to watch the Blue Devils host a regional or cross-state rival. During the game there would be numerous ad hoc football games being played behind the bleachers or in the upper Doyle Field, with the dreams of one day playing high school football at stake.

Once the snow and freezing temperatures arrived, energy and exuberance shifted to the ponds and backyard rinks for ice hockey. At the time, the Big Bad Bruins had recently won the Stanley Cup and were on their way to a second championship during the 1971-1972 season. Pick-up hockey games would take shape at winter wonderlands like Rockwell Pond, Barrett Pond, Richardson's Pond at upper Litchfield Street, Lake

Samoset, Lake Whalom and several other neighborhood ponds. Most of us had perfected Bobby Orr's immortal mid-air flight after scoring a goal. Most of us wore rag-tag Bruins' black and gold colors. Others from Leominster's "French Hill" section were the *rouge, blanc et bleu* of the Montreal Canadiens.

    Joe Charielle laughed aloud when I asked if he remembered the summers of 1968 and 1969 when he, his brother Tony, my brothers Mike and Billy and I would spend day after day playing whiffle ball in the Charielle's back yard. The yard was anything but ideal for whiffle ball; however, we made up rules that were conducive to the yard. There was the tool shed that formed the backstop. On the door of the shed was a 3' x 3' square marked off in tape that represented the strike zone. The yard was narrow, no more than forty feet across from first-base to third-base. Second-base was located where shortstop would normally be due to a wall that bisected the infield from the outfield. Left-field was above a ten-foot wall that extended from the shed all the way to a driveway and the front yard. Right-field was to put it delicately, no-man's land, which was swampy quagmire of high grass and unknown dangers. A fly ball into the swamp was an automatic three outs, no questions asked, as nobody wanted to retrieve the ball. As a left-handed batter, this presented a problem for me as I was not allowed to pull the ball due to the 3-out automatic rule. Non-plussed, I learned how to hit right-handed.

    I submit the dimensional details of this backyard field only to make the point that every back yard had its own character which determined the ground rules and other quirks to make competition possible. Without knowing it at the time, I learned to hit to the opposite field while playing whiffle ball. Without a coach. Without a parent. Without any conscious thought about doing so. Fast-forward to my Babe Ruth, high school and American Legion baseball career. As a left-handed batter, my specialty was to sucker a team into playing for me to pull the ball to right-field. I accomplished this ruse during my warm-up swings in the batter's box. As the pitcher entered his wind-up, I would shift my feet and my body weight, and drive the ball down the left-field line which frequently led to extra bases. Where did I learn that skill? In the Charielle's back yard.

What Joe also laughed about was that we would literally field lineups that were comprised of the then current line-ups from of each and all National and American League Major League Baseball clubs. We kept statistics in a notebook. When speaking with Joe as part of my research for this book, he shared that he had recently found some of those rosters and statistics after over fifty years.

The five of us - Joe and Tony Charielle, my younger brothers Mike and Billy and I, were inseparable during those years. We rotated through the seasons based on the calendar. In hindsight, playing multiple sports certainly made us better athletes when we grew into organized sports. By playing "off-the-wall" with a tiny Super-Ball, we developed hand-eye coordination. When we played basketball we developed our legs and our quickness. The same for street hockey and football. We were all better baseball players because we played other sports.

Joe and Tony's dad, Egidio Charielle, was a baseball junkie. He coached his sons and volunteered his time as an umpire. When he'd come home from work, Mr. Charielle would bellow "well if it isn't the 'Lu-FAY" boys" to anyone who was within ear-shot. I'm sure he took great satisfaction in those scenes. Until he saw that we broke another window on the door of his tool shed that is.

Leominster High School class of 1973 graduate and good friend Steve McCumber recalls growing up on the corner of Green Street and Main Street next to Kentucky Fried Chicken. Due to the proximity to Doyle Field, Steve and his neighborhood friends Dave Sicard, Gary Brow, Rich Hildreth, Jimmy Mitchell, Joe DeStadio, John Boissoneau, and Jimmy Coleman would descend on the upper field of Doyle to play baseball every day for several months out of the year. They too transitioned to football and basketball (at Priest Street School) during colder weather months.

Baseball was so popular during Steve's childhood that on any given Sunday morning, there would be three games in progress at Doyle Field. The main event was held on the high school/Legion baseball diamond and two other fields at opposite corners of the Priest Street side of the park.

McCumber recalled, "We used to gather and wait at the gates that were locked overnight. When the city parks department worker opened the gates at 7:30 Sunday mornings, there would be a mad dash to the varsity field where the first eighteen players to reach the infield would earn their right to play at the big field. By 9:00 all three fields were full" (S. McCumber, February 26, 2022).

Doyle Field hosted a New England Regional Babe Ruth Tournament game in 1966 when the popularity of the Puerto Rico team forced the game to be moved from the Lancaster Street Field to Doyle to accommodate the crowd.

Doyle Field was also home to the Leominster Pop Warner football teams that played on the infield of the track loop. At that time there were wooden bleachers that would be filled on Sunday afternoons in the Fall when the Leominster Dolphins, Giants and Rams would play. On Sunday mornings several football games - both touch and tackle - were underway in various corners of the field. Occasionally Leominster native and Cleveland Browns tight-end Milt Morin would be working out on the field and would join the neighborhood kids in the fun.

McCumber also recalls that summer basketball at Bennett School was a big deal during 1970's where city and regional high school-aged players were drafted to play in summer leagues. Webber Lumber sponsored a team trip to New York City to play inner-city teams.

John Crawley, my former Babe Ruth all-star teammate and high school friend, remembers Pop Warner football and Bennett School basketball. "Leominster had the Giants and Dolphins. Bennett's School basketball was emerging as a playground for developing players. And after our Babe Ruth playing days were over, Leominster High baseball, football and soccer teams were emerging as powerhouse teams in the state with lineups filled with the players emerging from our Babe Ruth all-star team, winning titles and ranking high in state and national polls. Ex-Babe Ruth stars Bobby Angelini, Stevie Tata, and Richie Kelly went on to star in baseball, football and basketball while at Notre Dame High School. Paul and Peter Gamache were three-sports stars at St. Saint Bernard's High School as well. Those Babe Ruth all-star teams planted the seeds for high school success throughout north central Massachusetts. Every single player from the 71-73 teams went on to drive success in high school sports teams from the area." (J. Crawley, June 10, 2021).

John Lieneck, former Leominster Babe Ruth, Leominster High School, and Leominster American Legion star, and older brother of 1971 Babe Ruth star Pete Lieneck, recalls growing up in North Leominster off Prospect Street. "Me and my and friends Jim Beauregard, Mike Caisse and others would play switcheroo baseball in the Monoosnock Golf Club parking lot every Sunday from 10:00 AM until dark, often using golf balls instead of baseballs," said Lieneck (J. Lieneck., February 21, 2022). John went on to play Division 1 baseball as a walk-on at the University of Michigan before ending his baseball career after his freshman season. One of the highlights of his baseball career was playing against former Detroit Tiger pitcher and 1976 American League Rookie-of-the-Year Mark Fidrych when Lieneck starred for the Acton A's semi-pro baseball team.

Growing up on Lindell Street in Leominster's west end, Ron Patry would become a left-handed ace pitcher of the 1971 Leominster High School and 1971 Massachusetts state champion American Legion teams. "1971 was a great summer, enthuses Lieneck's former teammate Ron Patry. "We'd play ball at an empty neighborhood lot or ride our bikes to Doyle Field," said Patry. "What became known as Cook's Field would attract neighborhood kids from all over including Jay DiGeronimo, Eddie and Joe Cataldo, Billy Bateman and Eric Legere" (R. Patry, March 3, 2022). Legere would become a three-year varsity starter for LHS football and earned North Worcester County All-Star and LHS Hall of Fame honors.

Patry remembers riding his Schwinn 10-speed bike all over the city to play ball with his friends and classmates. "Pierce Pond (also referred to by locals as Roache Pond) was the go-to venue for ice hockey. And we'd always find 12-14 kids at the Ringer's field. We'd never give a second thought about riding our bikes to any neighborhood to play ball."

Patry played in the National Little League for Borden Chemical in the minors and Dupont in the majors. Leo Conway was his coach. Tim Conway, Eric Legere, Rick O'Malley, and Ricky Marchand were his Dupont teammates. Coach Bob Boissoneau drafted Ron to play for TAG in the Leominster Babe Ruth League and became an all-star during his final season.

Former Leominster baseball star and Leominster High School baseball coach Don Freda recalls growing up playing baseball at what was known in the 1960's and 1970's as the Eugene Street playground which was actually at the end of Lisa Drive at the upper end of Pleasant Street. The playground was in Freda's words, "a hotbed of activity for many kids who came to play baseball, basketball, or just hang around. What was unusual about the Eugene Street field was that it actually had grass" (Do. Freda, April 9, 2021).

Also making the Eugene Street playground interesting was the enormous boulder in shallow left-center field, and the very short distance to the woods in right-field. Left-handed slugging Dave Malatos was known to have developed his ability to go to the opposite field at this playground according to Freda.

During the summers of the early 1970's there were plenty of opportunities for neighborhood kids to band together to compete with cross-town neighborhood rivals in a city recreational league comprised of 12 playground teams. Lancaster Street School, Crossman Ave, Northwest School, Bennett School, Priest Street, Spruce Street, Pierce School, Carter Field, North Leominster, Lincoln School, Upper Doyle Field, and Fallbrook School all fielded street hockey and/ or softball teams. Our parents would refer to these venues as "camps." Our counselors would refer to these camps as babysitting. We kids would refer to the concept of being outdoors and away from our parents for the whole day as heaven.

In March of 1972, the Leominster Recreation Department projected up to 3,000 of the city's youth to enroll in summer programs.[1] In addition to the playground programs, the city also created summer swimming camps at Barrett Park and the F&L beach at Lake Whalom. Summer basketball tournaments were also in the works.

Figure 1: Dick and Don Freda, 1968 (photo credit: Don Freda)

In the summer of 1972, my family relocated to a new home on Glenwood Drive located at the upper end of Union Street. From the top of our street we could walk a dirt path through to a house lot across the street from the original Holy Name Church. Behind Holy Name Church was Fall Brook School, one of the newer elementary schools serving neighborhoods on the southwest side of Leominster. Future Leominster City Councilor Mark Pickford was our camp counselor and coach. To say our playground street hockey and softball teams were stacked was a vast understatement. As 13–15-year-olds, future LHS stars Steve Ringer, Rick L'Ecuyer, Dick Freda, Charlie Kirouac, and Jim Normandin were among a rag-tag group of kids living in what was at that time the most rural section of the city. My brother Mike and I, Matt DiNardo, Tom Tefft, Terry Mullen, Anthony DePasquale, Bennie DiNardo, Steve Longo and Charlie Ciccone filled out the rosters of our street hockey and softball teams, both of which won that summer's Leominster Summer Recreation League city championship.

Not only were kids active in these summer recreational programs, during this era local newspapers routinely provided coverage of the results. From the August 23, 1972, *Fitchburg Sentinel*:

Fallbrook Playground won the city playground championship in street hockey by defeating Carter in a best of three game series, winning the first two games. Fallbrook's record for the summer was 10-1.... Fallbrook Playground also won the city playground softball league championship Friday by taking two out of a three game series from North Leominster Playground. They clinched it by taking the rubber game 6-4. During the season, the Fallbrook club compiled a 13-2 record.[2]

These playground teams required no adult supervision except for perhaps a high school-age instructor and rides to/from playgrounds across the city. I look back at the commitment of the neighborhood kids in their early teen years with pride and astonishment. Where many of today's teenage athletes tend to major on one or two sports, or in some cases play year-round on AAU club teams in one sport, the kids of my youth tended to participate in any activity that would provide a bit of competition and exercise. The result was a pipeline of well-rounded athletes to fill the rosters of organized leagues and future high school teams.

Today Leominster offers a much broader set of Recreation Department-sponsored programs for a wide variety of age-appropriate groups. Per the department's web site, ..."over 100 programs are offered over the course of the year, serving over 3,000 participants."[3]

Chapter Three: Leominster is (Also) a Baseball Town

When people think of Leominster and its rich and storied sports history, football, specifically high school football, tends to top the list. With numerous Massachusetts Super Bowl championships, the trans-generational Thanksgiving Day rivalry with Fitchburg, and the stunning victories over Brockton, it is no surprise that the city of Leominster is captivated by high school football. This popularity has led to hundreds of young boys taking part in the local football tradition. On any given crisp fall afternoon during the 1970's, Leominster fielded varsity, junior varsity, Gallagher Junior High, Carter Junior High, and three Pop Warner teams. Rivalries were forged across town between the two junior high school squads. The younger players learned the fundamentals of football during the heyday of Leominster Pop Warner football when three teams - the Rams. Dolphins and Giants – would compete against each other and regional teams. And of course we had the much-heralded rivalry between Leominster and Fitchburg High Schools.

Figure 2: Kinsey's of Leominster Summer Baseball League, Doyle Field circa 1946 (photo credit: Don Freda)
Front Row: Louis Picucci, Arthur Pignata, Rocco Spinelli, Dieco Pignata, Billy Wheeler, Angelo "Stiff" Picucci, John "Moose" McDermott, batboy Bobby Perla
Back Row: Joseph Davenport, Candido Torcoletti, Barney Ward, Lavoie, Armand "Fatty" Vivoamore, Joseph Kinsey (Manager/Sponsor)

That said, in terms of the sheer numbers of leagues, teams, players and tournaments, baseball can also claim its rightful place as a sport that defined the city of Leominster. This was especially true from the mid-1960's through the 1970's. During this period, Leominster had three Little League organizations - American, National and North Leominster leagues, each with major and minor league divisions. The Leominster Babe Ruth league expanded to two divisions in 1968 due to the number of players and the opportunity to offer younger players the chance to gain valuable game experience.[4] Both Carter and Gallagher Junior High Schools offered baseball programs with games against neighboring towns such as Fitchburg, Marlboro, Lunenburg, Milford, Nashua and others.

Figure 3: Fred Bergeron of the 1930 Leominster Rovers (photo credit: Dave Bergeron)

Former *Boston Globe* sportswriter and ESPN baseball analyst Gordon Edes grew up in Lunenburg, and recalls that in Leominster, northern Worcester County and the state of Massachusetts as a whole, there was no shortage of recreational programs that provided youngsters with opportunities to develop relationships, especially when it involved youth sports. Edes in fact played for Russo's, Lunenburg's Division 2 entry in the Leominster Babe Ruth League. Edes graduated from Lunenburg High School in 1972, and while a student he worked for the *Fitchburg Sentinel, Leominster Enterprise* and the *Worcester Telegram*, mostly covering Lunenburg school sports, men's softball leagues in both Lunenburg and Leominster, as well as semi-pro football.

"We moved to Lunenburg when I was nine, and Little League was central to my existence," Edes shares. "In January, if there was no snow on the ground on Sunnyhill Road, my brother Lionel and I would go out and throw ground balls to each other on our rock-hard yard. I lived for those Little League games, and I remember what a big deal the All-Star tournaments were, and following along in the Sentinel as the Fitchburg and Leominster teams advanced. I think Babe Ruth ball in Lunenburg at that time had two tiers; I played in the lower level for a year, but I knew all about the legendary Babe Ruth League coach Herb Hill, and Emile Johnson, the Leominster American Legion coach" (G. Edes, August 20, 2021).

Edes recalls being dazzled by Leominster star Gregg Picucci who became the baseball coach and athletic director at Gardner High School, and "who I first saw playing softball in Lunenburg. I think he starred in baseball at Leominster High. He had a ridiculously strong arm at shortstop, and I remember my dad and I going to see him play for the semi-pro Acton Braves." Edes also recalls going to the New England Babe Ruth League tournament in Nashua, and loving the Puerto Rico team and their fans who were loud, energetic and made every game a party.

No one benefited more from the popularity of youth baseball than the legendary Emile Johnson, coach of the Leominster High School and Leominster American Legion baseball squads. In 2020, Coach Johnson was named by MaxPreps as the greatest coach in Massachusetts high school history.[5] Not baseball coach, but the greatest high school *coach* in Massachusetts history. MaxPreps is a CBS Sports property which tracks high school and prep school athletics and serves as a recruiting tool for college programs.

Let that settle in for a moment. Of all the legendary coaches in Massachusetts history, across all sports, and for over a century of record keeping, Coach Johnson was selected as the best of all time. The numbers speak for themselves. Johnson was the all-time winningest baseball coach with 725 wins, and three state championships. He never had a losing season in 43 years, and he reached the district tournament 42 times. In his spare time, Johnson also coached varsity soccer with 429 wins and led the girls basketball team to three state tournament entries.

Former Leominster baseball star and coach Don Freda has perhaps spent more time alongside coach Johnson than anyone over the decades. Freda remembers that playing baseball for coach Johnson was intense and at times unforgiving. "You could not have thin skin, especially when you got in his doghouse," recalls Freda. "Many talented players from Leominster did not even try out for the team for fear of playing based on what they heard."

I can personally attest to coach Freda's assertion. While a junior at Leominster high school in 1975, I started in left field for the entire season. I was eager, I was teachable, and I did all of the things that coach Johnson expected of me. During my senior year, however, I was indeed in coach Johnson's doghouse, and I sat for most of the season. I was distracted, I couldn't find my swing, and simply there were better players on the field ahead of me. I did manage to redeem myself with coach Johnson during that summer when I hit .311 while batting third and playing left-field during my final year of Legion baseball.

The summer of 1971 was a special one for Leominster baseball. Freda played for the Leominster American Legion team that defeated Milford for the 1971 American Legion state championship. John Lieneck, Mike Pananos, Dave Antocci, Ed Cataldo and Ron Patry all played for that championship team. During that same summer, the 1971 Leominster Babe Ruth all-stars won the Massachusetts state championship, its first since the 1952 Leominster all-stars won the title. Emile Johnson played for that 1952 Massachusetts Babe Ruth state championship team as a 15-year-old.

The following op-ed piece appeared in the *Leominster Enterprise* on August 17, 1971:

Leominster - Baseball Town

Let's all stand up and cheer for our young baseball players. The Leominster All-Stars of the Babe Ruth League and the Leominster Post of the American Legion baseball have done a superlative job.

The All-Stars who finally went down to defeat against the Puerto Rican team made a very good showing. The top-rated Puerto Nuevo, Puerto Rican team will probably go on to the World Series. It is always a thrill to see our own players do so well.

The Leominster Post No. 151 team is proving of championship quality also. Steve Fredette's no-hitter made for extra merit on the part of our boys. As of this writing, they have yet to play the game in the State Championship. But we know they will represent Leominster well. Leominster can really be proud of these young men. A good job, well done.[6]

Leominster American Legion Post 151 indeed went on to win its first and only State Championship under the direction of coach Emile Johnson. In Babe Ruth action that summer, Puerto Nuevo not only went to the 1971 New England Regionals in Nashua, but they also went on to win the 1971 World Series in Albuquerque, NM. Thus, it took two defeats at the hands of the eventual 1971 Puerto Rican world champions to eliminate the mighty 1971 Leominster team from competition.

Coach Johnson demanded much of his players. He taught us to be prepared for any game situation, and we practiced these situations repeatedly. Repetition, mental preparedness, skills development...over and over and over again until making the proper play became rote. There were many players and would-be-players who were turned off by Johnson's abrasive and sometimes border-line abusive style. However, coach Johnson created a standard of excellence and a culture of success that has never been matched.

Looking back, coach Freda summed it up best. "Playing for Emile

Johnson was quite an experience. He could make you laugh. He could piss you off. All he wanted was to win and to find a way to motivate his players to play the best we could possibly play. He would learn how close to the line he could go when pushing certain players. Some dropped out. Others who possessed very good talent, but had poor character, got cut."

Figure 4: 1954 Leominster High School Varsity Baseball Team (photo credit: Don Freda)
Front Row: Ernie Sawin, Larry Boissoneau, Dave Chester, Frank Novak, Henry Lanza
Second Row: Bill Lewis, Dom Angelini, Paul Padovano, Rich Mazzaferro, Ding Cormier, Danny Hill, Al Menard (Mgr.)
Third Row: Carmine Picucci (Coach), Carl Agnew, Bimbo Montaquila, Bob Morgan, Frank Swett, John Thomas, Don Deitzel, Emile Johnson, Lou D'Innocenzo

I caught up with Emile Johnson in the spring of 2021. "I remember fondly the quality of the players coming up from the Babe Ruth League over the years. Rich Kelly decided to play at Notre Dame High School in

Fitchburg, but we got Ted Rockwell to transfer to Leominster. Pete Lieneck was a great shortstop. Steve Jackson had a great glove at second-base. Dick Freda, boy he got a lot of outs for us with his stretch at first-base. Dave Malatos was a fierce competitor and a damn good right fielder.

Figure 5: 1975 LHS Varsity Baseball Team (photo Credit: 1975 Leominster High School Magnet Yearbook).
Front Row: Bob Antocci, Doug Girouard, Dave Arsenault, Dave Malatos, Rick Comeau, Dick Freda, Ted Rockwell, Bob Koch
Back Row: Coach Emile Johnson, Rick Gallien, Mike Pignata, Mark Lefebvre, Mike Leclair, Mike Bergeron, Rick Daigneault, Coach Dick Labelle (Missing: Mike Gasbarro)

Rick Comeau won a lot of games for us as did Mike Leclair. Mike Pignata was tough as nails at third-base. And you were a great hitter and left fielder for us in high school and Legion as well. And all of you were so well-prepared for Leominster High School and American Legion baseball. All I had to do was reinforce the fundamentals and coach situational baseball" (E. Johnson, April, 21, 2021).

Figure 6: Clockwise from top left: Ted Rockwell on the mound, the author laying down a drag bunt, Mike Pignata pitching, and Rick Daigneault on deck for the 1976 LHS Blue Devils (photo credit: Leominster High School Magnet Yearbook).

Chapter Four: Leominster Little Leagues

Baseball in Leominster during the 1960's and 1970's was so popular that three Little League organizations operated in separate sections of the city. The American Little League attracted kids from the southeastern part of the city, while the National Little League and North Leominster Little League represented west and north Leominster communities, respectively. All three leagues provided both Minor and Major league teams, affording kids the opportunity to play competitive baseball at the appropriate age and skill level.

The Leominster National Little League played games at Northwest School Field on Stearns Avenue and featured two fields. The league in the late 1960's and 1970's was comprised of four teams – Tilco, DuPont's, Kingman's and Foster Grant. Many of my future Babe Ruth, Leominster High School and American Legion teammates were stars from this league including Rick Daigneault, Ted Rockwell, Lou Piano, Mike Brown, Jim Normandin, Steve Shaw, Bob Angelini, Dave and Mike Bergeron, and Peter Gamache. During this period, the league had a membership of nearly 100 players.[7]

The North Leominster Little League played games at the Bernice Avenue field off Main Street in North Leominster. During the 1960's and 1970's, the league was composed of Duval, Gagnon, King's Corner, and Federals. The league also offered minor league competition for 8-year-olds assigned to two teams, D'Onfro Construction and Victory Markets. Many future Leominster baseball standouts including John and Pete Lieneck, Jim Donnelly, Paul D'Onfro, Bryan Beaudette, Steve McCumber, and Bill and Mike Pananos came from the North Leominster Little League. Over 50 youngsters played ball in North Leominster during any given season during the 1960's and 1970's.[8]

Figure 7: The 1965 Duval team of North Leominster Little League (photo credit: Steve McCumber)
Front row: Peter Rudnicky, Dan Donnelly, Dan Hanley Russell Grubb, Paul Roger, Gary Jones, Mike Beauregard, Mike Donnelly.
Back row: Coach Valera, Paul Grubb, Lou Beauregard, Steve Mahoney, coach Mahoney, Paul Fiffy, Steve McCumber, Jack Siciliano, coach Rudnicky.

Figure 8: 1970 Kingman infield (photo credit: Dave Bergeron)
Front row: Benny Butkiewicz, John Moynihan, Ron Storro
Back row: Mike Secino, Doug Pulsifer, Jay Connors, Dave Bergeron

Figure 9: The 1969 Kingman team of Leominster National Little League (photo credit: Leominster Historical Society)
Front Row: Ron Storro, Rick Comeau, Pat Mason, Rock O'Malley, Mario Acerbi, Jamie Marchand
Back Row: Coach Maurice Marchand, Paul Bouvier, Tony DiNardo, Steve Preville, Rick Marchand, Joe Cataldo, Ray Bissonnette, Mgr. Al Steinmetz

Figure 10: 1966 Tilco of the Leominster National Little League (photo credit: Steve Tata)

Figure 11: Mike Bergeron of the 1970 Kingman team of Leominster National Little League (photo credit: Mike Bergeron)

Figure 12: Steve Tata of the 1966 Tilco team from Leominster National Little League (photo credit: Steve Tata)

The American Little League played their games on Twelfth Street up on French Hill, offering two fields for Major and Minor league competition. In March of 1970, then American Little League president, Bernard LaPointe expected 232 youngsters to register for the American Little League alone.[9] Between the three Leominster Little Leagues, it is not a stretch to estimate that over 400 kids played Little League in Leominster that summer.

The Leominster American Little League was a shining example of the positive impact to the community through service and volunteerism. And the face of that selflessness was Vern Brideau. In the early 1970's, Brideau was Leominster's Ward 2 City Councilor, and went on to serve as president of the Leominster American Little League for 40 years. He was instrumental in making the Twelfth Street American Little League Field one of the best in the area, and the first to have lights for night games. The Twelfth Street Field was dedicated as the Ronnie Bachand Memorial Field under his watch in 1968 in honor of the neighborhood boy and American League standout who passed away earlier in the year.

All three Leominster Little Leagues were non-profit organizations operating on revenues collected as dues from player families, community and business contributions, raffles, and collections from concessions at the game. The league officers, committee heads, coaches, umpires and concession workers were all volunteers. One particularly effective way the leagues raised funds was through "Tag Days," where players were distributed across the city in full uniform to ask patrons of local businesses for contributions. In my three years of Little League, I was stationed at Rockdale's on Water Street and the downtown Dunkin' Donuts at the intersection of Central and Lancaster Streets. Tag Day was typically held prior to the upcoming season, often early March. I recall it snowed in 1969.

Don Freda shared his experiences playing in the American Little League beginning in 1963. Freda played for Crossman's Minor League team which was sponsored by then Leominster Mayor Ralph Crossman. Mayor Crossman, who owned a neighborhood market on Merriam Avenue, also sponsored a Crossman's in the Leominster American Little League Majors. At that time in Leominster, both Major and Minor League teams played in an intercity championship playoff for the city crown. Freda's Little League idol, the future Leominster High School Hall of Fame inductee Gregg Picucci played on Crossman's Major League team and would be then shortstop Freda's infield partner at second-base for over twelve years, joining Freda on the Leominster High School, Leominster American Legion, Fitchburg State and the Acton A's semi-pro entry of the Stan Musial League baseball teams.

Figure 13: 1963 Crossman Minors of the Leominster American Little League (photo credit: Don Freda)
Front Row: Don Freda, Billy DiGregorio, Anthony Dellechiaie, Bob Caisse, Dave Brideau,
Bobby DiNardo, Alan Rouleau.
Back Row: Manager Hawk Decarolis, Mike Proietti, Melanson, Morrison, Eugene LaChance, Unknown,
Don Baril, Assistant Coach Mr. Eugene LaChance, Charlie "Rip" DiGloria Jr., Assistant Coach Charlie DiGloria, Sr.

My entry to Little League was relatively late as I entered the league as a 10-year-old, and therefore played my first two years in the minor league. As an 11-year-old I played with my brothers Mike (10) and Billy (8) for Leominster Credit Union. The practice at the time was to group brothers on the same team to minimize travel to games and practices for parents. That year in 1969 was the first time I experienced the thrill of having a new uniform. We opened that season with a parade down Mechanic Street with all of the league players, the Joanettes marching band and city luminaries. As a 12-year-old, I tried out and made the 1970 American League Ranchers along with brothers Mike and Billy.

Figure 14: Opening Day 1969 American Little League (photo credit: Mark Lefebvre)
From left to right: Mark, Billy and Mike Lefebvre

In 1970, we had a very good team led by the arm and the bat of returning ace Mike Leclair. We won the first half-season with a 6-1 record, while finishing in second behind Holdet Vise for the second half. Holdet Vise, led by Mike Gasbarro, Kevin Buckley and Alan Quiet won the American League championship defeating us in a best-of-three playoff. Three seasons later, my late brother Billy batted .710 for the 1973 Ranchers, a record that I imagine still stands to this day.

My first taste of local renown came in the summer of 1970 when I was a member of the American Little League All-Stars that went on to the Massachusetts Little League State Tournament in Oxford. Future Babe Ruth All-Star teammates Mike Leclair, Dave Arsenault, Doug Girouard, Jay Burke, and Mike Gasbarro were also on that team of 12-year-olds. Rick Gallien, Kevin Buckley, Alan Quiet, Paul Aubuchon, Buddy Vaillancourt, Scott Paquette, Dennis Moquin and Elijah Rodriquez were also selected for the team. After capturing the district and sectional championships, the local American Leaguers joined Parkway (of Roxbury), Wilmington, and Weymouth for a double-elimination tournament in Oxford, MA.

Figure 15: 1970 Ranchers team of the Leominster American Little League (photo credit: Mark Lefebvre)
Front Row: Mike Leclair, Scott Landry, Billy Lefebvre, Glen Fasquel, Pete Tellier
Back Row: Coach Landry, Mike Lefebvre, Elijah Rodriguez, Rick Gallien, Bob Gaudette, coach Pete Iacobone, Ed Cuddahy, Denis Moquin, Rick Iacobone, Mark Lefebvre, Coach Dick Gallien

Although the entire all-star season lasted a little more than a month, the summer seemed endless. On our way to the state tournament we defeated Lunenburg, Fitchburg East, Gardner, the Barry League stars of Worcester, and Great Barrington behind the dominant pitching of Mike Leclair and Jay Burke, and the bats of Burke, Leclair, and Alan Quiet who all hit home runs during that all-star run.

As good as we were, we were soundly defeated in consecutive games at the hands of the Wilmington and Weymouth stars. Parkway National of West Roxbury won the tournament and was crowned 1970 Massachusetts Little League State Champions.

Figure 16: 1970 Leominster American Little League All-Stars (photo credit: Leominster Enterprise, July 1970)
Front row: Elijah Rodriguez, Rick Gallien
Second row: Coach Paul Aubuchon, Scott Paquette, Denis Moquin, Kevin Buckley, Mark Lefebvre, Doug Girouard, Coach Paul Paquette
Third row: Buddy Vaillancourt, Jay Burke, Dave Arsenault, Alan Quiet, Mike Gasbarro, Paul Aubuchon, Mike Leclair

I recall fighting back tears in the back seat on the ride home from Oxford following the completion of the state tournament. After weeks of being swept away by the comradery, the community support, and yes, the attention, it was suddenly over. I felt empty and exhausted.

My dad and mom were up in the front seat when one of them sensed that I was crying. My mom leaned back over the front seat and tousled my hair and said, "we are very proud of you. And you'll have another opportunity."

In the weeks leading up to school that summer, the team was honored with an awards banquet hosted by the city. We each received warm-up jackets and trophies. One could spot one or several of us in the schoolyards and hallways of 7th grade later that fall by the yellow and blue warm-up jackets we all wore.

Figure 17: 1970 Little League Tournament Guide (photo credit: Mark Lefebvre)

That fall I met Leominster High School baseball coach Emile Johnson for the first time. In 1970, "Mr. Johnson" was my shop class instructor at Gallagher Junior High School, and apparently he was aware of our team's success over the previous summer. At our first class he passed around blank index cards and asked the students what sports we played. He also asked those of us who played baseball if we threw left-handed or right-handed, or batted left or right. When I said I threw right and batted left, Mr. Johnson looked at me sideways above his glasses and told me I'd be playing outfield for him at Leominster High School someday in the future.

Chapter Five: A Brief History of Babe Ruth Baseball

February 9, 2022, marked the 71st anniversary of the founding of what is known today as Babe Ruth Baseball. In 1951, ten citizens of Hamilton Township, NJ gathered to discuss the need for baseball for boys aged 13-15 for at that time there was a three-to-four-year gap between completion of Little League and the start of high school. Initially the league was called the Little Bigger league and in 1954 was renamed in honor of Babe Ruth through the kindness and support of the slugger's widow, Claire Ruth. With the re-branding, Babe Ruth League, Inc. became recognized both nationally and internationally.

From that first 10-team league in Hamilton Township, NJ, the league has grown to over one million players on over 59,000 teams in over 10,000 leagues across the world including Babe Ruth Baseball, Babe Ruth Softball, Cal Ripken Baseball, and Bambino Buddy-Ball. Notable milestones include the first BRL World Series in 1952, establishment of the 16-18-year-old division in 1966, formation of a 13-year-old Babe Ruth Prep League in 1974, establishment of the Babe Ruth Softball league for girls ages 4 through 18, and recognition of Boston Red Sox star Carl Yastrzemski as the first BRL graduate inducted into Major League Baseball's Hall of Fame in 1989.

Today Babe Ruth Baseball (13-15 years-old) is divided into 8 regions. The New England Region is comprised of Eastern and Western Massachusetts, Vermont, New Hampshire, Maine, Rhode Island and Connecticut. The other seven regions are Middle Atlantic, Southeast, Southwest, Ohio Valley, Midwest Plains, Pacific Southwest and Pacific Northwest. Canada is divided into three regions and competes in the Pacific Northwest, Midwest Plains and Middle Atlantic Regions. Puerto Rico and other Caribbean islands participate in the Southeast Region. China joined in the World Series in 2019.[10]

Chapter Six: Babe Ruth Baseball in Leominster

Any expectations that my participation on the American Little League All-Stars being a predictor of immediate success at the Babe Ruth level were immediately dashed shortly after I suited up for my rookie year playing for Donnie Bigelow and United Transportation (U-Trans). Traditionally, 13-year-olds didn't see much game time participation in Babe Ruth as there was a wide gap of abilities and especially size between 13-year-olds and 15-year-olds. Coaches, with player safety in mind, rightly eased the younger players into the mix.

My fragile ego and I were introduced to Babe Ruth via my first at-bat as a 13-year-old member of U-Trans. This at-bat took place during a so-called "mercy" inning when we were on the losing end of a one-sided affair against rival Tanzio Park. On the mound was perhaps one of the most feared pitchers at the time in all of Massachusetts, Rich Kelly. To say Kelly threw heat was a vast understatement.

With the bases empty and one out in the top of the seventh inning, Coach Donnie Bigelow snarled into the dugout, "Lefebvre, grab a bat. You're on deck." As I trudged up to the on-deck circle, trying to act like I actually belonged there, I pondered my dilemma. The game was out of reach, so there would be no pressure to advance a runner, I thought to myself. But before I had any time to mentally prepare myself, I heard the unmistakable pop of ball on leather and umpire Deico Pignata's shout, "Strike three! You're out!" It was now my turn at bat. Dead man walking.

With two outs I made my way to home plate like a prisoner on death row. My grandparents offered their encouragement from the stands. I soon realized that all of my accomplishments in Little League and what was left of my ego were non-factors as I meekly tapped my bat on home plate. With my mouth as dry as the summer air, I looked out to the mound and tried to gulp. My knees were shaking. I made eye contact with Kelly as he looked in to his catcher for the signal. He was a giant. At that moment, he and I both knew the outcome of this brief encounter as if it was pre-ordained by the creator. Needless to say, the bat never left my shoulder and I watched, or I should say, I *felt* three fastballs hit the mitt for a sudden and merciful end to the at-bat and the game. A lesson in humility for me and respect for Kelly would be my only takeaways from the experience. That lesson would serve me well as I doubled down on my commitment to grow as an athlete and as a person.

I shared this experience with Rich Kelly in an exchange about his experiences and this book. He commented that it was the same for him when he played as a 13-year-old and that he sympathized with that experience. He also acknowledged that his experiences from the 1971 all-star season were some of his most cherished memories from childhood.

Don Bigelow recalled my rookie year with a chuckle when I met with him and his wife Jackie recently in Leominster. "As coaches we tried to make it all about the kids, and to ease the transition given the age and physical disparities of kids 13-15 years old. I wouldn't have sent you up to bat against Kelly if I did not think you could handle it" (D. Bigelow, June 3, 2022). I only wish I shared his confidence in me when I trudged back to the dugout after that three-pitch whiff.

As a Babe Ruth League rookie, I was in awe of the 14–15-year-olds who made the 1971 all-star team. Pete Lieneck and Joe Cataldo were teammates of mine on U-Trans, and I saw first-hand the carnage they laid on opposing pitchers throughout that season. Steve Tata and Bryan Beaudette from TAG; Kelly, Dave Malatos, Joey Hamilton, Joe DePasquale and Jim Donnelly from Tanzio Park; Paul D'Onfro from Solar Chemical; Terry McNally and Steve Wentworth from Werner's Sporting Goods; and Paul Gamache and Bob Healey from Elks – all of these players exemplified the characteristics my impressionable 13-year-old mind sought out. Each of these players consistently displayed great skill, commitment, experience, teamwork, and leadership - traits that I would call upon throughout my own years as an athlete and continuing on throughout my adult life.

The Leominster Babe Ruth League was founded in 1952 and the league's reputation was established immediately as the local all-star team from that year went on to win the 1952 Massachusetts State Championship. Several familiar names and faces appear in the team photo below including future LHS baseball coach Emile Johnson.

Figure 18: 1952 Massachusetts State Champion Leominster Babe Ruth All-Stars (photo credit: 1972 Massachusetts Babe Ruth State Tournament Program Guide)
Front row (l-r): Doug White, James McNeil, William Smith, bat boy Harry McHugh
Middle row: Emile Johnson, Carl Baker, Louis Lambert, Paul Padavano, Dick Picucci, Phil White
Back row: Richard Cormier, Phil Fallon, Dan Hill, Don Deitzel, Dave Chester, Larry Boissoneau, Earl Divoll

Former Leominster Babe Ruth star and coach Mike Pavilaitis and I discussed some of the reasons Leominster had such a storied organizational history, and we both agreed that it was the volunteers who established and organized the Leominster Babe Ruth League. These volunteers included names like Jack McLaughlin, Bob Lamothe, Ray

Racine, Donnie Bigelow, Jim Marrone, Bob Boissoneau, and all of the managers, coaches, umpires, officials and volunteers who drafted and coached the players, organized the league schedules, coordinated the administrative activities with the state and regional BRL offices, groomed the fields, staffed the concessions, ran the scoreboard, liaised with the local media, and countless other functions behind the scenes. And we also acknowledged parents during that era who committed the time to transport their kids to practices and games, who showed up at the games, and who supported the league financially.

Up until around 1961, Leominster Babe Ruth games were played at Doyle Field. In 1961, the league acquired land at the current Lancaster Street location and immediately started construction of the original field which was completed in time for the 1962 season. Lights were added in 1966 and for most of us from that generation of players, playing on that field was the first opportunity to play night games. The land for the lower field was acquired in 1980 and constructed a few years later. By the mid-1980's games were being played at both fields.

Former Leominster police chief and original Leominster Babe Ruth president George Smith appointed Jack McLaughlin as league president in 1955 and McLaughlin served until 1998.[11] Under McLaughlin's stewardship, the league won fourteen state titles and made three BRL world series appearances as New England Regional champions.. In 1985, the Lancaster Street complex was named after McLaughlin for his dedication and service. He was also inducted into the Babe Ruth Hall of Fame in 2001.

Jack, or "Mr. McLaughlin" as he was respectfully referred to by the players, was a constant presence at the field. He would be seen raking the infield before games, lining batters' box and base baths, passing the tambourine during the games for donations, and talking with coaches, umpires and players before, during and after games. A lasting image that burns in my memory when I think back to the games at Lancaster Street was the sight of Jack McLaughlin chasing down foul balls that left the playing field, often outrunning any of the youngsters looking to score a free baseball.

Ray Racine, Sr. was another pioneer of the league and volunteered hundreds of hours of his time as a coach, and helping with field construction and maintenance. According to his son Ray, Jr., "my dad did quite a bit of work on Lancaster Street and he and Pin Cannavino were major contributors to the construction of the lower field. My dad had a construction background, and he built the old dugouts and block buildings."

Luis "Pin" Cannavino had been involved in Leominster Babe Ruth Baseball as a manager and coach for over 30 years. In 2007, the lower field at McLaughlin Park in Leominster was named the "Pin Cannavino Field" to commemorate his service to the league.

Since 1968, two divisions of Babe Ruth were in operation. Division 1 teams included United Transportation (U-Trans), Tanzio Park (formerly Minuteman), Solar Chemical, TAG, Werner's Sporting Goods of Lunenburg, Elks, and Sterling Lumber of Sterling. In 1968 the league added the second division to meet the demand and to offer younger players a chance for more playing time.

Division 2 teams included ACWA, Leominster News, Modern Tool, Moose, AFL-CIO, and Russo's for Lunenburg kids. During the period between 1971 and 1973 there were at least 180 youngsters playing Babe Ruth baseball in any of those seasons. Practices were typically held during the weekend, usually on Saturday mornings at the park. Towards the end of the 1960's, Leominster Babe Ruth League managers included Charlie DiGloria (Solar), Bob Boissoneau (TAG), Bob Lamothe (Minuteman), Don Bigelow (U-Trans), John Campobasso (Elks), and Herb Hill (Werner's).

Figure 19: John "Jack" McLaughlin at Babe Ruth League Hall of Fam Induction, 2001 (photo credit: Babe Ruth Baseball Hall of Fame)

Figure 20: Volunteer Bob Boissoneau mowing the Lancaster Street Field circa 1967 (photo credit: Leominster Historical Society)

Don Freda recalls his days playing Babe Ruth baseball. "I played on the Minuteman Sand & Gravel team coached by the legendary Bob Lamothe, the knowledgeable Frank Nass, and the grandfatherly Alton Harris. Lamothe was fun to play for and even though he coached his son, our catcher Bobby, Lamothe coached and volunteered his time long before and after his sons had aged out." Lamothe's other son, Ron, who went on to become the head baseball coach at Lunenburg High School, coached to 250 wins, and was inducted into the Massachusetts Baseball Coaches Association Hall of Fame.

"Coach Lamothe's practices were simple, focused on fundamentals, and involved everyone," continued Freda. "One way we conducted batting practice was to take the field while a batter got his turn in the box, and with another on deck. After the first hitter completed his turn, he moved to right-field. The right-fielder then moved to center-field, while that player went to left, and everybody else rotated through the positions. This gave me the opportunity to not get pigeon-holed into one position. It kept the practices interesting, and it allowed me chances to play these other positions I was not used to. All hits were 'live,' so we had to make the plays from each position instead of just fielding and tossing the ball back to the mound. I was fortunate in my youth baseball career in Leominster to actually play every position on the field in real games. This experience was invaluable to me when I started my coaching career."

Dave Bergeron who also played for Lamothe, but from 1971-1973, recalls fondly the lessons learned on the playing field from the countless volunteers and parents who supported the league. Dave's father Fran was the league treasurer for over 10 years and handled all of the financial affairs for the league. His grandfather was awarded "Fan of the Year" in 1983 in honor of his dedicated service to the league.

Figure 21: 1969 Minuteman team (photo credit: Don Freda)
Back row (l-r): Lance McCarthy, Mike Nutting, Dave Antocci, Dave Bilodeau
Front row (l-r): Donny Freda, Timmy Hulecki, Tommy Kelly, Jimmy Malatos, Tony Dinardo, Steve Corliss, Billy Pananos

"You could always tell when Coach Lamothe arrived for practice or for a game. He drove an enormous Buick convertible loaded with players he picked up along the way," mused Bergeron. Dave also pointed out that the success of the league over the years was especially due to the leadership of Jack McLaughlin. "His leadership, his demeanor and his commitment set the example for league officials, volunteers, coaches, umpires and players."

It was not unusual to see over a hundred fans on a given weeknight during those summers in the late 1960's and early 1970's. Many of these fans would come from across town just to enjoy competitive baseball on such a beautiful field. It was common to see folks from the Lancaster Street and Willard Street neighborhoods flock to the field carrying lawn chairs and of course, bug spray.

Figure 22: 1967 Leominster Babe Ruth All-Stars (photo credit: Don Freda)
Front row: Greg Picucci, Ken Goss, Dick Ingemie, Tim Hannon, Brian Kane, John Cormier, Kevin Haverty
Back row: Coach Larry Boissoneau, Coach Bob Lamothe, Randy Bigelow, Billy Ruggles, Fred Salvatelli, Tony Piermarini, Steve Mahoney, Tom Fraturelli, Tony Pandiscio, John Fraturelli, Manager Len Warner

The mosquitoes at the Lancaster Street fields were legendary, especially once the lights came on. The fields border the Nashua River, and the surrounding area is heavily wooded. Playing in the outfield without bug spray was a losing proposition. If a player didn't spend the inning in the outfield swatting bugs, he was spitting out mosquitoes that were inhaled from the cloud surrounding his head. It was no better in the stands. Cans of OFF! were as ubiquitous as Bazooka Joe bubble gum.

Section 2: Insane Talent - 1971 Babe Ruth All-Stars

Figure 23: 1971 Leominster Babe Ruth All-Stars (photo credit: 1972 Massachusetts BRL State Tournament Guide)
Front row: Bat Boy Chuck Marrone, Dave Malatos, Terry McNally, Paul Gamache, Joe DePasquale, Steve Tata. **Middle row**: Jim Donnelly, Bob Healey, Joe Hamilton, Bryan Beaudette, Paul D'Onfro, Rich Kelly.
Back row: Manager Jim Marrone, Joe Cataldo, Steve Wentworth, Coach Bob Boissoneau, Pete Lieneck, Coach Paul Harris.

Chapter Seven: The Team

Coach Jim Marrone

Today I can close my eyes and still see Coach Jim Marrone standing on the top step of the dugout, surveying the game situation. He'd be conferring with coaches Paul Harris and Steve Campobasso regarding his options and weigh the risks in his mind. One could almost hear the gears turning as he ran out to the field to instruct his charges to be alert for a given situation. "Gamache, grab a bat," Marrone would bark. "Arsenault, keep your head down on the ball," he'd shout after a swing and a miss.

During the 1973 state tournament, I had singled and was on first-base. The opposing team had a left-handed pitcher on the mound, and I fell for his clever footwork resulting in me being picked off first-base for the out. "Lefebvre, get your shit together," I heard Marrone shout from the 3rd base coaching box as I dusted off my pants and nursed my bruised ego.

My teammate Dave Bergeron recalls Marrone as a confident mentor who "treated us all with honesty and respect. We were always prepared for any game situation by practicing live scenarios on a regular basis."

Throughout his all-star coaching tenure from 1971-1973, all of Marrone's players could hit, field, run and play numerous positions. What Coach Marrone instilled in us was a work ethic and team first attitude. There were no teams more prepared in any of those tournaments than the Leominster all-star teams.

Jim Donnelly who played on the 1971 and 1972 all-stars recalled that he was approached by Marrone before the first game of the 1972 state tournament versus Lawrence. Donnelly, as a returning all-star and one of the best players on that team, fully expected to make his usual start at second-base. Marrone pulled Donnelly aside and told him that he would be starting Steve Jackson at second-base for that game. He explained that Jackson had been performing better at practices and had earned the start. While Donnelly at that time was clearly disappointed, he now appreciates that Marrone was honest and up front with him regarding his decision. Because of Marrone's communication style, Donnelly recalls shrugging it off and assumed that the decision was best for the team. "Coach Marrone was a great communicator," said Donnelly. "It really struck me over the years that he cared about us all, and made decisions that gave us the best chance for success."

James Joseph (Jim) Marrone was born in Brooklyn, N.Y., and was a 1953 graduate of Leominster High School, where he played football, baseball, basketball, and swam for the LHS swim team. He was a classmate of my mom in high school, a fact that escaped me until conducting research for this book. Following high school, he served in both the Korean and Vietnam wars as an Air Force technician. [12]

Figure 24: Jim Marrone, LHS Class of 1953 (photo credit: 1953 LHS *Magnet* Yearbook)

1972 and 1973 all-star Jay Burke recalls fishing for bass with Coach Marrone years later up at Hy-Crest Pond, a few miles from the Sterling town line. "We'd paddle in a canoe on hot summer evenings when the bass were active. One night I caught a 6-lb largemouth in a canoe with Marrone."

Burke also recall Marrone as a tremendous in-game tactician. "Coach would walk down the base line to the fence and back to the dugout with me after pre-game warm-ups to discuss game strategy. These talks included how he wanted us to pitch certain hitters. He was always looking for an edge."

Marrone coached for Elks in the Leominster Babe Ruth League for several years and led the All-Stars to 3 consecutive Massachusetts State Championships in from 1971-1973. We lost coach Marrone in 2003 after he was stricken ill.

Rich Kelly

A block from May A. Gallagher Jr. High and a stone's throw to Northwest School Field, the neighborhood of Orchard Street and the surrounding 2-block area consisting of Merriam Avenue, Walnut Street, Grove Avenue and Washington Street, was the essence of residential city life. Tall and majestic Victorian, Colonial, and New Englander homes were connected via back yard fences and front yard sidewalks whose surfaces were rutted by the roots of ancient elm, maple and oak trees.

Rich Kelly grew up on Orchard Street in a neighborhood that included future all-stars and Notre Dame teammates Ted Rockwell and Steve Tata. Throw in Leominster High School baseball, basketball, hockey, and football stars such as Rick Comeau, Rick Daigneault and Jack O'Donnell, and you might have asked, "what's in the water up on Orchard Street?"

It was within this neighborhood where a young Rich Kelly spent his summer days playing whiffle ball, baseball, street hockey and basketball. As Kelly recalls, "just on Orchard Street alone where I grew up the neighborhood was loaded with some of the city's best athletes across all sports - Kelly, Rockwell, Daigneault, and O'Donnell. Around the corner was Tata, Marchand and Comeau. Outside of Little League we spent hundreds of hours playing baseball at Northwest Field. We spent much of our time playing basketball and other activities at the Leominster Recreation Center right down the street, and countless hours playing football on Orchard Street, right on the street."

Kelly played for Tilco in the Leominster National Little League at Northwest Field, Pop Warner with the Giants, St. Leo's for parochial league basketball, and Leominster Rec Center for city-league basketball. As a grade-schooler, he went to St. Leo's for grades 1-8 and then Notre Dame High School in Fitchburg where he starred in baseball, basketball and football. In 1972 Kelly earned Offensive Player of the Year honors at Notre Dame.

During the summers between his high school years, Rich played American Legion baseball for Leominster under the tutelage of coach Emile Johnson. After graduating from Notre Dame High School, Kelly went to pitch for the Minutemen of UMass.

"Those Babe Ruth years were some of the best playing days of my life," muses Kelly. "Not only were we an exceptional team at every position, but we also had a lot of fun both on and off the field. Ironically, but not surprisingly, our most difficult games were against local teams, especially Fitchburg. Aside from the 'anomaly' of a 16-15 comeback win in the State Tournament, we pretty much had our way with everyone else. Our time spent in Lynn with the most gracious host families was a great experience. I stayed connected with my host family (the Lords) for a few years after our time there. As far as the regionals held in Nashua, we had even an easier time with the other New England state champions, averaging I believe runs in the teens. The team from Puerto Rico that we and the other two Leominster teams unfortunately lost to in the finals, in my opinion, should never had participated in the New England region which is a 5-hour flight away. I understand that Puerto Rico has since been repositioned to another, much closer region after the 1973 season which is where they belong. It certainly would have accomplishment never to be replicated again, for one city to represent the region three straight years at the Babe Ruth World Series" (R. Kelly, June 15, 2021).

Steve Tata
Steve Tata also hailed from the same neighborhood as Kelly, growing on Walnut Street and playing baseball at Northwest School with other neighbors Rich and Tom Kelly, Ted Rockwell, Bob Angelini, Billy Grady, and Ricky Marchand. A typical summer day for youngster Steve Tata was playing whiffle ball with Rich Kelly in his backyard, using a folding chair set up as a strike zone, followed by basketball at Bennett School at night.

Tata dominated in hoops from a very young age, playing basketball for St. Ann's in the grammar school league, and starring for the Bullets in the Leominster Rec League. He made the Rec League all-star team in 1966 and 1967 playing in that youth league that was hosted at Carter Junior High School. He, like many of his friends, played Pop Warner football for the Leominster Dolphins.

In Little League, Tata played for Tilco and made the National Little League all-stars. He recently shared one of the highlights of his Little League career when I interviewed him for this book. "I had just hit a home-run in the districts and was interviewed by local sportswriter and reporter, Ken Albridge on WLMS radio after the game," Tata recalls. Here I was, 12-years-old and on the radio!"

Tata was drafted by coach Bob Boissoneau to play for TAG in Leominster's Babe Ruth League, and as a lead-off hitter, quickly developed a reputation for his bat and his speed on the bases. During that magical summer of 1971, Tata would play second-base and bat lead-off for Marrone's all-star squad, leading the team in stolen bases during that all-star run.

"What stands out for me thinking back to the summer of 1971 was the hospitality of the Nashua community and host families who took us in. I roomed with Bryan Beaudette, and they treated us great," recalls Tata. "And can't say enough about the following of the Leominster crowd, even folks from Fitchburg. Playing against Puerto Rico was overwhelming. Coach Marrone was great guy, and I learned a lot about character and commitment from the likes of coaches Paul Harris, Bob Boissoneau and umpire Deico Pignata. These men and many others in the extended Babe Ruth community helped us all build character."

After attending Gallagher Junior High school for grades 7 and 8, Tata transferred to Notre Dame High School in Fitchburg where he excelled in both baseball and basketball, earning team MVP honors in 1972. During the 1970's, Notre Dame basketball was dominant, often being among the top teams in the state. Tata, Rich Kelly and Bob Angelini joined Marty Caron and Jim "Soup" Campbell as among the best players during that dynasty run. During those high school summers, Tata played American Legion baseball for Leominster Post 151 with most of his Babe Ruth all-stars teammates playing along with him. After graduating from Notre Dame, Tata attended Nichols College in Dudley, playing three years of baseball and four years basketball averaging 16 points per game and earning all-conference recognition.

Steve still lives in Leominster with his wife Sally and splits his time between Leominster and Florida, (S. Tata, July, 26, 2022).

Paul Gamache
Paul Gamache is the third of six sons of Roger and Jeanne Gamache. I had come to know Paul and his youngest brother Danny through my friendship with brother Peter, who was my Babe Ruth all-star teammate and roommate in Lynn for the 1973 New England Regionals.

The Gamache's spent their early childhoods living on Grafton Street just past the intersection of Route's 2 and 12 (N. Main Street) on the northwest side of Leominster. Paul recently shared that the Gamache boys and the Tucker boys (future and legendary Nashoba Regional High School football coach Ken Tucker, and future LHS star Don Tucker) would play baseball and football on the hilly street where they lived. They would bat uphill and then switch sides. For football, offense would run uphill, and again, they would switch sides.

The family moved to upper Union Street later during their youth which gave the Gamache boys more room to roam and play in the Fall Brook school area. On Sundays, I would often see the brothers lined up between their mom and dad in their usual pew at Holy Family Church.

Paul played Little League for Dupont in the National Little League with future Leominster Babe Ruth Baseball stars Mike Pignata, Rick Comeau, Greg Carchidi, Steve Jackson and future LHS and Holy Cross standout Rick Daigneault. Following Little League, Paul was drafted by Jim Marrone to play for Elks. A standout pitcher and infielder, Paul was one of the rarest of players to play for two Massachusetts State Champion Babe Ruth all-star teams.

Paul was a three-sport standout at Saint Bernard's High School in Fitchburg where he starred as a running back for the football team, guard for the hoops team, and shortstop for the baseball Bernardians. He went on to play basketball at Merrimac College. Paul currently lives near Venice, Florida with his wife Janet and enjoys golf and the beach (P. Gamache, May 20, 2022).

Dave Malatos
There were very few athletes in my experience who played with the intensity and fearlessness that Dave Malatos brought to his game. Whether it was baseball, football, or ice hockey, Malatos always showed up to play. It didn't matter if was a tryout, practice, or game, he had one objective in mind and that was to win.

Dave Malatos is the son of late long-time city councilor James

Malatos and mother Janet. He batted and threw left-handed and often displayed his cannon of an arm from right-field. In 1967 he made the Leominster American Little League all-stars. Following Little League he was drafted by Bob Lamothe to play for Tanzio in Babe Ruth.

Following Babe Ruth he was a 3-year starter for Leominster High School S baseball, playing right-field and occasionally pitching in relief. He hit for power, could lay down a sacrifice bunt, steal bases, and hold runners on base with his defensive reputation. I was privileged to be his teammate at LHS. During his senior year in high school he batted .311 with 3 homeruns and 23 RBI's in 22 games. Later that summer he led the Leominster American Legion squad with a with a ridiculous .484 average.

In addition to baseball, Malatos also starred for the LHS football and hockey teams. He started all three years of his high school football career under the tutelage of Huck Hannigan. As a linebacker and special teams player, he scored the winning touchdown following a blocked punt in overtime over Chicopee for the 1974 Central/Western Massachusetts Division 1 Super Bowl championship. Following high school, he joined LHS teammate Dick Freda and attended Eckerd College in Florida for the 1977 team that finished runner-up for the NCAA Division II World Series championship. Other Eckerd teammates included future Major League Baseball all-stars Joe Lefebvre (Concord, NH) and Steve Balboni (Manchester, NH).

Steve Wentworth
Steve Wentworth starred as the centerfielder for the 1973 Babe Ruth all-stars, and joined Werner's Sporting Goods teammate Terry McNally as the Lunenburg representatives for the team. As a youngster, Steve played for the P.J. Keating Mets in the Lunenburg Little League, where he pitched and played outfield. In addition to baseball, Steve played hoops for Fitchburg Paper in the Lunenburg Park Department Junior Basketball

League.

Following Babe Ruth, Steve attended Lunenburg High School where he starred as a tight end, defensive end and punter for the football Blue Knights. He earned Wachusett League All-Star honors in football for 1973 season. In baseball, he played center-field for the division leading Lunenburg High School team.

Terry McNally
Terry McNally was the oldest of five kids and grew up on Rennie Street in Lunenburg. With three boys (brothers Kevin and Brian), plus two sisters (Maureen "Mo" and Kathy), life at the McNally home was anything but boring. Mom Jeanette (Jinx) and dad Bob were Lunenburg town favorites, always there for their kids, and known for their witty repartee around the kitchen table. As a frequent guest of the McNally's (Brian was one of my best friends during my teen years), I could not help but think of the Kramden's on the Honeymooners TV show.

Terry and his brothers were each three-sport standouts, and were always up for a game whether it was playing ice hockey on the rink behind the Demers' house or at the pond at the end of Pratt Street. They played football and whiffleball in their back yard, or pick-up baseball at nearby Lesure Field with the "West Street Gang."

"There was always a game to be played - every day and all day," mused Terry when I caught up with him for this book. "The West Street crew would bike up to Marshall field to play the Whalom gang and there would always be enough players to put together two full teams."

The West Side gang would play hoops at Wallis Park. Terry also played for the Apothecary Celtics in the Lunenburg Junior Basketball League in 1969 with brothers Kevin and Brian, and coached by his dad Bob.

In summer, Terry played Little League baseball for the Lunenburg Cardinals with his younger brother Kevin. The Cardinals were also coached by their dad Bob McNally. Terry was dominating on the mound, once striking out 17 of 18 possible batters against the PJ Keating Mets. He made the 1968 Lunenburg Little League All-Stars with future Babe Ruth All-Star Jeff Johnson. In Babe Ruth he played for Werner's and credits coaches Herb Hill and Tim Hillman for his development as a baseball player.

In high school, Terry was a standout 3-sport athlete playing football, hockey, and baseball. During his senior year he had a 7-1 record for the 16-1 Lunenburg Wachusett League regular season champions. He played defense for the Blue Knights hockey team and was again joined on-ice by brothers Kevin and Brian. Terry recently shared when on the power play lineup, Kevin was a forward, Terry was a defenseman and freshman Brian was the other defenseman. He wondered aloud how it would have been like for his dad Bob to see the three McNally boys on the ice at the same time for Lunenburg High School hockey.

Terry played American Legion baseball for Leominster in 1974 and went on to play at Fitchburg State. He continues to work as a sales rep in the Information Technology sector, selling fiber-optic systems. He currently lives in Leominster and enjoys time with this three grandchildren (T. McNally, March 13, 2022).

Joe Cataldo
Joe Cataldo and his older brother Eddie would practically live at the Northwest School field during the spring and summer days of their youth, so much so that their mom, Genevieve, would often bring them lunch at the field. Joining the Cataldo boys would be neighborhood friends Rick Marchand, Rich Kelly, Rick Comeau and Tim Conway as part of Orchard Street gang. "I was living every boy's dream." Cataldo remembers. "We had everything we needed, everything we wanted in the safety of our neighborhood."

The Cataldo's lived on lower Washington Street, a stone's throw from the Northwest School which offered basketball courts and two baseball diamonds. Joe, the future three-sport star at St. Bernard's High School, developed into a special baseball talent who could hit for power, play flawless defense, and steal a base on demand.

Older brother Eddie was two years Joe's senior and they both played for Kingman in the Leominster National Little League for coach Al Steinmetz. Joe made the National League All-Stars in 1968 and was drafted by coach Don Bigelow to play on the 1969 U-Trans squad of the Leominster Ruth League. Once again, Joe would join older brother Eddie who played first-base for U-Trans.

Joe was selected to play third-base for 1971 Babe Ruth All-Stars and would bat 3rd in the lineup for manager Jim Marrone. Following his Babe Ruth success, Joe went on to star at St. Bernard's where he played varsity baseball (third-base), basketball (guard, forward), and football (quarterback, defensive back, kicker). He also played for Emile Johnson on the 1973 and 1974 Leominster American League squad. He eventually played baseball at the University of Miami.

Joe and his family currently reside in Fitchburg, and he remains active on the local athletic scene having run softball camps, coaching softball and baseball, and was the former Wachusett High girls' softball coach. He founded Cat Inspection Services in 1997, and ran the city of Leominster's Office of Planning Development for 33 years. He is an avid outdoors-man and hunter, spending his free time in the woods of Sterling (J. Cataldo, March 7, 2022).

Pete Lieneck
Pete Lieneck and his family lived in North Leominster on Prospect Street a few hundred yards up the hill from Pete's Coffee Shop. He recently shared with me that he and his brothers Marty and John liked to play baseball in the parking lot of Monoosnock Country Club, much to the peril of cars in that lot.

Pete played for King's Corner of the North Leominster Little League at Bernice Avenue with his brother Marty. Following Little League, U-Trans coach Don Bigelow drafted Lieneck to pitch and play shortstop during the 1969 draft. During my rookie season for U-Trans, Lieneck and Joe Cataldo were the team leaders and terrorized opposing pitchers.

Lieneck attended Leominster High School and started all three years in baseball and football. He also played basketball and ran indoor track at LHS from 1971-1973. During the summers, he played three years of American Legion ball for Leominster Post 151. Coach Emile Johnson shared that Lieneck was one of his best players ever when I interviewed him for this book.

After graduating from Leominster, Lieneck attended Nichols College in Dudley, MA, with fellow Babe Ruth and Legion teammate Steve Tata, at which he played both football and baseball. At Nichols, he was inducted in to the Nichols College Athletic Hall of Fame. He also played semi-pro baseball for the Acton A's.

Today, Lieneck lives in Florida where he founded and operates a retail furniture business (Pete Lieneck, February 21, 2022).

Joe Hamilton
Joe Hamilton was drafted by Coach Bob Lamothe to play for Tanzio Park as a pitcher and catcher. During his final year of Babe Ruth eligibility, Hamilton and teammate Rich Kelly would frequently pitch to or catch each other, providing Lamothe with a formidable battery.

Hamilton's arm and bat were major factors for Leominster's state championship run in 1973. Against Concord, New Hampshire, in the New England Regional tournament in August of 1973, Hamilton drove in 8 runs in that one game.

Following Babe Ruth, Hamilton attended Leominster High School where he played three years of football as a defensive back and fullback. He also played baseball (catcher) and basketball (guard) at LHS.

Bob Healey

Bob Healey grew up on North Street in North Leominster near King's Corner, playing neighborhood ball with the Jim Donnelly and Donnelly's brothers. He played for Duval's in the North Leominster Little League and joined future Leominster Babe Ruth all-star teammates Paul D'Onfro, Jim Donnelly, Bryan Beaudette and Pete Lieneck on their all-star team.

Coach Jim Marrone drafted Healey to play for Elks in the Leominster Babe Ruth League, and to pitch and play outfield. Bob was a versatile player for Elks, capable of hitting for power and laying down a bunt.

Following Babe Ruth he played baseball and football for the LHS Blue Devils. As a gifted punter for the Blue Devils, Healey was a key piece of the 1974 Super Bowl Champion team under coach Huck Hannigan.

Perhaps most notable is that Bob Healey served on Leominster's police force from 1978 until his retirement in 2015, and was Leominster's Chief of Police from 2011 until his retirement.

Jim Donnelly

Jim Donnelly spent his childhood playing ball with this three older and two younger brothers in the North Street neighborhood near Kings Corner in North Leominster. One of nine children, Jim and his siblings were never seeking companionship for any extended period of time. Whalom Park and Lake were walking distance from the Donnelly home. The North American Little League field was a short bike ride. On any summer day there would always be a game to be played.

Jim, his brothers, and the Perkins boys (John, Mike and Pat) would also play hardball in one of the sandlots in the neighborhood. They'd play tackle football on the grass fields and touch football on the street. In the winter they would sling their skates over their hockey sticks and shovels, and head off to the small pond in the woods nearby. Sometimes future Babe Ruth League all-star teammate Terry McNally and some of the other guys from Lunenburg would join in the scrum.

Donnelly played for Duval's in the North American Little League and made the all-stars his final year. Bob Lamothe, the legendary Tanzio Park manager drafted Jim to play Babe Ruth baseball. Jim chuckles when thinking about coach Lamothe. "Bob was kind of a surrogate father for me during those years. My dad was rehabilitating from an illness and coach would drive me to and from practice and games. It was not unusual for Bob to make multiple stops to pick up the Nutting's, Corliss's and other teammates along the way. He pretty much ran a bus service."

At the age of thirteen Jim badly injured his right wrist playing baseball, diving for a ball that resulted in damaged tendons and nerves in his throwing hand. This injury stayed with him throughout his three years in Babe Ruth, affecting throws to first and plaguing him with a lack of confidence when making those throws. As a result, his interest in baseball began to wane by the team he reached high school.

At St. Bernard's, Donnelly starred in football where he was a team MVP running back. He also played on the inaugural St. Bernard's ice hockey team which only a few years later made it to the old Boston Garden for the Massachusetts state hockey championship game. After graduating from St. Bernard's in 1975, Donnelly spent a year at UMass Amherst and the Fitchburg State College where he played ball alongside Terry McNally and Steve Jackson.

Jim is retired and living at the Cape with his wife of 40 years, Mary Ann. The Donnelly's have two daughters and three grandchildren. He spends his time cross-fit training and enjoys running sprint triathlons (J. Donnelly, May 23, 2022).

Joe DePasquale

Joe DePasquale played for Tanzio Park as an outfielder and was known for his glove and speed. He was particularly feared by opposing base runners for the strength and accuracy of his arm.

Following Babe Ruth Baseball, Joe graduated from Leominster High School, class of 1973, and was a proud member of the football team for which he played safety and kicker for coach Huck Hannigan.

Sadly, Joe DePasquale passed in 2017.[13]

Bryan Beaudette

Bryan Beaudette was a magnetic presence wherever he went, and it seemed that he was always smiling and always having fun, especially when playing baseball, soccer or ice hockey. Bryan grew up in North Leominster and was a regular at the Pierce School playground and the North American Little League Field on Bernice Avenue. He would often be joined by other neighborhood friends and fellow all-star teammates Paul D'Onfro, Jim Donnelly, Bob Healey, and Pete Lieneck.

Bryan played for Barone's in the North Leominster Little League as a pitcher and first-baseman. He batted and threw from the left side. Along with Healey, Lieneck, Donnelly, and D'Onfro, Bryan made the 1968 North Leominster Little League all-stars.

During the 1969 Leominster Babe Ruth League draft, Coach Bob Boissoneau of TAG drafted him to play first-base and pitch. During the 1971 season Bryan was consistently among the top ten hitters in the league. Former umpire Joe Charielle remembers Beaudette in the batter's box. "Bryan had had the sweetest swing and in hindsight reminded me of Ken Griffey, Jr," he mused. "Bryan never lost control of his bat speed, yet when he made contact, that ball was drilled."

Bryan played varsity baseball, soccer and ice hockey for the LHS Blue Devils and graduated in 1974. Following high school, Bryan owned and operated a number of coin-op businesses in the community. He was a star softball player in the Leominster Men's Softball League. I recall playing softball for Hospital Road in that league, and playing against Bryan, who then played for Tam 'O Shanter, in the 1979 league championship finals. My brother Billy had passed a couple of days earlier and the game was in the evening of day we laid Billy to rest. After the last of our extended family and friends departed the reception at our home, my parents convinced me that I should join my teammates for the game. After we won the championship game, Bryan pulled me aside and gave me a big hug and said he knew how difficult it was for me to be playing that game. It was a very kind gesture from a great man.

Bryan Beaudette passed in 2009 and is missed dearly by his family and friends.[14]

Paul D'Onfro
Paul D'Onfro grew up on Main Street in North Leominster, and spent his childhood year's playing ball with his brother Steve and their neighborhood friends at Pierce School, the North Leominster Little League field on Bernice Avenue, and Monoosnock Country Club. He was a star player for Barone's in the North Leominster Little League and was an all-star teammate of Bryan Beaudette, Jim Donnelly, Pete Lieneck, and Bob Healey.

Following Little League, Paul played for TAG as an outfielder and occasional pitcher. He earned a spot on the 1971 Leominster Babe Ruth all-stars and made significant contributions in the field and at bat for that state championship team. He was a favorite of coach Jim Marrone due to his speed, versatility to play multiple positions, and his patience at the plate.

Paul was a 3-sport star at Leominster High School, playing football, running track, and wrestling. On the football field, Paul started at quarterback and safety during his senior year, but saw his season cut short as a result of a shoulder separation suffered during a win over Marlboro.

Paul graduated in June of 1973 and went on to study at University of Massachusetts Amherst and Albany Law School.

I got to know Paul through my friendship with his younger brother Steve who also played quarterback and safety for LHS. I recall many ice-fishing excursions on Spec, Fort, and Stuart ponds with Paul, Steve, Kevin Buckley, Rick Daigneault and many other Leominster men during our high school and college years.

Paul D'Onfro passed away in 2018 at the age of 62. He was predeceased by his brother Steve in 2008.[15]

Chapter Eight: The Games

Athol vs. Leominster, Friday, July 9, 1971
The 1971 Leominster Babe Ruth All-Stars kicked off their season at home with a convincing 7-1 victory over Athol on Friday night, July 9, under the lights at the Lancaster Street Field. Rich Kelly got the nod on the mound for the locals with Joe Hamilton behind the plate as his battery mate. Kelly held Athol to one hit and only 3 base-runners in total in a dominating performance.

Leominster got on the board in their half of the first inning when lead-off batter and second-baseman Steve Tata drew a walk and immediately stole second. After right-fielder Dave Malatos went down swinging, third-baseman Joe Cataldo flied out to left field. With two outs, shortstop Pete Lieneck laced a double to the right-center-field gap bringing in Tata with the game's first run.

Leominster struck again in the third inning when both Tata and Malatos walked with one out. Cataldo then launched a towering home run over the left-field fence increasing Leominster's lead to 4-0.

In the fourth inning Leominster pushed two more runs across the plate. Catcher Joe Hamilton got the offense going with a single followed by his theft of second-base. After center-fielder Steve Wentworth struck out, left-fielder Bob Healey homered over the left-center-field fence for a 6-0 Leominster lead.

Athol finally got on the scoreboard in the sixth inning when center-fielder Pete Cetto walked, stole second and scored on an infield error. Leominster added an insurance run in their half of the sixth when left-fielder Paul D'Onfro, substituting for Healey, walked, stole second and scored all the way from second on a throwing error by the catcher. Final score Leominster 7, Athol 1.[16][17]

Leominster	AB	R	H	RBI
Tata, 2b	1	2	0	0
Donnelly, 2b	0	0	0	0
Malatos, rf	2	1	0	0
Cataldo, 3b	4	1	1	3
Lieneck, ss	4	0	2	1
Kelly, p	3	0	1	0
Beaudette, 1b	3	0	0	0
McNally, 1b	1	0	0	0
Wentworth, cf	2	0	0	0
DePasquale, cf	1	0	0	0
Healey, lf	2	1	1	2
D'Onfro, lf	0	1	0	0
Totals	**23**	**7**	**5**	**6**
Athol	**AB**	**R**	**H**	**RBI**
Ainsworth, 2b	2	0	0	0
Burnett, 1b	3	0	0	0
Niedzwiedz, ss	3	0	0	0
King, cf-p	3	0	0	0
Kistler, lf	3	0	0	0
Godin, 3b	2	0	0	0
Tie, c	2	0	0	0
Cetto, cf-p	1	1	0	0
Lavigne, p-cf	1	0	1	0
Phelps, rf	2	0	0	0
Totals	**22**	**1**	**1**	**0**

Fitchburg vs. Leominster, Sunday, July 11, 1971

Two days following the win over Athol, the 1971 all-stars took on the Fitchburg nine at Leominster's Lancaster Street field. Joe Hamilton got the nod to start on the hill with Tanzio teammate Rich Kelly behind the plate as his battery mate. Hamilton did not disappoint with a stellar two-hit complete game shut-out performance as the locals defeated their rivals 6-0, thereby advancing to the district finals to face West County.

Leominster scored the only run they would need in the second inning as shortstop Pete Lieneck worked Fitchburg starter Don Lemieux for a walk and stole second. Lieneck scored on a double down the right field off the bat of Kelly, giving Leominster a 1-0 lead after two innings.

In the bottom half of the fourth inning Leominster broke the game open with a four-run outburst. Third-baseman Joe Cataldo got things going with a single and a stolen base. U-Trans teammate Lieneck singled Cataldo to third and promptly stole second putting men on second and third with no outs. Kelly walked to load the sacks with pitcher Hamilton coming to the plate. Following a short trip to the mound by the Fitchburg manager, Hamilton walked forcing in the second Leominster run.

Pete Maggs came in to relieve Lemieux but immediately threw a wild pitch past catcher Mark Chartrand scoring Lieneck, and advancing runners to second and third with no outs. Following a walk to center-fielder Steve Wentworth to again load the bases, left-fielder Bob Healey forced Kelly out at home. However, an error on the part of Chartrand allowed Hamilton and Wentworth to score the fourth and fifth Leominster runs. Healey advanced to third-base on the error. With one out, Bryan Beaudette lofted a sacrifice fly to right field which scored Healey. After four innings Leominster led 6-0.

Leominster managed only 6 hits in the contest with second-baseman Paul Gamache, Malatos, Cataldo, Lieneck and Hamilton hitting singles. Kelly had the only extra-base hit in the game with his double. Fitchburg managed only two singles off Hamilton, coming off the bats of left-fielder Rich Viens and right-fielder Gary Linder.[18]

Leominster	AB	R	H
Tata, 2b	3	0	0
Gamache, 2b	1	0	1
Malatos, rf	4	0	1
Cataldo, 3b	2	1	1
Lieneck, ss	2	2	1
Kelly, c	2	0	1
Hamilton, p	1	1	1
Wentworth, cf	1	1	0
DePasquale, cf	1	0	0
Healey, lf	2	1	0
D'Onfro, lf	1	0	0
Beaudette, 1b	1	0	0
McNally, 1b	1	0	0
Totals	**22**	**6**	**6**

Fitchburg	AB	R	H
Pelletier, cf	3	0	0
Linder, rf	3	0	1
DePasquale, 2b	2	0	0
Viens, lf	3	0	1
Dame, 3b	3	0	0
Pelland, 1b	1	0	0
Boudreau, 1b	2	0	0
Rivers, ss	2	0	0
Finn, ph	1	0	0
Chartrand, c	2	0	0
Stone, c	0	0	0
Lemieux, p	1	0	0
Maggs, p	0	0	0
McCluskey, p	1	0	0
Totals	**24**	**0**	**2**

West County vs. Leominster, Wednesday, July 14, 1971

Leominster now faced the West County Babe Ruth All-Stars at home. Operating on five day's rest, Rich Kelly was again immense as he scattered three hits over seven innings for a 2-0 shutout victory, striking out seven and walking only two West County batters. As a result of the victory, Leominster advanced to face Oxford on Monday, July 19 at Billy Mundie Field in Fitchburg for the Area 2 championship.

The locals got things going in the bottom of the fourth inning when first-baseman Bryan Beaudette worked West County starter, Gary Sanborn, for a walk. Catcher Joe Hamilton laid down a perfect bunt single, advancing Beaudette to second-base and putting runners on first and second with no outs.

Leominster	AB	R	H	BI
Tata, 2b	3	0	3	0
Malatos, rf	3	0	0	0
Cataldo, 3b	2	0	2	0
Lieneck, ss	3	0	0	0
Kelly, p	3	0	1	0
Beaudette, 1b	1	1	0	0
Hamilton, c	3	1	2	0
Wentworth, cf	2	0	1	0
Healey, lf	2	0	0	1
Totals	22	2	9	1
West County	**AB**	**R**	**H**	**BI**
Oliver, 3b	3	0	0	0
Worthington, cf	3	0	1	0
Sasseville, lf	3	0	1	0
Parker, rf	3	0	0	0
Crozier, 1b	1	0	0	0
Simakauskas, c	3	0	0	0
Snow, 2b	3	0	1	0
Martinez, ss	3	0	0	0
Sanborn, p	1	0	0	0
Totals	23	0	3	0

Pitcher	IP	H	R	ER	BB	K
Kelly, W	7	3	0	0	2	7
Sanborn, L	6	9	2	0	2	6

Center-fielder Steve Wentworth in turn dropped a perfect sacrifice bunt which advanced Beaudette and Hamilton to third and second-bases, respectively. Beaudette scored the first Leominster run on a wild pitch which also advanced Hamilton to third-base. Continuing with the "small ball" approach, left-fielder Bob Healey executed yet another sacrifice bunt which brought in Hamilton with the second run. Leominster threatened again in the sixth inning when Hamilton singled, stole second, but was thrown out by West County catcher Allan Simakauskas attempting to steal third-base.

West County mounted its only threat in the top of the seventh inning when first-baseman Steve Crozier led off with a walk, advanced to second on a passed ball and stole third. However, Kelly bore down to strike out the next three West County batters to preserve the win.

Leominster second-baseman Steve Tata paced the local offense with three singles. Hamilton and third-baseman Joe Cataldo had two singles apiece with Kelly and Wentworth both having a single each.[19][20][21]

Oxford vs. Leominster 1, Tuesday, July 20, 1971
Coming off a long break since their victory over the West County Americans, the Leominster Babe Ruth All-Stars defeated Oxford in a nail-biter, 1-0 at Billy Mundie Field in Fitchburg. The win sent Leominster to the Massachusetts state championship tournament at Fraser Field in Lynn.

Leominster ace Rich Kelly pitched a sparkling 2-hitter, striking out eight and walking three. Kelly provided all the offense he would need with a solo homerun off Oxford pitcher Skip Giza in the second inning. Kelly had a single in addition to his round-tripper while second-baseman Steve Tata (two singles), third-baseman Joe Cataldo (single), and first-baseman Bryan Beaudette (single) provided the rest of the Leominster offense. Oxford threatened in the top of the fourth inning when first-baseman Rick Charbonneau doubled with one out. However after advancing on a passed ball, he was stranded on third-base as Kelly bored own and retired the next two Oxford hitters.

Leominster	AB	R	H	BI
Tata, 2b	3	0	2	0
Malatos, rf	3	0	0	0
Cataldo, 3b	3	0	1	0
Lieneck, ss	3	0	0	0
Kelly, p	3	1	2	1
Beaudette, 1b	3	0	1	0
Hamilton, c	2	0	0	0
Healey, lf	1	0	0	0
Wentworth, cf	2	0	0	0
Totals	**23**	**1**	**6**	**1**
Oxford	**AB**	**R**	**H**	**BI**
Giza, p	2	0	0	0
Polis, 2b	3	0	0	0
Charbonneau, 1b	3	0	2	0
Vancelette, 3b	2	0	0	0
Groh, c	3	0	0	0
Coleman, ss	3	0	0	0
Gomes, rf	3	0	0	0
Robideaux, lf	1	0	0	0
Viel, cf	2	0	0	0
Totals	**22**	**0**	**2**	**0**

Pitcher	IP	H	R	ER	BB	K
Kelly, W	7	2	0	0	2	8
Giza, L	6	6	1	1	1	3

Leominster's journey to the state championship tournament included wins over Athol (7-1), Fitchburg (6-0), West County (2-0). Kelly was the winning pitcher for three of the four wins with Joe Hamilton picking up the win over Fitchburg.[22][23]

Leominster vs. Lynn, Wednesday, July 28, 1971
Massachusetts State Tournament, Fraser Field, Lynn, MA

The Leominster all-stars made the trip Lynn, MA, for the Massachusetts State Tournament which was held at Fraser Field. Leominster was scheduled to face the host team from Lynn on July 28, 1971 in the tournament opener, with Wakefield and Pittsfield rounding out the tournament slate.

Figure 25: 1971 Massachusetts Babe Ruth League State Tournament Score Book (photo credit: Jim Donnelly)

Rich Kelly got the starting nod in the opener with eight days of rest since his last start. The rest of the starting lineup for the locals included Steve Tata at second-base and batting lead-off, followed by Dave Malatos in right. Third-baseman Joe Cataldo batted third, shortstop Pete Lieneck batted clean-up with Kelly batting fifth. Bryan Beaudette batted sixth and started at first-base. Center-fielder Steve Wentworth hit seventh, left-fielder Bob Healey batted eighth, and catcher Joe Hamilton batted ninth.

Leominster took a 1-0 lead in the top of the second inning when Kelly singled over Lynn pitcher Rick Kane's head into center-field, but was forced at second-base on a fielder's choice off the bat of Bryan Beaudette. Beaudette, however, advanced to second-base on a passed ball. Following a walk to Steve Wentworth, Bob Healey bounced a hopper to second-base, forcing Wentworth at second. Beaudette scored the unearned run when the throw to third sailed wide. Leominster led 1-0 after 2 innings.

The locals added to their lead in the top of the third when Steve Tata walked and stole second. Dave Malatos then launched an opposite field homerun over the left field fence for a 3-0 Leominster lead. However, in the bottom half of the third, Lynn would strike back when third-baseman Paul King drove in a pair of runs with a one out double.

Figure 26: 1971 Lynn BRL All-Stars (photo credit: Jim Donnelly)
Front row: Tommy Rowe, Clark Crowley, Dave D'Archangelo, Bernie Young, Vinnie Morabito, John Nelson, Donny McGuish. (bat boy Michael Connors)
Back row: Manager Tom Marino, Coach George Cronin, Phil Cassidy, Rick Kane, Tim Simpson, Paul King, Lou Terrelli, Frank Pike, Tom Bourque, Coach Rick Jackson

Leominster broke things open in the top of the sixth when Kelly led off with his third single of the game. After Beaudette again walked,

Wentworth lined a single into right field scoring Kelly and advancing Beaudette to third. Wentworth then stole second-base putting Leominster runners on second and third with no outs.

Lynn	AB	R	H	BI
Young, cf	3	1	1	0
Crowley, c-p	2	1	0	0
King, 3b	3	0	1	2
Cassidy, rf	3	0	0	0
Torelli, ss	3	0	0	0
D'Arcangelo, ph	1	0	0	0
Nelson, lf	1	0	0	0
Bourque, lf-c	2	0	0	0
McGuish, c	1	0	0	0
Simpson, 1b	2	0	1	0
Anderson, 2b	1	0	0	0
Kane, p	2	0	0	0
Maribito, ph	0	0	0	0
Totals	24	2	3	2
Leominster	AB	R	H	BI
Tata, 2b	2	2	0	0
Malatos, rf	4	1	1	2
Cataldo, 3b	4	0	2	0
Lieneck, ss	3	0	0	1
Kelly, p	4	1	3	0
Beaudette, 1b	2	1	0	0
Wentworth, cf	1	1	1	1
Healey, lf	2	0	0	1
Hamilton, c	3	0	0	0
Totals	25	6	7	5

Pitcher	IP	H	R	ER	BB	K
Kelly, W	7	3	2	2	5	10
Kane, L	5.1	6	6	4	4	2
Crowley	1.2	1	1	1	1	2

Lynn starter Keane was relieved by Clark Crowley with Bob Healey coming to the plate. Healey then laid down a perfect squeeze bunt to score Beaudette from third with Wentworth advancing to third on the play. Wentworth then scored on a wild pitch making the score 6-2 in favor of Leominster after five and a half innings.

Leominster added an insurance run in the seventh when Pete Lieneck drove in Steve Tata from third with a sacrifice fly.

Ace Kelly, operating on eight days rest, struck out ten Lynn hitters, walked three and surrendered only three hits. By virtue of the victory, Leominster moved to the winners' bracket and awaited the outcome of the Wakefield vs. Pittsfield tilt. [24] [25] [26] [27]

Wakefield vs. Leominster, Thursday, July 29, 1971
For the first time during the 1971 All-Star playoff run, Leominster found itself trailing by multiple runs late in a game. As a result, Leominster had to rally from a six-run deficit going into the bottom half of the fifth inning, and a five-run hole in the bottom of the seventh to pull out a wild victory against the stars from Wakefield. Leominster eventually found a way to win this game, largely due to the depth of talent and performance of the subs.

Pete Lieneck got the start for Leominster and promptly found himself in trouble as Wakefield plated two runs in the top of the first. Leominster cut that lead to 2-1 in the bottom half of the inning when right-fielder Dave Malatos singled, advanced to second-base on an error and scored on a single by third-baseman Joe Cataldo.

Leominster tied the game in the bottom of the second inning when first-baseman Bryan Beaudette walked, gained second on a sacrifice bunt by Steve Wentworth, stole third, and scored on a base hit by left-fielder Bob Healey. After two innings the score was 2-2.

Figure 27: 1971 Wakefield Babe Ruth All-Stars (photo credit: Jim Donnelly)
Front Row: Ralph Romeo, Chris Bigger, Robert Trudeau, Bat boy Mike DeMarco, Mark Classen, John Hurley, Chester Crocker
Back row: Coach Travis Goodchild, Coach Picky Walsh, Chuck Campbell, Al Yelba, James Crocker, Bruce Canty, Paul Murphy, David Herook, Bob Perry, Chuck Strong, Manager Rick Pruneau

In the bottom of the third Cataldo doubled to deep center and took third-base on a sacrifice fly by Lieneck who had moved to shortstop. Cataldo scored in a fielder's choice cutting the deficit to 6-3 after three.

After a scoreless fourth inning, Wakefield poured it on in the top of the fifth, scoring three unearned runs following a series of Leominster errors. Bob Healey came in to replace Hamilton on the mound and Leominster manager Jim Marrone, hoping for a spark, began to substitute freely. Leominster now trailed 9-3 coming to bat in their half of the fifth and managed to put another run across the plate when Cataldo singled and hustled to third on a Pete Lieneck single. Cataldo scored on a perfectly executed delayed double steal making the score 9-4 Wakefield after five.

With the remaining innings and outs dwindling, the local stars found themselves down 12-4 entering the bottom of the sixth inning as Wakefield continued its relentless attack and scored three more runs in the top of the sixth. Paul Gamache and Joe Hamilton singled to put men on first and second. With two outs, Lieneck drove in Gamache and advanced Hamilton to third with a single. After Lieneck stole second putting men on second and third, Paul D'Onfro drove in both runners with a single of his own, and ended up on second-base as the throw to home missed the cut-off.

Now with the score 12-7, Beaudette lofted a fly ball to deep left which was muffed resulting in him advancing to second with two outs. Joe DePasquale singled Beaudette home with the eighth Leominster run and also took second on an overthrow to the plate. Bob Healey promptly lined a single down the left-field line scoring DePasquale and he too advanced to second on the throw to the plate. Wakefield's lead was now cut to 12-9 with Healey on second. Gamache singled for the second time in the inning to drive home Healey with the tenth Leominster run. Wakefield was barely hanging on after six 12-10.

But the fireworks were not over yet. Wakefield ran their lead to 15-10 with three more runs in the top the seventh. Down to their last three outs, Marrone sent Terry McNally to bat in the bottom half of the seventh. McNally came up big with a single, but was forced at second when Cataldo chopped a ground ball to second-base. Cataldo, standing on first-base as a result of the fielder's choice, advanced to third by yet another single by Lieneck, putting runners on first and third with one out. Executing another delayed double-steal allowed Cataldo to score. It was now 15-11 Wakefield with Lieneck on second and still only one out.

Paul D'Onfro beat out an infield hit sending Lieneck to third-base. Marrone put on the hit-and-run with Bryan Beaudette at the plate and as D'Onfro broke for second, Beaudette laced a single into right-center which scored both Lieneck and D'Onfro, cutting the lead to 15-13. With Beaudette on second-base, Joe DePasquale fanned, and things looked bleak for Leominster, even though Beaudette stole third-base on the strikeout. With two outs, Healey walked, and Jim Donnelly was hit by a pitch which loaded the bases. Down to their last out with bases loaded,

Joe Hamilton walked on five pitches to send Beaudette home binging Leominster to within one run of Wakefield. McNally kept the rally alive and forced in the tying run with yet another walk.

With bases still loaded, two outs and the score tied after six-and-two-thirds innings, Joe Cataldo watched the first three pitches sail outside of the strike zone. With the count 3-0, Cataldo was obviously taking the next pitch which was over the plate for strike one. The fifth and final pitch of the at-bat was low and outside and the jubilant Cataldo trotted to first-base and brought Jim Donnelly in with the winning run. After the dust settled on this marathon of a game, the final score was Leominster 16, Wakefield 15.

Marrone claimed after the game, "our super subs won it for us. Those kids did the job. They were unreal!"

Since Lynn went on to defeat and eliminate Pittsfield, Leominster again faces Lynn with a chance to win the state championship on Saturday, August 1.[28][29]

Author's note: There is no box score on record for this game. My guess is that the official scorer gave up after multiple innings when Leominster or Wakefield batted around the order within an inning.

Leominster vs. Lynn, Sunday, Aug 1, 1971
Massachusetts State Championship Game

As a result of Saturday's rain-out, Leominster's ace hurler Rich Kelly got the starting nod in the championship game on three full days rest. With this extra day's rest for the star pitcher, Leominster felt good about their chances in the Massachusetts State Championship finals despite the fact that their opponent from Lynn would be playing in front of a home crowd at Fraser Field.

What the local nine did not anticipate, however, was to be trailing Lynn after the first inning. Lynn's lead-off hitter, center-fielder Bernie

Young, walked to open the bottom of the first inning, and promptly stole second- and third-bases. Lynn's second batter of the inning, left-fielder Frank Pike brought Young in with first run of the game on a long sacrifice fly to left-field.

Lynn's lead was short-lived as Leominster would tie the game in the top of the second by way of an in-the-park home-run off the bat of Kelly. Kelly's lead-off laser-like line drive into right field skidded on the wet grass past the diving Lynn right-fielder Tom Bourque, which allowed Kelly to hustle his way around the bases to score the tying run.

Lynn would threaten again in the bottom of the second when catcher Clark Crowley reached on an error with one out. Right-fielder Bourque popped out to Leominster catcher Joe Hamilton for the second out. Lynn first-baseman Tim Simpson then hit a slow roller to third which Leominster third-baseman Joe Cataldo bobbled, resulting in Crowley advancing to second and Simpson beating Cataldo's throw to first. However, Kelly bore down and retired Lynn pitcher Vin Maribito who grounded out to Cataldo at third. The score remained tied 1-1 at the end of two innings.

Kelly again helped his own cause by knocking in the go-ahead run in the top of the third, but it would come at a cost. With one out, Cataldo roped a sharp single between short and third. Taking a hefty lead off first, Cataldo bolted on the first pitch and successfully stole second-base. However, while attempting a hook slide to avoid the tag, Cataldo caught his cleats on the bag bounced his head on the ground which rendered him unconscious for a few scary moments. He was carefully stretchered to a waiting ambulance which took him to Lynn Hospital where it was determined he suffered a mild concussion.

Paul D'Onfro took Cataldo's place on second-base and advanced to third on a wild pitch. Kelly then slapped a single into right field scoring D'Onfro with the go-ahead run. D'Onfro remained in the game at third-base in place of the injured Cataldo.

Leominster added to their lead in their half of the fourth inning when center-fielder Steve Wentworth singled to left and advanced to second on a beautifully executed sacrifice bunt by left-fielder Bob Healey. Joe Hamilton grounded out to first with Wentworth advancing to third on the fielder's choice. Wentworth scored when second-baseman Steve Tata hit a clutch single to center. After three-and-a-half innings, Leominster had a 3-1 lead.

In the meantime, Lynn continued to threaten with baserunners in the fourth and fifth innings; however, Kelly's dominance on the mound and Leominster's stingy defense kept those runners from scoring. One play of note was Joe Hamilton gunning down Lynn's Bernie Young who was attempting to steal second in the fifth. Kelly's no-hit bid was busted in the bottom of the fifth inning when Lynn left-fielder Frank Pike drilled a solid single into center-field.

Leominster added to their lead with a 2-run outburst in the top of the seventh. With one out, right-fielder Dave Malatos and Paul D'Onfro hit back-to-back singles putting runners on first and third. D'Onfro stole second without drawing a throw putting both runners in scoring position. After Pete Lieneck struck out, Kelly hit a pop-up just past second-base which was misplayed for an error sending both Malatos and D'Onfro in to score the fourth and fifth Leominster runs.
With Lynn down to their last three outs, Kelly took the mound with a chance to seal the championship.

Those last two Leominster runs scored in the top half of the seventh inning seemed to take the wind out Lynn's sails as they went down in order. Dave Malatos made the last put-out of the game with a dazzling running catch of a shot hit off the bat of Lynn pinch-hitter Rick Kane. The Leominster players mobbed Malatos as they celebrated Leominster first Massachusetts state championship since the 1952 team accomplished the same outcome.

Lynn	AB	R	H	BI
Young, cf	1	1	0	0
Pike, lf	3	0	1	1
King, 3b	3	0	0	0
D'Archangelo, 2b	3	0	0	0
Torelli, ss	2	0	0	0
Anderson, ss	1	0	0	0
Crowley, c	2	0	0	0
Bourque, rf	2	0	0	0
McGuish, rf	1	0	0	0
Simpson, 1b	2	0	0	0
Maribito, p	1	0	0	0
Kane, ph	1	0	0	0
Totals	**22**	**1**	**1**	**1**

Leominster	AB	R	H	BI
Tata, 2b	4	0	1	1
Malatos, rf	3	1	1	0
Cataldo, 3b	2	0	1	0
D'Onfro, 3b	2	2	1	0
Lieneck, ss	4	0	0	0
Kelly, p	4	1	2	2
Beaudette, 1b	4	0	0	0
Wentworth, cf	2	1	1	0
Healey, lf	2	0	1	0
Hamilton, c	2	0	0	0
Totals	**29**	**5**	**8**	**3**

Pitcher	IP	H	R	ER	BB	K
Kelly, w	7	1	1	1	5	3
Maribito, L	7	8	5	3	5	5

Playing in the winner's bracket paid off handsomely for Leominster, enabling them to win the state title in only three games. The state championship sent Leominster to the New England Regional

Tournament in Nashua, New Hampshire to battle the other New England state champions as well as Puerto Nuevo of Puerto Rico.[30]

Leominster vs. Maine (Bath), Saturday, Aug 7, 1971
New England Regionals, Holman Stadium, Nashua, NH
The week between the conclusion of the Massachusetts State Tournament and the New England Regionals must have seemed interminable for Leominster's players and coaches. After a week of honors, celebration, and yes, practice sessions, the Leominster squad could finally get down to business and seek its first New England BRL Regional title.

Figure 28: 1971 New England Babe Ruth Tournament Program (photo credit: Jim Donnelly)

Nashua, New Hampshire was the host city which allowed scores of Leominster fans to make the daily trek up Routes 13, 119 and 111 to Holman Stadium. In addition to Leominster representing Massachusetts, Fairfield (Connecticut), Brattleboro (Vermont), Bath (Maine), Concord

(New Hampshire), Lincoln (Rhode Island), and Puerto Nuevo (Puerto Rico) rounded out the tournament field.

I was in the stands for this and all of the New England Regional Games, having made the trek with my grandparents Gus and Susie Lanciani, both of whom were avid Leominster baseball fans. Then, as a 13-year-old rookie in the Leominster Babe Ruth League, I knew all of the players and considered them personal heroes of mine as a result of their accomplishments.

Joe Cataldo, after suffering a mild concussion in the Massachusetts State Championship game against Lynn, was cleared to play. However, center-fielder Steve Wentworth was ruled out for the duration of the season after an emergency appendectomy upon his return to Leominster from Lynn. Slugger Bob Healey got the starting nod from manager Jim Marrone and patrolled center-field.

There would be no real drama in the opening contest as the locals trounced their opponents from Bath, Maine 13-3. This win was their 8th consecutive all-star win, and once again placed Leominster into the all-important winners bracket for the tournament. Leominster batters drew 14 walks and cranked out 10 timely hits, making the most of their offensive opportunities.

Leominster ace Rich Kelly picked up his sixth win of the all-star season, but struggled a bit with command as he walked a season-high of 8 batters. However, he only surrendered five singles and Leominster's defense managed to keep Maine's offense in check. In all, Bath left 10 runners on base.

Bath would take an early, but brief lead in the bottom of the first inning when right-fielder Leo Hill drew a walk and advanced to second when third-baseman Dan Hart beat out an infield single. Hill scored easily on a two-out single by first-baseman Mike Torrey. Kelly bore down and retired starting pitcher Hal Lovett. The score after one inning was 1-0, Bath.

Bath	AB	R	H
Jumpel, ss	2	0	0
Marco, cf	2	0	0
Hill, rf	3	1	0
Hart 3b	3	0	1
Torrey, 1b-p	4	1	2
Lovett, p-c	2	1	1
Wallace, 2b	2	0	0
Oliver, 2b	1	0	0
Gilliam, c	2	0	0
Pilgrim, 1b	1	0	0
Wagg, cf	2	0	1
Charbuck, lf	0	0	0
Totals	**24**	**3**	**5**

Leominster	AB	R	H
Tata, 2b	3	0	1
Gamache, 2b	0	0	0
Malatos, rf	1	1	0
McNally, rf	1	0	0
Cataldo, 3b	4	1	0
Lieneck, ss	3	1	2
Kelly, p	4	1	1
Beaudette, 1b	3	2	3
D'Onfro, lf	3	3	1
Healey, cf	1	1	1
Hamilton, c	2	3	1
Totals	**25**	**13**	**10**

Pitcher	IP	H	R	ER	BB	K
Kelly, W	7	5	3	3	8	6
Maribito, L	6	9	10	8	8	1
Torrey	1	1	3	2	6	0

Leominster answered the bell in the top of the second inning, pushing across four runners and taking a lead that would not be squandered. First-baseman Bryan Beaudette singled down the right field line and advanced to second-base on a walk to left-fielder Paul D'Onfro. Center-fielder Bob Health loaded the bases with a single. With no outs, third-base coach Paul Harris wisely held Beaudette up at third.

This conservative approach paid off as catcher Joe Hamilton roped a long double off the right field fence scoring both Beaudette and D'Onfro, and sending Healey to third. Healey scored the third Leominster run on an infield error on a ball Joe Hamilton hit into the hole between first-and second-base. That error proved to be key as Hamilton advanced to third-base with one out, and eventually scored on a long sacrifice fly by right-fielder Dave Malatos. This run was the fourth of the inning which held up as the eventual game winner. Leominster led 4-1 after one-and-a-half innings.

Leominster and Bath traded runs in the third and fourth innings giving Leominster a 6-3 lead entering the fifth. All hell broke loose in the fifth when Malatos, third-baseman Joe Cataldo, shortstop Pete Lieneck, Kelly, Beaudette and D'Onfro all scored. Leominster took a 12-3 lead into the Bath half of the fifth inning, and led 13-3 after scoring another run in the sixth.

Beaudette (three singles) and Lieneck (double, single) led the Leominster offense which also capitalized on four Bath errors. Leominster advanced to face Concord, New Hampshire in the next round of the tournament.[31]

Leominster vs. New Hampshire (Concord), Monday, Aug 9, 1971
If there were any remaining doubts about Leominster's offensive prowess, those uncertainties were obliterated as the locals shocked Concord, New Hampshire, 26-1 in their second game of the tournament. Let that sink in for a moment. At the highest levels of New England Babe Ruth baseball, and against the top team from the Granite State, Leominster pounded out 17 hits, 8 of which were for extra bases including four home-runs, and scored 26 runs of which 19 were earned. Coupled with Leominster's

opening 13-3 victory over Bath, Maine two days prior, the local contingent pounded out 27 hits and 39 runs against elite opponents. They advanced in the winner's bracket, improving their tournament record to 2-0.

Leominster pitcher Joe Hamilton breezed through seven innings of 4-hit ball, giving up a lone run in the bottom of the fifth inning. Leominster's defense was stellar as they turned two double-plays to keep the Concord offense in check. Only a single runner for Concord reached second-base. Hamilton certainly helped his own cause by driving in an astonishing eight runs.

Figure 29: 1971 Concord NH Babe Ruth All-Stars
Front row: Batboy Charlie Kelley, Tom Painchaud, Richard Cochran, Peter Cassavaugh, John Marchand, Richard Flanders, Dwight, Pflundstein, Brian Stebbins, Joe Lefebvre
Back row: Manager Philip King, Coach Terry Gregg, Coach Stephen Robie, Brian Sabean, Michael Curry, John Flanders, John Merrill, Stephen DeStefano, Richard Lancellotti

Shoddy defense on the part of Concord led to four Leominster runs in the top of the first inning. Second-baseman Steve Tata opened the game with a four-pitch walk. Dave Malatos pushed Tata to second-base with the first of his three hits, a solid single to center-field.

Third-baseman Joe Cataldo reached on an error by Concord first-baseman John Merrit, which loaded the bases. Shortstop Pete Lieneck popped to second-base for an infield fly rule and the first Leominster out. Rich Kelly, shifting battery positions with Hamilton as catcher, lofted a sacrifice fly to left-field, sending Tata home with the first Leominster run and advancing Malatos to third-base. After Cataldo stole second, first-baseman Bryan Beaudette drew a walk, re-loading the bases for Leominster. Malatos scampered home with the second Leominster run on a passed ball which advanced Cataldo to third and Beaudette to second. Left-fielder Paul D'Onfro walked to re-load the bases once again. Center-fielder Bob Healey reached on a two-base error which sent Cataldo and Beaudette home with the third and fourth runs. Leominster had a 4-0 lead without yet having taken the field for defense.

Concord starting pitcher and future New York Yankee Joe Lefebvre (no relation) retired Leominster in order in the second inning; however, the floodgates opened in the top half of the third as Leominster sent fourteen batters to the plate, scoring eleven runs in the process. Pete Lieneck opened the inning with a single to center-field. Rich Kelly followed with a line-drive home-run over the right-center-field fence scoring Lieneck. Not to be outdone, Bryan Beaudette then launched another homer to the same spot as Kelly's blast, ending the day for Concord starter Lefebvre and bringing reliever Rich Cochran to the mound.

Paul D'Onfro worked Cochran for a walk and advanced to third on a single down the left-field line by Bob Healey, with Healey racing to second on the throw to third. With runners on second and third with only one out. Hamilton lofted a long sacrifice fly to deep left which scored D'Onfro and the hustling Healey all the way from second. After Tata singled and Malatos doubled, Concord's Cochran was lifted in favor of the second reliever of the inning Steve DeStefano. Joe Cataldo greeted DeStefano with a monstrous shot over the left-field fence scoring Tata and Malatos ahead of him for a 12-0 Leominster lead. Lieneck singled for his second hit of the inning and ended up on third-base after consecutive walks to Kelly and Beaudette. A wild pitch scored Lieneck with Kelly and Beaudette advancing. After D'Onfro grounded out for the second out of the inning, scoring Kelly from third. Beaudette then scored on a bloop single by Healey. 15-0 Leominster after two and a half innings.

Joe Hamilton continued to cruise through four innings when Leominster struck again in the top of the fifth. Rich Kelly doubled to center-field and scored on an error. The score was 16-0 heading into the bottom of the fifth when Concord scored its only run as DeStefano walked and scored on consecutive base hits by Rick Lancellotti and Tom Flanders. The score was 16-1 after five innings.

Leominster added to its commanding lead by striking for four more runs in the top of the sixth. Cataldo opened with a single, Kelly walked and Beaudette singled to load the bases. Terry McNally, subbing for Paul D'Onfro in left-field walked in a run. With two outs and a 3-2 count, Hamilton cleared the bases with a solid single in the left-center-field gap. 19-1 Leominster.

After Hamilton shut Concord down in the bottom of the sixth, Leominster scored the final six runs of the game with the big blows being a two-run single by Beaudette and a three-run homer by Hamilton. Final score 26-1.[32]

Concord	AB	R	H	RBI
Sabean	1	0	0	0
Marchand	2	0	0	0
Stebbins	2	0	0	0
T. Flanders	1	0	1	1
Curry	3	0	0	0
Pflundstein	3	0	0	0
Lefebvre	0	0	0	0
Robie	2	0	1	0
Merrit	3	0	1	0
Cassavaugh	0	0	0	0
R. Flanders	1	0	0	0
Painchaud	1	0	0	0
Cochran	0	0	0	0
DeStefano	1	1	0	0
Lancellotti	3	0	1	0
Totals	**23**	**1**	**4**	**1**
Leominster	**AB**	**R**	**H**	**RBI**
Tata, 2b	2	2	1	0
Donnelly, 2b	3	0	0	0
Malatos, rf	7	3	3	0
Cataldo, 3b	7	3	2	3
Lieneck, ss	5	3	2	0
Kelly, c	3	4	2	3
Beaudette, 1b	3	5	3	3
D'Onfro, lf	1	1	0	0
McNally, lf	1	2	0	1
Healey, cf	3	1	2	1
DePasquale, cf	3	1	0	0
Hamilton, p	3	1	2	8
Totals	**41**	**26**	**17**	**19**

It should be noted that Brian Sabean, Concord's lead-off hitter, went on to various Major League Baseball roles. He was a scout for the NY Yankees and drafted as amateurs the likes of Derek Jeter, Mariano Rivera, J. T. Snow, Jorge Posada and Andy Pettitte. He went on to become the general manager of the San Francisco Giants and retired in 2014 as the executive vice president of baseball operations for the 2014 Giants. He's largely responsible for building the Giant's teams that won the MLB World Series in 2010, 2012 and 2012. He was recognized as major league baseball's Executive of the Year in 2003.

Also of note, both Lefebvre and Sabean would be future Eckerd College teammates of Leominster All-Stars Dave Malatos (1971) and Dick Freda (1972). (D. Freda, December 11, 2021).

Puerto Rico (Puerto Nuevo) vs. Leominster, Wednesday, Aug 11, 1971
Rich Kelly, Leominster's ace through the sectional and district rounds, in the Massachusetts state tournament in Lynn, and up to now in the New England Regional Tournament in Nashua, had been nearly untouchable. In the six games that Kelly started, he had six complete game wins, gave up only 15 hits, yielded only 7 runs of which 6 were earned. Coupled with the offensive barrage in their first two games of the tournament, the locals were confident that they matched up well against Puerto Nuevo. Why wouldn't they? Leominster scored 39 runs in their first 2 games and had their ace on the hill. This was the match-up that was anticipated by fans of both teams since the tournament began.

Both Leominster and Puerto Nuevo entered the game each 2-0 and the sole undefeated teams midway through the tournament. The Puerto Rico lineup was stacked with elite hitters who could certainly catch up to Kelly's fastball. And their pitching staff was dominant.

With rain threatening from the west, Leominster took the field at 2:00 in the afternoon as the home team. Kelly warmed up with his catcher Joe Hamilton as the grandstands on both sides of Holman Stadium filled up. Scores more fans in lawn chairs lined the outfield fence as the PA announcer asked those in attendance to stand and remove their hats for the National Anthem.

Puerto Nuevo wasted no time showing they were on to Kelly's

fastball when center-fielder and lead-off hitter Edwin Lopez belted a double into the right-center-field gap and scored on a base hit from left-fielder Jesus Valdosa. After shortstop Carlos Rodrigues doubled to right, Kelly retired right-fielder Rene Quinones to end the inning.

After Leominster went down in order in the bottom half of the first, Puerto Nuevo added another run in the second. Catcher Rene Atilano doubled and advanced to third on a single by first-baseman Carlos Garcia. Atilano scored on a passed ball making the score 2-0 with Leominster coming up in their half of the second inning.

Figure 30: 1971 Puerto Nuevo, Puerto Rico Babe Ruth All-Stars
Front row: Rene Atilano, Edwin Lopez, Juan Jose Quinones, Santiago Aldrey, Alexis Firpi, Jesus Barbosa, Jesus Barbosa, Daniel Ortiz, Oscar Negron
Back row: Pedro Roman (league official), coach Gerry Cruz, Rene Quinones, Richard Rodriguez, Ruben Suarez, Samuel Torres, Carlos Rodriguez, Carlos Ruben Garcia, Manuel Lopez, coach Freddie Muniz, Manager Alfredo Carlo Toro, Gilberto Graulau (league official)

Leominster bats could not solve making contact off Puerto Nuevo's starter Juan Jose Quinones and the locals went down silently in the bottom of the second. Kelly retired Puerto Nuevo in order in the third; however, Leominster did the same in the bottom half of the inning.

Puerto Nuevo increased their lead to 4-0 with a pair of runs in the top of the fourth. Quinones roped a double and scored on another two-bagger from Atilano who was thrown out at the plate trying to score on a base hit by Garcia. Pitcher Quinones reached on a fielder's choice and scampered all the way home when Lopez tripled making it 4-0 Puerto Nuevo entering the bottom of the fourth.

After Leominster was again retired in their half of the fourth, Puerto Nuevo put the game completely out of reach with a four hit, four run attack in the top of the fifth. Perhaps mercifully, the skies finally opened, and the game was eventually halted and scheduled to be resumed the next day with the score 8-0.

Quinones had taken a no-hitter through 4 innings and again took the mound when the game resumed on Thursday, August 12. His no-no was broken up in the bottom of the sixth when Leominster second-baseman Steve Tata drove a solid single past second-base for Leominster's only hit. Final score Puerto Nuevo 8, Leominster 0. The victors pounded out fourteen hits off Kelly who suffered his first loss of the entire all-star season. Despite this loss, Leominster could still earn a trip to the tournament semi-finals with a second win over Concord.[33][34][35]

Leominster vs. New Hampshire (Concord), Thursday, Aug 12, 1971
It was either elimination or advancement to the championship game for the Leominster All-Stars in a rematch against Concord NH at Holman Stadium in Nashua, NH. Leominster earlier this week had crushed Concord 26-1, but none of that mattered as the winner would advance, and the loser would go home.

Joe Hamilton got the nod to start for Leominster with Rich Kelly catching, Bryan Beaudette at first, Steve Tata at second, Pete Lieneck at short, and Joe Cataldo at third-base. The outfield was patrolled by Paul D'Onfro in left-field, Steve Wentworth in center and Dave Malatos in right. Given that this was an elimination game, Leominster manager Jim Marrone was prepared to empty the bench if necessary.

Leominster wasted no time in the top of the first, taking advantage of control problems for Concord starter Mike Curry as the first five of the first seven Leominster batters drew bases on balls. Lead-off hitter Steve Tata drew a walk and immediately stole second. After Malatos and Cataldo were retired, Curry issued free passes to Lieneck, Kelly, Beaudette and D'Onfro giving Leominster a 2-0 lead with Concord coming to bat.

In the bottom half of the first Concord's Brian Sabean singled and came around to score on a bases-loaded walk to Joe Lefebvre. Leominster led 2-1 after one inning.

Hamilton helped himself with a base hit in the top of the fourth inning which represented Leominster's first hit of the game. With Hamilton on second-base and two outs, Steve Tata laced a long double to the fence in right-center which scored Hamilton who was running on contact, extending Leominster's lead to 3-1.

That lead was short-lived, however, as Concord stormed back to take the lead in their half of the fourth on a wild pitch that scored Joe Lefebvre from third-base, and a two-out, two-run clutch single off the bat of second-baseman Brian Sabean. After four innings, Concord had a narrow 4-3 lead.

Concord took that lead into the top of the seventh; however, Leominster would bring the top of the order to bat. To this point, Concord pitcher Mike Curry had struck out thirteen Leominster hitters. Steve Tata opened the inning by popping out to Sabean at second for the first out. Right-fielder Dave Malatos hustled out an infield hit and attempted to steal second on the first pitch. When the throw sailed into centerfield, Malatos scampered the third base. With third-baseman Joe Cataldo up to the plate, everyone in the park expected that Marrone would call a squeeze bunt with one out and Malatos on third. Sure enough, Cataldo dropped a bunt between the mound and third-base, and Malatos scored easily to tie the game at 4. The hustling Cataldo reached first without a throw and the hundreds of Leominster fans on hand were ecstatic.

Still with one out, shortstop Pete Lieneck drew a walk putting runners on first and second. The ever-clutch hitting Rich Kelly crushed a long fly ball over the reach of right-fielder Lancellotti for a triple, bringing home both Cataldo and Lieneck for a 6-4 Leominster lead.

In the bottom of the seventh, Concord threatened with a lead-off pinch-hit double by Rich Cochran. Marrone replaced Hamilton with southpaw Terry McNally since Concord had a left-handed batter next up. Unfortunately, McNally walked Lancellotti, which brought Marrone back to the mound to bring in Malatos from right-field in relief. With runners on first and second with no outs, Malatos bore down and retired the next three batters on ground outs to clinch the game and send Leominster to face Puerto Nuevo once again for a chance at the title.[36]

Author's note: there were no box scores provided for this game.

Puerto Rico (Puerto Nuevo) vs. Leominster, Friday, Aug 13, 1971
With the New England Tournament championship on the line, Leominster faced Puerto Nuevo for the second time in three days. Since Leominster ace Rich Kelly pitched only two days prior in that 8-0 loss, and since Joe Hamilton pitched the day prior in the win over Concord, NH, manager Jim Marrone was forced to go deeper into his pitching rotation for this game. Paul Gamache, the 14-year-old star from Marrone's regular season Elks team got the starting nod, but knowing that his team faced elimination, the Leominster manager knew that everyone was available to step up if

necessary.

Puerto Nuevo wasted no time jumping on Gamache when the first two batters, center-fielder Ed Lopez, and left-fielder Sam Torres both doubled, and both scored on a single to left-field by second-basemen Santiago Aldrey. Aldrey took second-base on the throw to home plate and advanced to third on a single by Jesus Barbora. After Carlos Rodriguez walked on four pitches to load the bases with no outs, Marrone made it to the mound and replaced Gamache with second-baseman Steve Tata. Gamache remained in the game at second-base.

With the score 2-0, bases loaded and no outs, Tata tried valiantly to stem the onslaught of the hot Puerto Nuevo bats. However, right-fielder Ray Quinones greeted Tata with a solid double to right-field which scored two more Puerto Nuevo runs, with runners now on second and third with no outs. Catcher Rene Atlano then singled to left-center scoring two more runs making the score 6-0, still with nobody out. Tata escaped further damage as the Leominster infield turned a double-play followed by a grounder to Beaudette at first for the final out. Leominster trailed 6-0 before picking up a bat.

Hoping to cut into the lead, Leominster failed to score in the first two innings. However, right-fielder Paul D'Onfro started a Leominster rally in the bottom of the third inning when he hustled to first-base following a passed ball third-strike. Left-fielder Bob Healey forced D'Onfro at second for the first Leominster out of the inning. First-baseman Bryan Beaudette lined a double to right-center, scoring Healey all the way from first. Steve Tata then bounced a chopper to third-base, but the wild-throw from Barbora enabled Beaudette to score the second Leominster run. The score was now 6-2 after three innings.

Puerto Nuevo struck back in the top of the fourth with another run when first-baseman Carlos Garcia led off the frame with a solid single to center-field and advanced to third on a ground-rule double by pitcher Rodriguez. Center-fielder and lead-off hitter Lopez lined to center-field and Leominster center-fielder Dave Malatos made the catch on the run. However, Garcia scored on an errant throw to home giving Puerto Nuevo a 7-2 lead with Leominster coming to bat in the fourth.

Leominster clawed back in the bottom of the fourth when Rich Kelly launched a long home-run over the left-center-field fence, thus narrowing the Puerto Nuevo to 7-3 after four.

Puerto Nuevo pitcher Dick Rodriguez led off the top of the sixth inning with a walk off reliever Steve Tata who managed to keep the game in reach. However, center-fielder Lopez doubled down the right-field line which scored Rodriguez all the way from first for the 8th Puerto Nuevo run.

But manager Jim Marrone's squad would not lay down as they put another pair of runs across the plate in the bottom of the sixth. Dave Malatos drew a lead-off walk and safely swiped second-base. When Puerto Nuevo catcher Atilano threw a pick-off attempt into center, Malatos hustled into third. After Joe Cataldo fanned, Pete Lieneck also struck out on three pitches, but Atilano could not hang on to the ball, sending the speedy Lieneck safely to first without a throw. The error put runners on first and third with one out. With Rich Kelly at the plate and Malatos at third as a major distraction, Rodriguez threw a wild pitch the enabled Malatos to score and Lieneck to hustle all the way to third-base. Kelly then lofted a long fly to right-field scoring Lieneck with the fifth Leominster run. Puerto Nuevo led after six innings, 8-5.

With the game within reach, Marrone brought his ace Rich Kelly to the mound with hopes to keep things close. After giving up a lead-off double off the bat of Puerto Nuevo second-baseman Aldrey, Kelly bore down, Kelly fanned Barbora, got shortstop Rodriguez to ground out to second-base and retired Quinones on an infield pop fly. Leominster now had just three outs to avoid ending their fairytale season.

Bryan Beaudette got the Leominster bench and the crowd right back into the game with a lead-off walk and the top of the Leominster order coming to bat. Steve Tata lofted a fly ball to left-center field for the first out. Joe Hamilton came on to pinch-hit for Paul Gamache and went deep into the count before he too flied out to the outfield. Leominster's season came down to the steady and hard-hitting Dave Malatos. With the crowd on its collective feet, the scene was tense. However, Puerto Nuevo prevailed when Malatos gallantly stood in the batter's box, stared down Rodriguez, but ultimately went down swinging. Final score: Puerto Nuevo 8, Leominster 5.[37][38][39][40]

    I was in the crowd that day and stood with my grandparents cheering along with the rest of the fans who made the trip to Holman Stadium. I had traveled to Lynn to see the team win the state championship. I made the trek from Leominster to Nashua for the New England regionals and didn't miss an inning of that tournament. As a fan, I wasn't ready for this amazing season to end. Leominster had never made it to the Babe Ruth World Series. We all desperately wanted this year to be our year, especially given the talent, coaching and amazing depth of this team. But it wasn't it be. Looking at the pitching line, Puerto Nuevo had struck out only once. This meant that Puerto Nuevo batters put the ball in play for all but a single out. Given Leominster made only one error in this game, one could say that it was their defense that kept them in it despite the 12 hits that Puerto Nuevo banged out in the game

    The city of Leominster embraced these 14- and 15-year-olds upon their return home. They were feted at home with a parade and a banquet. Red Sox former ace, Jim Lonborg presented the team with trophies and warm-up jackets. They were honored at Fenway Park before a Sox game.

    Through all of this I soaked it all in. I wanted to experience first-hand what these players before me had experienced. Little did I know at the time that this scene would repeat itself for the next two all-star seasons. The city of Leominster was in for one hell of a ride.

Leominster	AB	R	H
Tata, 2b, p	2	0	0
Hamilton, ph	1	0	0
Gamache, p, 2b	4	0	0
Malatos, cf	4	1	1
Cataldo, 3b	3	0	0
Lieneck, ss	3	1	0
Kelly, c	2	1	1
D'Onfro, rf	2	0	0
Healey, lf	3	1	0
Beaudette, 1b	2	1	1
Totals	**26**	**5**	**3**

Puerto Nuevo	AB	R	H
Lopez, cf	4	1	2
Torres, lf	4	1	1
Aldrey, 2b	4	1	2
Barbora, 3b	4	1	2
C. Rodriguez, ss	1	1	0
Quinones, rf	4	1	1
Atilano, c	3	0	1
Garcia 1b	3	1	1
Suarez, 1b	0	0	0
D. Rodriguez, p	2	1	2
Totals	**29**	**8**	**12**

Pitcher	IP	H	R	ER	BB	K
Rodriguez, W	7	3	5	2	4	7
Gamache, L	0	4	6	6	1	0
Tata	6	7	2	2	1	0
Kelly	1	1	0	0	0	1

Figure 31: Babe Ruth Day at Fenway Park (photo credit: Leominster Enterprise)
(l-r) Paul Gamache, Rich Kelly, Bob Healy, Joe DePasquale, Joe Hamilton, Massachusetts Babe Ruth League Director George Lally, Red Sox pitcher Ray Culp.

A little over a week later, Puerto Nuevo would become the first non-US team to win the Babe Ruth World Series with a perfect 4-0 record in the tournament, which was held in Albuquerque, NH. In the championship game, Puerto Nuevo rallied for six runs in the sixth inning and routed Mount Healthy, Ohio, 12-3. Leominster had been eliminated by the eventual World Series champs.

Leominster Babe Ruth League Inc.

ALL STAR BANQUET

JOHN McLAUGHLIN, President
CHARLES CONEFREY, Vice-President   NORMAN GLASHEEN, Secretary & Treasurer

HEAD TABLE GUESTS

Tom Dowd GUEST SPEAKER	James Fitzgerald M.C.
MAYOR Ralph Crossman	SUPERINTENDENT Martin Moran
REPRESENTATIVE Angelo Picucci	George Lally STATE DIRECTOR
PRESIDENT John McLaughlin	Robert Curran REGIONAL DIRECTOR
REVEREND Peter Inzerillo	Burr Jacobsen AREA DIRECTOR
Clarence Daniels	Norman Glasheen SEC. & TREAS.
Charles Conefrey VICE-PRESIDENT	Stanley Zioneck MEMBER NATIONAL BOARD

Leon Hannigan ATHLETIC DIRECTOR L.H.S.

ALL STAR TEAM

James Marrone – MANAGER   Paul Harris – COACH
Robert Boissoneau – COACH   Ted Rockwell – BAT BOY

PLAYERS

Richard Kelly	Joseph Cataldo
Joel Hamilton	Peter Lieneck
James Donnelly	Stephen Tata
David Malatos	Bryan Beaudette
Joseph DePasquale	Paul D'Onfro
Paul Gamache	Terence McNally
Robert Healey	Steven Wentworth

SPECIAL PRESENTATIONS

Tom Dowd   James Marrone

Figure 32: 1971 Leominster Babe Ruth All-Star Banquet Program

Chapter Nine: 1971 Leominster Post 151 Legion Team

Not to be outdone by the success of the 1971 Babe Ruth state champions, the 1971 Leominster American Legion Post 151 squad also won the Legion state championship under the leadership of coach Emile Johnson.

Like many of my contemporaries from that era, I was glued to the radio and scoured the local papers for their coverage of the exploits of Post 151. Many of the players of the 1971 team had younger brothers with whom I played Little League or Babe Ruth ball. Needless to say, the summer of 1971 was special for Leominster baseball fans.

Figure 33: 1971 Massachusetts State Champions - Leominster Post 151 (photo credit: Dick Freda)

Front Row: Dan Danley (St. Bernard's), Steve Corliss, Mark Gagnon (Athol), Don Freda, Steve Brown, Bill Vitello (Athol), Wayne Hancock (Gardner)
Back Row: Dave Bilodeau, Dave Antocci, Ron Patry, John Lieneck, Ed Cataldo
(St. Bernard's), Steve Fredette (Athol), Bob Langlois (Gardner), Dave Chaisson (Athol), Gary Anderson (Oakmont) Ed Bryce, Emile Johnson, Jr.

Section 3: Home Cooking –1972 Babe Ruth All-Stars

Figure 34: 1972 Leominster Babe Ruth All-Star Team (photo credit: 1972 Massachusetts Babe Ruth State Tournament Program)
Front row: Peter Gamache, bat boy
Middle row: Bob Koch, John Cantatore, Paul Gamache, Mike Gasbarro, Greg Carchidi, Steve Jackson, Mike Pignata
Back row: Manager Jim Marrone, Coach Cary Noels, Jeff Johnson, Jim Donnelly, Dick Freda, Rick Comeau, Jay Burke, Mike Leclair, Charlie Richard, Steve Szymkiewicz, Coach Paul Harris, Coach Vinnie Campobasso

Chapter Ten – The Tournament

Although each of the 1971 all-stars with the exception of returning veterans Paul Gamache and Jim Donnelly had graduated from the league since their highly successful 1971 all-star run, manager Jim Marrone was again blessed with a deep and talented pool of all-stars representing all seven teams of the Leominster Babe Ruth League.

Since the 1971 team's success was largely due to a combination of great pitching, speed, hitting and defense, manager Jim Marrone selected the 1972 team with those very same characteristics in mind. Each player on this team was capable of stealing bases and attempting an extra base, thus forcing the opposing players to make the play.

The city of Leominster was selected as the site of the 1972 state tournament which meant that the 1972 Leominster Babe Ruth all-star team would participate as the host team. Volunteers from across the community stepped up to provide the necessary support and services that were required to host a tournament of this magnitude. Organizing host families for the players, field maintenance, scheduling, official tournament duties and reporting, concessions, program design and publication, umpires, and a myriad of other activities required a small army to plan and execute.

Being the host team is both good and bad. On one hand, the team would have an automatic bid and avoid the single elimination road to the tournament on which every section champion in the state would need to travel. However, those teams who would make their way to the tournament would be battle-tested, whereas Leominster would risk coming into the tournament rusty and untested in competitive play. All that said, it was special for Leominster to participate as defending Massachusetts state champions on its home field.

In addition to Leominster as host, Longmeadow (Section 1 champion), Burncoat of Worcester (Section 2 champion), Parkway of West Roxbury (Section 3 champion), and Greater Lawrence (Section 4 champion) filled out the slate of Massachusetts teams for the 1972 tournament. Participating teams arrived in Leominster on Tuesday, July 25, 1972, and were hosted by "foster-families" during the tournament.

Fran and Rachel Arel were great friends of the Leominster Babe Ruth League in the early 1970's. Fran was a retired lieutenant of the LPD, and an accomplished amateur photographer. Both were almost daily visitors to the ball park as baseball fans.

Fran took many of the photographs that were used in the 1972 Massachusetts BRL State Tournament program. Rachel was often heard cheering for her nephews on countless summer evenings at the park. Their daughters Nancy and Patricia Arel were team hostesses during the 1972 tournament.

Fran and Rachel are now in their 90's and still recall that summer of 1972. "The community support for the tournament was amazing," replied Fran when asked what he remembered most from that summer. "The city really came together that summer" (Arel, F., July 15, 2021).

Figure 35: 1972 Tournament Team Hostesses (1972 Massachusetts Babe Ruth State Championship Program)
(l-r) Nancy Arel, Sue Paquette, Patricia Arel, Janice LaRoche, Mary Kelly

Figure 36: 1972 Longmeadow Babe Ruth All-Stars (photo credit: 1972 Massachusetts State Championship Program)
Front row: bat boy Scott Williams.
Middle row: James Peys, Mark Meserve, Brian Durocher, Robert Petroff, Gary DeStephano, Steve Hurwitz.
Back row: coach Peter Sarant, Stephen Williams, Paul Gutermann, Frank Maddux, Scott Aye, coach Louis Peys, Donald Howard, John Fleming, John Sadler, Wes Atwood, manager Raymond Sadler

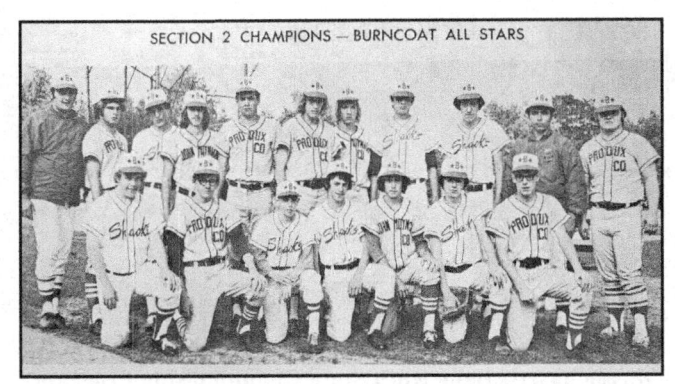

Figure 37: 1972 Burncoat (Worcester) Babe Ruth All-Stars (photo credit: 1972 Massachusetts Babe Ruth State Championship Program)
Front row: James Olson, Pat Remington, bat boy James Masterson, Walter Sands, Martin Hastings, William Gibbons, John O'Brien.
Back row: manager Michael Simmarano, Mark Killeen, Tim Dunn, Brad Cutty, Jim Powers, Jon Shepeluk, Mike Quinn, Gary Lamoureux, Michael Eressy, coach James Pedone.

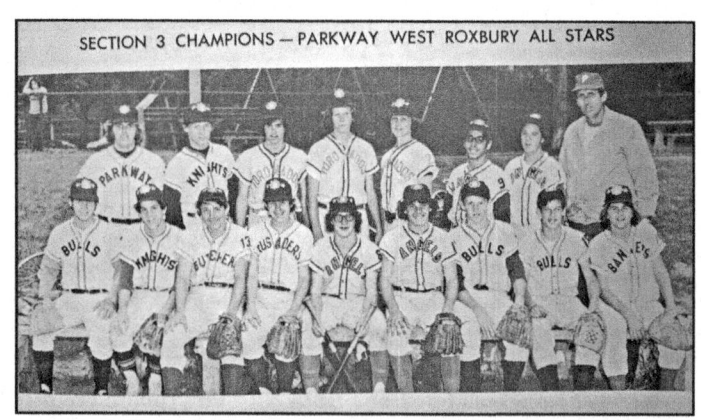

Figure 38: 1972 Parkway (West Roxbury) Babe Ruth All-Stars (photo credit: 1972 Massachusetts Babe Ruth State Championship Program)
Front row: Mark Sullivan, Matt Kelleher, Joe Nelligan, Phil Olsen, Chris Farrell, Joe Celeste, Kevin Rose, Ron Perry, Mitch Kaltsunas.
Back row: coach Ed Donnelly, Bill Daugherty, Dave Foley, Paul Knox, Jim Conroy, Mike Thomas, John Neill, manager Charles Kiley.

Figure 39: 1972 Greater Lawrence Babe Ruth All-Stars (photo credit: 1972 Massachusetts Babe Ruth State Championship Program)
Front row: Donald Saab, James Loffredo, David Robinson, Sam Milone, Dave Mosher, Fred Simm.
Middle row: Steve Camparone, Robert Hajjar, Ricky Redman, Keith Verrette, Jeff Weinhold.
Back row: coach Tom Heenan, manager Charles Beaudette, Brian Smith, John Doherty, coach Charles Larouque, league president Nick Carter.

Chapter Eleven: The Team

Steve Jackson
Steve Jackson lived on Richardson Street between North Main Street and Grove Avenue, and in a neighborhood that included future Leominster High School teammate Lou Piano. He is the oldest of five children of Aubrey and Marcia Jackson. Steve recently shared that on every day of his childhood there was a game of baseball, whiffle ball, basketball or football going on. He'd shoot hoops with Lou Piano or play baseball with the guys from his neighborhood in the Elks Club parking lot down the hill from his home, often competing against other neighborhoods from across that side of the city. He now recalls that life was simple back in those days with the only concern being which sport and which playground would host the action.

Steve and I became teammates on the 1975 Leominster American Legion team; however it was during the summer of 1973 that I got to know Steve as a result of my friendship with his sister Laura who was a classmate of mine. I recall Steve as being very fast and athletic, and exceptional in both baseball and football. He always seemed to make the right play. He attributes his skills to the hours that he and his dad played catch and held batting practice at Doyle field with his brothers Brad, Barry and later, Mark.

Like many of the boys growing up in that section of Leominster, Steve played in the Leominster National Little League at the field behind Northwest School, making the all-star team his final year. He played for Tilco with future teammates Rich Kelly and Ted Rockwell. He also played Pop Warner Football for the Leominster Dolphins where he was known for his speed and hands. Steve attended Priest Street School for elementary school and went to Gallagher Junior High School where he played baseball and football.

Steve was a second-baseman while playing Babe Ruth baseball

and he played for Solar Chemical with all-star teammates Jay Burke, John Cantatore, and Greg Carchidi. He narrowly missed making the 1971 Babe Ruth All-Star team but was selected for the 1972's.

At Leominster High, Steve was a stellar defensive back for the 1974 Blue Devils football team and set a team record for most interceptions in a season. He was a two-year starter for the LHS baseball team and played for the 1973, 1974 and 1975 Legion teams, all for coach Emile Johnson.

After graduating from Leominster High, Steve played a year at Cushing Academy in Fitchburg, and then for the Falcons of Fitchburg State College where he was the captain of that baseball squad. Steve resides in Leominster today and works at Leominster High School as a paraprofessional after many years working at Digital Equipment Corporation (S. Jackson, May 6, 2021).

Paul Gamache
Paul Gamache is the third of six sons of Roger and Jeanne Gamache. I had come to know Paul and his youngest brother Danny through my friendship with brother Peter, who was my Babe Ruth all-star teammate and roommate in Lynn for the 1973 New England Regionals.

The Gamache's spent their early childhood living on Grafton Street just past the intersection of Route's 2 and 12 (N. Main Street) on the northwest side of Leominster. Paul recently shared that the Gamache boys and the Tucker boys (future and legendary Nashoba Regional High School football coach Ken Tucker, and future LHS star Don Tucker) would play baseball and football on the hilly street where they lived. They would bat uphill and then switch sides. For football, offense would run uphill, and again, they would switch sides.

The family moved to upper Union Street later during their youth which gave the Gamache boys more room to roam and play in the Fall Brook school area. On Sundays, I would often see the brothers lined up between their mom and dad in their usual pew at Holy Family Church.

Paul played Little League for Dupont in the National Little League with future Leominster Babe Ruth Baseball stars Mike Pignata, Rick Comeau, Greg Carchidi, Steve Jackson and future LHS and Holy Cross standout Rick Daigneault. Following Little League, Paul was drafted by Jim Marrone to play for Elks. A standout pitcher and infielder, Paul was one of the rarest of players to play for two Massachusetts State Champion Babe Ruth all-star teams.

Paul was a three-sport standout at Saint Bernard's High School in Fitchburg where he starred as a running back for the football team, guard for the hoops team, and shortstop for the baseball Bernardians. He went on to play basketball at Merrimac College. Paul currently lives near Venice, Florida with his wife Janet and enjoys golf and the beach (P. Gamache, May 20, 2022).

Charlie Richard

For as long as he can remember, Charlie Richard could run fast, perhaps faster than all of his Healey Street neighborhood friends. Being close to the Northwest School playground, Charlie would often be found playing pick-up baseball or basketball with many of his future National Little League and Babe Ruth Baseball teammates.

Charlie played for Leominster News in Division 2 of the Leominster Babe Ruth League, and made the 1972 team based on his speed, hustle and raw talents. Following Babe Ruth, he played basketball at Leominster High School and starred in center-field for the 1974 Leominster Post 151 American Legion baseball team.

Jim Donnelly

Jim Donnelly spent his childhood playing ball with this three older and two younger brothers in the North Street neighborhood near Kings Corner in North Leominster. One of nine children, Jim and his siblings were never seeking companionship for any extended period of time. Whalom Park and Lake were walking distance from the Donnelly home. The North American Little League field was a short bike ride. On any summer day there would always be a game to be played.

Jim, his brothers, and the Perkins boys (John, Mike and Pat) would also play hardball in one of the sandlots in the neighborhood. They'd play tackle football on the grass fields and touch football on the street. In the winter they would sling their skates over their hockey sticks and shovels, and head off to the small pond in the woods nearby. Sometimes future Babe Ruth League all-star teammate Terry McNally and some of the other guys from Lunenburg would join in the scrum.

Donnelly played for Duval's in the North American Little League and made the all-stars his final year. Bob Lamothe, the legendary Tanzio Park manager drafted Jim to play Babe Ruth baseball. Jim chuckles when thinking about coach Lamothe. "Bob was kind of a surrogate father for me during those years. My dad was rehabilitating from an illness and coach would drive me to and from practice and games. It was not unusual for Bob to make multiple stops to pick up the Nutting's, Corliss's and other teammates along the way. He pretty much ran a bus service."

At the age of thirteen Jim badly injured his right wrist playing baseball, diving for a ball that resulted in damaged tendons and nerves in his throwing hand. This injury stayed with him throughout his three years in Babe Ruth, affecting throws to first and plaguing him with a lack of confidence when making those throws. As a result, his interest in baseball began to wane by the team he reached high school.

At St. Bernard's, Donnelly starred in football where he was a team MVP running back. He also played on the inaugural St. Bernard's ice hockey team which only a few years later made it to the old Boston Garden for the Massachusetts state hockey championship game. After graduating from St. Bernard's in 1975, Donnelly spent a year at UMass Amherst and the Fitchburg State College where he played ball alongside

Terry McNally and Steve Jackson.

Jim is retired and living at the Cape with his wife of 40 years, Mary Ann. The Donnelly's have two daughters and three grandchildren. He spends his time cross-fit training and enjoys running sprint triathlons (J. Donnelly, May 23, 2022).

Mike Pignata

I have such fond memories of Tiggy throughout my Babe Ruth Baseball experience, but especially as a good friend in high school. For three years Mike Pignata, shortstop Rick Gallien, and I would collectively get a frequent eye roll from Coach Emile Johnson over our shenanigans. All of that foolishness would end when we left the dugout, crossed the baseline and onto the field where it was all business. Coach Johnson would hit ground ball fungoes to Pignata at 3rd base, each grounder hit harder than the one before. It was a battle of wills between the two of them. Pignata was a fierce pull hitter in the batter's box, often times hitting a frozen-rope line drive down the left-field line, or a searing grounder past the opposing third-baseman. Most of these hits were for extra bases as Pignata had exceptional speed.

While playing for Foster Grant in the Leominster National Little League and the National LL All-Stars, Mike was brutal against opposing pitchers and was among the league leaders in batting average, home runs and runs-batted-in.

Mike was a standout baseball and football player at Leominster High School and was inducted into the LHS Athletic Hall of Fame in 2016. Sadly, Mike Pignata passed away in 2019. He was a life-long resident of the city.[41]

Jay Burke

Jay Burke remembers playing off-the-wall behind Spruce Street School with some of the boys from Leominster's French Hill section of the city, named for the community of French-Canadian immigrant families who relocated to the community during the rise of Leominster's renown plastics industry. Off-the-wall was game with automatic baseball rules that involved bouncing a tennis or rubber ball off the wall of a building which was fielded by the team on defense. If the defensive team did not field the ball cleanly it was a single. If the ball crossed a pre-determined boundary it was a double. If the ball went over the head of the outfield, it was deemed a home-run. Rules could vary and often times we would use a super-ball rather than a tennis ball. As Jay grew older, his playground of choice shifted to Saxton Trade Field up off Mill Street, and the Ronnie Bachand Little League field on 12th street. Jay also loved to play street hockey behind Spruce Street School with Sheehan brothers, Guy Gagnon, the Richards brothers, and Rick Gallien.

"We were perhaps the only Irish family living on French Hill at the time," he recalls. "We lived on Fourth Street which is about a mile out of downtown Leominster heading east on Mechanic Street." His dad, George, was a construction worker and his mom, Jane, a nurse at Leominster Hospital.

Jay was used to standing out in a crowd. Ever since his early playground days behind Spruce Street School, Jay would tower over his friends. This phenomenon continued as he migrated up through Little League, Pop Warner football, and Babe Ruth Baseball. I faced Jay in what was my first at-bat for Ranchers in the American Little League in April of 1970. Jay was on the mound for Crossman's and as I walked up to the plate I thought he was so tall, and the mound was so close to the plate that he would literally hand the ball to his catcher. Nonetheless, I made contact and shot a ground ball up the middle and into centerfield for my first Little League Majors hit. In addition to baseball, Jay played football for the Dolphins in the Leominster Pop Warner football league and played hoops in the St. Ann's Parochial Basketball League. He went on to play football and basketball at Gallagher Junior High.

When not on the mound, Jay could be found behind the plate as an all-star catcher and was my teammate on the 1970 American Little League all-star team that advanced to the Massachusetts Little League state tournament in Oxford. He was drafted by Solar Chemical by coach Ray Racine and made the Babe Ruth all-stars at both 14- and 15-years old.

Looking back, Jay claims that his three years playing Babe Ruth were the best years of his youth, and he especially enjoyed playing for coach Jim Marrone who Jay claimed was like a second father to him.

Following Babe Ruth, Jay played Leominster High School and Leominster Post 151 American Legion baseball leading up to a great collegiate experience playing for the Lancers at Worcester State College. He currently lives with his family on the Massachusetts south shore (J. Burke, April 21, 2021).

Rick Comeau

As a kid, Rick Comeau spent much of his time at Northwest School playing pick-up baseball, and at George Street School for hoops. Both venues were close to his childhood home at the corner of High Street and Washington Street, and he would ride his bike to both playgrounds with childhood friends Jim Comerford, Tom Kline and Armand DiMauro.

Comeau played his first organized baseball for the Yankees in the Leominster National Little League Minors at the young age of 7. He eventually played for Kingman in the National Little League Majors division earning All-Star honors his last season there in 1969.

After finishing Little League, Rick was drafted by legendary Babe Ruth coach Bob Lamothe for what was then Minuteman and eventually Tanzio Park. As a 13-year-old, Rick had the great benefit of pitching in a staff that included 1971 All-Stars Rich Kelly and Joe Hamilton. During my second year playing for U-Trans, I stepped into the batter's box to face Rick for the first time. Rick had struck out the previous two batters with neither batter making contact. His first pitch was a fastball that sailed inside and drilled me in the back as turned from the pitch. Rick being a great sportsman, came rushing into the batter's box to make sure I was okay. A classy move by a classy guy.

During his Leominster High School and Leominster American legion baseball years, Rick was perhaps the most dominant pitcher in in Central Massachusetts and arguably in the entire state. I had the privilege of playing left-field for the Blue Devils and the Legion squad in 1975 as his teammate and I can recall his fierce competitiveness and commitment to his game.

For his junior and senior years at LHS Rick had a record of 15-2 and batted .307 his senior year. In 2018 Rick was recognized for his accomplishments by virtue of his induction of into Leominster High School Athletics Hall of Fame. A sampling of his achievements include being named to the 1975 North Worcester County Umpires Association All-Star Team, a 7-1 record in his senior year (6-0 in conference) with a 1.65 ERA, over 100 strikeouts per season from 1974 – 1975, 82 strikeouts in 51 2/3 innings during his junior year for the 1974 Blue Devils, an average of 12 strikeouts per 9-innings pitched over his high school career, and in 1975 games, threw 19 K's versus Fitchburg, 16 K's versus Gardner, and 14 K's versus Wachusett Regional High School.

I recall Rick being a great teammate and very appreciative of the run support he received. He was especially vocal about the play of the defense behind him. In 1975, my junior year at LHS, Rick was on the mound against conference rival St. Peter's of Worcester. I was starting in left-field with Teddy Rockwell in center. Former and future Red Sox star Rich Gedman, then a sophomore at St. Peter's, lined a fading shot to left-center-field, towards which Rockwell and I converged. Yelling to Ted, "mine!," I dove to my left and made the catch in the gap which ended the inning. Comeau rushed out to shallow left-field to pat me on the back thanking me for making the play. Again, this gesture of teamwork and sportsmanship made a lasting impression of me.

Comeau was the first player under Coach Emile Jonson to be drafted by a major league team when he was picked up in the 10th round by the Texas Rangers in the 1975 draft. He played college baseball for Manatee Junior College in Tampa and then for Quinsigamond Junior College in Worcester, earning a trip to the NJCAA College World Series in 1977.
Rick and his wife Carlene spend their winters in Myrtle Beach, SC and enjoy spending time with their grandchildren (R. Comeau, September 8, 2022).

Figure 40: Rick Comeau on the mound for LHS during the 1975 season (photo credit: Leominster Historical Society)

Dick Freda

Dick Freda recalls he was about 10 years old when he first grabbed a splintered baseball bat, barely safe enough to grip thanks to the half roll of electrical tape wrapped around the handle, and walked up to the plate. His brother Don was on the mound grinning as he clutched what was a poor excuse of a baseball, essentially a ball of tape. Don delivered his pitch, and the left-hand hitting Dick lofted a long fly ball toward the trees in right field. "Double!," shouted Dick as the ball fell from the branches back to earth, referring to the automatic ground rules negotiated by the neighborhood kids. Such ground rules were common in Leominster neighborhood lots that bordered homes, sheds, gardens, businesses and property boundaries.

Dick grew up on Tisdale Street which runs parallel to Manchester Street and Sylvan Avenue, up from Union Street. It is about a quarter mile from downtown Leominster. He and his older brother Don would gather with other neighborhood kids such as Steve and Mike Ringer, Terry Mullan, Mike Leclair, Mike Pavilaitis and Mark Adams to play baseball, football or hockey, depending on the professional sports calendar.

On this day, the boys from this neighborhood in the area between lower Union and Pleasant Streets were playing in the lot that connected the Mullan and Freda yards. Other times they would make their way over to Christine Street and join Bob and Dave Antocci for street hockey or touch football in the street, occasionally having to stop play and move the net from the street to allow a car to pass. Still other times they would trek up to the field between Hickory Road and Lisa Drive to play baseball on a field that boasted an enormous boulder between second-base and center field.

The Freda's had a rink behind the house with a net constructed of chicken wire and scrap lumber. When there were too many skaters showing up for the modest rink, the group would head down to lower Manchester Street to the Radicioni's who had a larger sheet of ice.

Dick went to Bennett Elementary School and played Little League baseball for Rancher's in the Leominster American Little League. His brother Don played for Crossman's. Dick's 1969 Rancher's team won the American league title and boasted a lineup of future Leominster Babe Ruth all-stars Mike Leclair, Bobby Koch and John Cantatore. Dick's dad Bob Freda, Jack Koch and Pete Iacobone coached the 1969 Ranchers.

After completing his championship Little League season for Ranchers, Dick was drafted to play for TAG in the Leominster Babe Ruth League. During his final year as a 15-year-old, Dick made the 1972 all-star team as the starting first-baseman. Because Leominster served as the host team for the 1972 state tournament, Dick would comment years later that he and his teammates sometimes felt guilty about participating in that tournament since they did not have to play their way in.

Dick would have tremendous success as a two-sport athlete at Leominster High School playing three years of varsity soccer and baseball, both teams coached by Emile Johnson. With his long arms and lanky physique, Dick accounted for countless put-outs at first-base with his spider-man-like stretches and deft glove hand. Dick also played American Legion baseball for Coach Johnson.

Dick went on to play division II baseball and soccer at legendary national baseball powerhouse Eckerd College in Florida. During his freshman year in 1977, the Tritons went 39-9 and made it to the NCAA Division II final, losing to UC Riverside 4-1. 1971 Leominster Babe Ruth star Dave Malatos also played for that team. Other Eckerd College teammates included future MLB stars Joe Lefebvre and Steve Balboni. Future NY Yankees and SF Giants executive Brian Sabean was the assistant coach of the 1977 team. Dick lives with his family in the Florida Panhandle area (Di. Freda, December 11, 2021).

Jeff Johnson

Jeff Johnson played for the St. Bonaface Cardinals in the Lunenburg Little League with future Leominster Babe Ruth all-star Terry McNally, and was drafted to play for Werner Sporting Goods in the Leominster Babe Ruth League. Following Babe Ruth ball, Jeff starred in football, basketball and baseball for the Lunenburg Blue Knights, and played legion ball for Cleghorn Post 429 of Fitchburg.

Bob Koch

Despite his wiry frame, Bob Koch had a cannon for an arm. I was fortunate enough to have Bob as a teammate in Babe Ruth, for Leominster High School, and Leominster American Legion ball. Bobby, as he was known to his friends, also pitched when he played for U-Trans in Babe Ruth, but was mostly known for his defensive skills behind the plate as a catcher. It was exceedingly rare for an opposing player to steal a base on him. And he was fearless chasing down foul pop-ups behind the plate and down either of the infield baselines.

Bob's dad Jack Koch was one of our U-Trans coaches in 1971 and 1972, and was a gifted teacher of the game to a lot of us youngsters who had some raw talent, but lacked in fundamentals. I recall fondly when Coach Koch would hit fly balls to the outfield or grounders to the infield during practice, or during pre-game warm-ups, he'd often stop to point out the correct way to make a play during any situation. Coach. Koch was generous with his time, often showing up early for games to rake and line the field.

At Leominster High, Bobby was a three-sport star, playing halfback in football, forward in basketball, and catcher in baseball. In 1975, which was Bobby's senior year, the LHS athletic department purchased a JUGS pitching machine. The unit sat on a tripod and was comprised of two rubber wheels that spun at various speeds to simulate a fastball, curve ball, slider, or even change-up to batters. During practice, coach Johnson would sometimes position the JUGS machine at home plate and point the business end of the machine toward the sky as a means of simulating foul pop-ups. No matter how high and no matter how much spin he'd put on the ball, Bobby would almost always make the play.

Bobby moved with his family to Florida in the ensuing years and has sadly passed. He is remembered for his flowing red hair, freckles, and tenacious competitiveness on the field.

John Cantatore
John Cantatore was born in New Brunswick, Canada and moved to Lancaster Street in Leominster at age eight. During his little league years, he lived on Twelfth Street next to Leominster American Little League Field, where he fondly remembers playing several pickup baseball games each summer day. His parents still reside at that address today and remain good neighbors to the Little League to this day. A two-time American League All-Star his final years in Little League, John played center-field for the 1969 city champion Ranchers with Bob Koch, Dick Freda and Mike Leclair, all of whom would again be his teammates on the 1972 Babe Ruth State Champion team. He played for Solar Chemical in the Leominster Babe Ruth Baseball League with all-star teammates Jay Burke.

John, or "Johnny" as I knew him as a kid, would often visit his cousins Gary and Peter Andries who lived on Longwood Avenue, which was a stone's throw from my home on Elm Hill Avenue. I remember Johnny as a tall skinny kid who enjoyed ice hockey, baseball and football. As grade schoolers, we frequently played ice hockey at the swamp beneath the railroad tracks off Litchfield Street. Heading up the ice carrying the puck, John would be bobbing and weaving with head fakes, starts, and stops. I struggle to remember anyone from my childhood who would spend so much energy moving the puck ten feet. Even at that young age he had a monster wrist shot, as evident from the small dent in my shin that I still sport to this day. It is a pleasant reminder of our afternoons playing ice hockey as kids.

John would also show up to play the weekly touch football games held in the Borden Chemical parking lot on Elm Hill Avenue. As a 10–12-year-old, he'd join his older cousin Gary Andries, the Tata's, the Hulecki's, Steve Martino, Victor Szewczyk, Charlie DiGloria, George Wallace, Joe Charielle and many other older kids of neighborhoods from across the Lancaster Street area. I recall watching safely from the chain link fence with a football in my hand and itching to get in the game. Being only 8 or so, the only action I saw was chasing the game ball after an incomplete pass.

As he grew older, John attended Lancaster St. School and then May A. Gallagher Junior High School where he played freshman football and baseball.. At Leominster High School, he played baseball from 1972-1974 and also wrestled his senior year.

John's love of baseball continued into his young adult life, when he coached several Little League and Babe Ruth teams. He also acquired baseball and softball umpire certification, officiating numerous Babe Ruth and high school baseball games and some slow pitch softball.

He later briefly played one year of Over-30 baseball for the Leominster Mets and subsequently co-founded and served as player/co-rep for the Leominster Diamondbacks of the Central Mass Over-40 Baseball League for ten years. During that period, he authored the league's first set of by-laws, and was able to rekindle numerous old friendships and make many new friends, several of whom continue to be some of his best friends in life.

Johnny recalls the 1972 Babe Ruth all-star run as one of the best summers of his youth and is proud to have been part of Leominster's winning baseball tradition. Today he is retired from Johnson Controls and still resides in Leominster with his wife Carol with whom he has two children and three grandchildren (J. Cantatore, April 27, 2021).

Mike Leclair

Mike Leclair and I spent most of the summer of 1970 together as best friends and teammates for Ranchers of the Leominster American Little League. Our friendship extended deep into the summer, cemented by the amazing ride of our Little League All-Star team which made it all the way to the Massachusetts State Tournament in Oxford that August. Mike was the superstar of that team, going 5-0 as a starting pitcher and terrorizing opposing pitchers with his bat.

At that time, Mike lived on Manchester Street with his mom, Janette, and his younger brother Danny. His dad was a police officer for the Leominster Police Department. Sleepovers were popular during that time, and we spent several days together going to practice, games, and playing at each other's houses in between.

Our American Little League all-star team was loaded and included several members of the 1972 and 1973 Babe Ruth state championship teams. In addition to Mike Leclair and me, Mike Gasbarro, Doug Girouard, Jay Burke and Dave Arsenault made that 1970 Little League all-star team.

Mike was drafted first overall in the 1970 Babe Ruth League draft, being snapped up by coach Donnie Bigelow of U-Trans. Mike Gasbarro and I would also be drafted by U-Trans in later rounds. Mike excelled as a 13-year-old rookie the following summer, both as a pitcher as well as an outfielder, which earned him Rookie of the Year honors for 1971.

Leclair carried this success into high school when he posted a sterling 5-0 record as a sophomore at Leominster High. He continued his success for the next two years playing for coach Emile Johnson for both high school and American Legion teams.

Mike is currently enjoying his retirement, playing golf and fishing in the Leominster area. When I caught up with him to interview him for this book, he shared that he recently golfed with Joe and Eddie Cataldo. (M. Leclair, May 12, 2021).

Mike Gasbarro

The sun was setting over the tree tops as 12-year-old Mike Gasbarro pedaled his Schwinn 5-speed stingray through the Monster Land woods located at the end of Old Mill Road in southeastern Leominster. Ever mindful of the roots and rocks that dotted the beaten path, Mike learned from many spills to keep his eyes on the pathway while simultaneously peddling with all his might to make his parents' curfew.

Mike recalls that Bel-Air Heights was a great neighborhood with lots of kids his age which provided many opportunities for pick-up games. He and his siblings would often head over to South End Market for penny candy and soda. The neighborhood kids would organize baseball, football, and basketball games with other nearby neighborhoods according to the seasons. His neighborhood team was named the Bel-Air Bombers and they played against the South End Lions and Litchfield Panthers. Games were played at Fall Brook School and without adult supervision. In the winter he and his friends would play ice hockey up at Lake Samoset where he swam and fished during the summer months.

Like many 11- and 12-year-olds of that era, Mike recalls going to the Lancaster Street field to watch Babe Ruth baseball games and dream of one day playing there. He and scores of other boys chased foul balls and returned them to the field thinking they were heroes. Because of his proximity to the fabled Monster Land forested area, Mike and his friends would ride their bikes on the paths worn down by generations of kids that preceded him.

When Mike was younger, his family lived on Longwood Avenue behind Archie's Shell Station and The Lazy A restaurant until he was 8-years old. The Lazy A eventually was sold and renamed to Gondola Restaurant right around the same time that my dad, Archie Lefebvre, sold the Shell station. The Gasbarro's then moved to the corner of Mechanic and Ninth streets which was a short bike ride to 12th Street American

Little League. It was at the 12th Street field that Mike, and his younger brother Mark would develop their passion for baseball.

While attending Fall Brook Elementary School, Mike played Little League for Holdet Vise and made the American Little League all-stars as my teammate in 1970. Holdet Vise would win the American Little League championship that same season.

"Looking back, at that time my life centered around baseball," Mike shared recently. He added, "great coaches and great tradition. At fifteen, I played for U-Trans, and we won the league championship. I was on top of the world that summer." Among his numerous and notable accomplishments that summer of 1973, Mike pitched a no-hitter in the opening game of that season's best-of-three league championship series against rival Tanzio Park. Mike Leclair and I were teammates of Mike's on that championship U-Trans team.

At Leominster High School, Mike played baseball and soccer. After graduating from LHS in 1975, Mike served in the US Coast Guard. He is enjoying his retirement and splits this time between Leominster and Myrtle Beach, South Carolina (M. Gasbarro, April 27, 2021).

Scott Szymkiewicz
Up until 1972, boys graduating from Sterling Little League had no organized options for continuing their youth baseball careers. In 1972, the Leominster Babe Ruth League expanded with Sterling Lumber joining U-Trans, Tanzio, TAG, Solar Chemical, Elks Club and Werner Sporting Goods as the seventh Division 1 team in the league. This was good news for boys like Scott Szymkiewicz who were able to join the league as a fifteen-year-olds.

Scott grew up on the northwest side of Sterling on Princeton Road, just a short mile out of the center of town. "I played hardball baseball almost every day when it didn't rain," he remembers. "There was a neighborhood field owned by a local farmer who generously let us kids play ball there all summer. My friends Greg Jones and George Reed would join a bunch of other kids and play homerun derby, pickle, or just hit the ball around to each other to pass the time and hone our skills. In the winter we'd play ice hockey on one of the many surrounding ponds." When Scott was old enough, he played Little League at what is now known as Rick Maypother Field, which is located near the Princeton line on Route 62 just west of the intersection of Route 140.

Figure 41: Scott Szymkiewicz (photo credit: Scott Szymkiewicz)

Scott recently shared about his first encounter with Coach Jim Marrone at the all-star tryouts late June of 1972. "I was the first player to show up for the practice and coach Marrone was on the field juggling a brand-new baseball back and forth between his left and right hands. As I entered the park he tossed the ball to me and asked me to take a look at it, saying, 'there are no grass stains on that ball, son. If you want to make the team, let's keep it that way.' That motivated me to do the best I could, and I ultimately was named to the team."

Scott had a cannon of an arm and used it effectively throughout his

Little League and Babe Ruth Baseball careers, often throwing runners out at home plate from his perch in center-field. His organized baseball career ended that 1972 season as he did not continue to play ball at Wachusett Regional High School from which he graduated in 1975.

After serving 37 years on the Boylston Police Department, Scott retired in 2015 and now lives in North Conway, New Hampshire. He spends his days motorcycling and snowmobiling throughout the White Mountains (S. Szymkiewicz, August 20, 2022).

Greg Carchidi

Greg Carchidi was fast on his feet. Very fast. It was impossible to cover him as a receiver during those cold November days of playing touch football on the pavement of Anthony Road at the upper end of Pleasant Street. Upper Pleasant Street area was a bountiful source of neighborhood kids who would somehow know when there was a game to be played. Future LHS football stars Charlie Kirouac, Steve and Ronnie Davis, Jack Celli, Rick L'Ecuyer, Tony DePasquale, Greg, and others would participate in this homegrown match-up of brawn, bravado and bragging rights.

Greg was also very funny, an animated storyteller, and a natural entertainer. He grew up on Anthony Road after his family moved from the corner of Pond Avenue and Pleasant Street. I lived a short distance from Greg through the woods at the bottom of Anthony Road to Glenwood Drive. On school days I would sneak through the woods and through one of the Anthony Road yards to catch the high school bus at the top of Anthony Road because it arrived later, and I could therefore catch an extra ten minutes of sleep. I remember how Greg would hold court at the back of the bus with all of us in stitches over his stories, his voice pitching higher as he got more excited.

Greg was a defensive back on the great 1974 LHS football team and a star basketball player over the winter. In the years leading up to his high school experience, he would frequently be seen at Fall Brook during summers playing for the Fall Brook playground softball and street hockey teams. In Little League, he played with future Babe Ruth League all-star teammates Mike Pignata and Rick Comeau on Foster Grants in the Leominster National Little League. When I recently spoke with Greg he still chuckled about his memories of playing for that team which was coached by Deico Pignata.

"My experiences playing for the Leominster Babe Ruth all-stars were wonderful," recalls Greg. "I made lifelong friends from my years in youth sports, especially rooming with Steve Jackson and Mike Gasbarro in Newport during the 1972 New England Babe Ruth all-star tournament."

Greg played a couple of years of baseball at Bridgewater State College, and is currently retired after a successful career as a corporate credit officer for various technology companies in Massachusetts including Lotus Software and IBM. Today he splits his time between Leominster and Myrtle Beach, SC, and enjoys playing golf and the piano (G. Carchidi, January 30, 2022).

Chapter Twelve - The Games

Leominster vs. Lawrence, Tuesday, July 25, 1972
With ace Rick Comeau on the mound for the state tournament opener against Lawrence, Leominster had every reason to be confident. Comeau was undefeated in regular season league play for Tanzio Park, including a complete game no-hit shutout. Like Rich Kelly from the 1971 team, Comeau was a power pitcher with tremendous command over his pitching repertoire. And judging by the fact that Comeau mowed down the first two Lawrence batters on six pitches, optimism was building for the hometown all-stars.

The Lawrence stars, however, had other plans, as pitcher Fred Simm, the third batter of the inning walked on four pitches. In a rare display of lack of control, Comeau threw consecutive wild pitches to Lawrence clean-up batter and shortstop Dave Robinson, sending Simm to third-base with two outs. Robinson chopped an infield ground ball which was misplayed resulting in an error that sent Simm home with the first Lawrence run.

Lawrence plated two more runs in the second inning when right-fielder Steve Comparone reached on another infield error and stole second. Catcher Bob Hajjar singled to center-field and scored Comparone when Leominster center-fielder Charlie Richard's throw was wide of home plate. Hajjar drew a throw from Leominster catcher Bob Koch on the play which sailed into the outfield, thus scoring Hajjar with the second unearned run of the inning.

Things went from bad to worse for Leominster as Lawrence put another two runs on the board in the third. Simm led off with a ground-rule double that hopped over the center-field fence. This was followed by a titanic home run by Robinson to left-center-field. After three innings, Leominster trailed 5-0.

Lawrence scored its final three runs in the fourth inning when Comparone doubled to center-field to open the inning. Dave Mosher bunted safely, but Comparone was held at second. The two runners executed a double-steal resulting in runners on second and third with no outs. Comparone scored on a John Doherty sacrifice fly to center, and Mosher scored when center-fielder Jim Loffredo's infield pop-up dropped behind the mound. A single by Simm advanced Loffredo to third. Comeau then intentionally walked slugger Dave Robinson to load the bases, thus creating a force situation to hopefully get out of the inning. However, Comeau threw his third wild-pitch of the game which plated Loffredo with the final Lawrence run. Lawrence now had an 8-0 lead after four innings.

Leominster did not go down quietly, however. Simm, who had shown remarkable control over the first five Leominster innings, opened the sixth by throwing 16 straight balls to Bob Koch, Jay Burke, Mike Pignata and Paul Gamache which scored Koch with the first Leominster run. Second-baseman Jim Donnelly cracked a single to drive in Burke with the second run. Simm uncorked a wild-pitch scoring Pignata with the third run.

Lawrence	ab	r	h	bi
Doherty, 2b	3	0	0	1
Loffredo, cf	4	1	1	1
Simm, p-ss	2	2	2	0
Robinson, ss-p	2	1	1	2
Redman, 1b	3	0	0	0
Smith, lf	2	0	0	0
Verrette, lf	1	0	0	0
Comparone, rf	3	2	1	0
Hajjar, c	3	1	1	1
Mosher, 3b	3	1	1	0
Totals	26	8	7	5

Leominster	ab	r	h	bi
Richard, cf	2	0	2	0
Freda, 1b	3	0	0	0
Koch, rf	2	1	0	0
Szymkiewicz, ph	0	1	0	0
Burke, lf	2	1	0	0
Cantatore, ph	0	1	0	0
Pignata, 3b	2	1	1	1
Gasbarro, ss	2	0	1	0
Gamache	1	1	1	2
Jackson, 2b	2	0	0	0
Donnelly, 2b	2	0	1	1
Carchidi, c	2	0	0	0
Leclair, ph	1	0	0	1
Comeau, p	1	0	0	0
Johnson, p	2	0	0	0
Totals	**24**	**6**	**6**	**5**

In the seventh inning, Leominster continued to claw back with three runs, but ultimately fell short, losing 8-6. Scott Szymkiewicz, pinch-hitting for starting catcher Greg Carchidi, drew a walk. This was followed by another walk to pinch-hitter John Cantatore putting men on first and second with no outs. Pignata punched a single up the middle into center-field which was misplayed by Lawrence center-fielder Jim Loffredo, and which allowed Szymkiewicz to score from second. Cantatore advanced to third on the error.

Lawrence starter Fred Simm was taken out of the game to a nice round of applause from the fans and switched positions with shortstop Dave Robinson. Paul Gamache, pinch-hitting for Mike Gasbarro, bounced a slow roller to third that was also misplayed, which scored Cantatore making the score 8-5. When Lawrence third-baseman Dave Mosher threw wildly to the plate, Pignata hustled home to make the score 8-6. With the potential tying run at the plate, Jim Donnelly and Mike Leclair both grounded out for the first two outs. Relief pitcher Jeff Johnson then struck out to strand Gamache and end the game and drop the home team into the tournament loser's bracket. Final score 8-6.[42][43]

Longmeadow vs. Leominster, Thursday, July 27, 1972
Finding themselves in a single-elimination scenario following their opening game loss to Lawrence, the Leominster all-stars roared back with a statement game against the Section 1 champions from Longmeadow. 14-year-old Mike Leclair took the hill for the home town team with regular season U-Trans teammate Bob Koch behind the plate as his battery-mate. Leominster's lineup included lead-off hitter and center-fielder Charlie Richard followed by first-baseman Dick Freda. Slugger third-baseman Mike Pignata batted third, left-fielder Jay Burke batted clean-up, and catcher Koch fifth in the order. Paul Gamache started at short and batted sixth. Second-baseman Jim Donnelly batted seventh, right-fielder Scott Szymkiewicz eighth, and pitcher Leclair closed out the starting line-up at ninth.

Leclair's arm and the bats of Charlie Richard and Mike Pignata were the key factors in a solid 9-2 victory over Longmeadow. Leominster scored the first run on of the game in the bottom of the first inning when Charlie Richard singled for the first of his two hits, stole second and advanced to third on a sacrifice bunt by Dick Freda. Richard scored on a sacrifice fly by Jay Burke.

Leominster exploded for three more runs in the third when Richards and Freda drew bases on balls off Longmeadow starting pitcher John Fleming. Mike Pignata wasted no time and launched a Fleming fastball over the left-field fence for a 3-run home run, putting Leominster up 4-0 through three innings. Leclair, in the meantime, had limited Longmeadow to a single base hit and no runs through five innings.

In the fifth, Leominster blew the game wide-open as Donnelly, Szymkiewicz, and Leclair all reached base, setting up Charlie Richard for a majestic grand-slam home run over the left-center-field fence to put

Leominster up 7-0 after five. Leclair lost his bid for a shutout when Longmeadow pushed across a pair of runs in the sixth inning as catcher Scott Aye walked and scored on a two-run homer off the bat of Wes Atwood.

Leominster	AB	R	H
Richard, cf	3	3	2
Freda, 1b	1	2	0
Pignata, 3b	3	1	1
Burke, lf	2	0	0
Cantatore, lf	0	0	0
Koch, c	3	0	0
Gamache, ss	2	0	0
Donnelly, 2b	2	1	1
Szymkiewicz, rf	1	1	0
Johnson, rf	0	0	0
Leclair	2	1	0
Totals	**19**	**9**	**4**

Longmeadow	AB	R	H
Meserve, 2b	2	0	0
Hurwitz, rf	4	0	0
Durocher, ss	3	0	0
Aye, c	1	1	0
Atwood, cf-p	3	1	1
Howard, 3b	2	0	0
DeStefano, 1b	2	0	0
Fleming, p	2	0	1
Sadler, ph	1	0	0
Williams, lf	2	0	0
Petroff, ph	0	0	0
Totals	**22**	**2**	**2**

Pitcher	IP	H	R	ER	W	K
Fleming (l)	2	3	4	3	3	2
Atwood	4	1	5	4	4	4
Leclair (w)	7	2	2	2	6	6

Leominster added a pair of insurance runs in the sixth inning and held on to win 9-2. The win earned Leominster the right to avenge its opening game loss against Lawrence within in only 24 hours.[44] [45]

Lawrence vs. Leominster, Friday, July 28, 1972 (Game 1)
Following the win over Longmeadow, Leominster needed a double-header sweep over Lawrence and Burncoat of Worcester to remain in the hunt for its second consecutive Massachusetts Babe Ruth League state championship. Mike Pignata went the distance on the mound in the opener and stymied the Lawrence hitters with a brilliant four-hitter, issuing five walks while striking out eight batters. Leominster's defense was stellar behind Pignata playing error-less ball and turning a bang-bang double-play to douse a Lawrence scoring threat.

For game 1, manager Jim Marrone started the fleet Charlie Richard in center-field and batting lead-off, followed by second-baseman Jim Donnelly. Shortstop Paul Gamache batted third, Pignata batted clean-up, and right-fielder Jay Burke hit fifth. Pignata's battery-mate Bob Koch batted sixth, first-baseman Dick Freda seventh, third-baseman Mike Gasbarro batted eighth, and left-fielder John Cantatore closed out the Leominster lineup in the ninth batting spot.

Lawrence sent three pitchers to the mound in an effort to thwart the Leominster offensive attack, but to no avail. Cantatore paced the Leominster offense with two hits, a run scored and an RBI. Richard chipped in with a two-run double and added a stolen base. Donnelly, Pignata, Freda and Gasbarro each contributed a base hit for the winning cause, with Donnelly and Gasbarro each scoring twice.

The only damage Lawrence could muster offensively was a solo home-run by Fred Simm in third inning, which at the time, tied the score at 1. Leominster quickly added seven runs in the top of the 4th to pull ahead for good.[46]

Leominster	AB	R	H
Richard, cf	3	1	1
Szymkiewicz, cf	0	0	0
Donnelly, 2b	2	2	1
Jackson, 2b	0	0	0
Gamache, ss	2	0	0
Pignata, p	3	1	1
Burke, rf	3	0	0
Koch, c	3	1	0
Freda, 1b	4	1	1
Gasbarro, 3b	2	2	1
Cantatore, lf	3	1	2
Totals	**25**	**9**	**7**

Lawrence	AB	R	H
Doherty, 2b	2	0	1
Lofredo, cf	2	0	1
Simm, p	4	1	1
Robinson, ss-p	3	0	0
Redman, 1b	2	0	0
Saab, lf	2	0	0
Smith, rf	2	0	1
Camparone, rf	1	0	0
Hajjar, c	2	0	0
Milone, rf	1	0	0
Verrette, p	1	0	0
Totals	**22**	**1**	**4**

Pitcher	IP	H	R	ER	W	K
Pignata (w)	7	4	1	1	5	8
Simm (l)	3.1	5	7	6	3	3
Robinson	1.2	2	2	1	3	0
Verrette	2	0	0	0	1	2

Burncoat vs. Leominster, Friday, July 28, 1972 (Game 2)
By virtue of its win earlier in the day versus Lawrence, the local nine earned the right to face Burncoat of Worcester in the night-cap. Rick Comeau, coming off his defeat in the tournament opener against Lawrence, got the start with three days' rest. Manager Jim Marrone shuffled the line-up as the prior game's winner Mike Pignata returned to third-base. The batting order featured Charlie Richard again leading off and playing center-field. Jim Donnelly batted second and returned to second-base, while shortstop Paul Gamache batted third. Pignata was slotted for clean-up followed again by Jay Burke in right-field. Dick Freda at first, John Cantatore in left, and pitcher Comeau filled out the bottom third of the batting order.

    The Leominster stars got off to a fast start with a run each in the first and third innings followed by an 8-run outburst in the fourth to blow the game wide open. Gamache led the Leominster hit parade with a double and a single, two runs scored and an RBI. Dick Freda and Bob Koch also contributed a pair of hits each. Charlie Richard hit a 2-run double for the second game in a row. Jim Donnelly and Gamache each stole a pair of bases to keep the pressure on the Burncoat infield throughout the game.

    Comeau regained his command and allowed only 4 singles. He fanned six and walked only three. For the second game of the day, Leominster played error-less defense behind their starting pitcher.

    Despite facing daunting odds as the host team, and after their crushing loss to open the tournament, Jim Marrone's squad now advances to the tournament semi-finals, awaiting the winner of Saturday's match-up between Parkway of Roxbury and Longmeadow as their next opponent.[47][48]

Leominster	AB	R	H
Richard, cf	2	1	1
Szymkiewicz, cf	1	0	0
Donnelly, 2b	2	2	1
Jackson, 2b	0	0	0
Gamache, ss	3	2	2
Pignata, 3b	3	0	0
Gasbarro, 3b	1	0	0
Burke, rf	2	1	0
Johnson, rf	1	0	0
Freda, 1b	3	1	2
Cantatore, lf	3	1	1
Koch, c	3	1	2
Comeau, p	2	1	0
Totals	**26**	**10**	**9**

Burncoat	AB	R	H
Powers, ss	3	0	0
Hastings, cf	2	0	0
Killeen, 1b	2	0	2
Quinn, rf	3	0	1
Shepeluk, p-c	3	0	0
Cutty, 3b	2	0	1
O'Brien, lf	1	0	0
Sands, rf	2	0	0
Lamaroux, c	1	0	0
Remington, p	1	0	0
Gibbons, 2b	2	0	0
Olson, ph	1	0	0
Totals	**23**	**0**	**4**

Pitcher	IP	H	R	ER	W	K
Comeau (w)	7	4	0	0	3	6
Shepeluk (l)	3.1	8	10	9	4	3
Remington	2.2	1	0	0	2	0

Leominster vs. Parkway, Saturday, July 29, 1972 (Game 1)
At 4-0, the Parkway Babe Ruth League All-Stars of West Roxbury entered the day undefeated in tournament play, while Leominster with its opening game loss to Lawrence brought a 3-1 tournament record. As a result, Parkway needed only one win to claim the championship, while Leominster needed to win its way into a winner-takes-all final in the nightcap.

Mike Leclair got the start for Leominster, but with this team facing elimination with a loss, manager Jim Marrone certainly planned to use whatever means necessary to force a second game for the title. Charlie Richard, as usual batted lead-off and patrolled center-field with second-baseman Jim Donnelly following in the second spot. The rest of the batting order and line-up had Paul Gamache at short and batting third, third-baseman Mike Pignata batting clean-up, right-fielder Jay Burke hitting fifth, first-baseman Dick Freda batting sixth, catcher Bob Koch seventh, left-fielder John Cantatore batting eighth and Leclair closing out the order in the ninth slot.

Leominster wasted no time getting on the scoreboard, plating two runs in the top of the first inning. Charlie Richard drew an opening walk and immediately stole second. An infield error off the bat of Donnelly's chopper sent Richard to third without a throw. With runners on first and third and no one out, Paul Gamache doubled to the fence in right-center, scoring both Richard and Donnelly for a quick 2-0 lead before any outs were recorded in the opening inning.

Leclair held Parkway scoreless in the first inning. Parkway starting pitcher Chris Farrell likewise held Leominster bats in check in the top of the second. In the bottom of the second, however, Farrell cut Leominster's lead in half with a long shot over the center-field fence for a solo home-run. 2-1 Leominster after two innings.

Leominster answered again the top of the third when shortstop Gamache grounded to the hole between short and third, beating the throw for a single. Gamache broke for second for a steal attempt and made it to third when Parkway catcher Joe Celeste's throw to second sailed wide of the bag. Lady Luck made her presence known as Mike Pignata's chopper to third took a strange hop over Parkway third-baseman Phil Olsen's head, scoring Gamache who was holding up on the play. 3-1 Leominster after three-and-a-half innings.

Parkway threatened again the fifth inning as Leclair began to show some fatigue. Center-fielder Kevin Rose and pitcher Farrell each singled to open the inning. First-baseman Jim Conroy walked to load the bases with no outs. Leclair then hit second-baseman Matt Kelleher with a pitch which forced in the second Parkway run. Fortunately for Leominster Leclair bore down and was able to escape the inning with a slim one-run lead.

That would all come apart in the bottom of the sixth inning when Parkway would take the lead. After retiring the first two Parkway batters, Leclair again tired as he walked four consecutive batters to force in the tying run. With bases still loaded and with two outs, manager Marrone made the pitching change and called on third-baseman Mike Pignata. Mike Gasbarro trotted out to take Pignata's spot at third. The crowd gave Leclair a great hand as he left the mound for the Leominster dugout.

Unfortunately, Pignata also struggled to find the plate and walked the first Parkway batter he faced which forced in the go ahead run for Parkway. Pignata escaped further damage by retiring right-fielder Mark Sullivan on fly out. At the end of six innings and with Leominster's season coming down to its last three outs, Parkway led 4-3.

The situation became even more dire as lead-off hitter Mike Gasbarro was retired. However, lead-off batter Charlie Richard, showing great discipline at the plate, worked Farrell for a walk. Every player, coach, umpire, and fan in the stands knew without a doubt that Charlie Richard would attempt to steal second-base on the first throw to the plate. Known for his tremendous speed, there was little if any chance that the catcher could throw him out at second. Farrell's only option was to check Richard at first-base with a few glances and perhaps then attempt a pick-off throw to keep Charlie close to the first-base bag.

It was all for naught, for as soon as Farrell's left toe pointed toward home plate and thus committing to the pitch, Richard broke for second and slid in safely without a throw from the catcher. Leominster now had the tying run at second-base with one out. Leominster second-baseman Jim Donnelly then hit a ground to the right side of the infield which advanced Richard to third. Unfortunately, Leominster was now down to its last out.

While Parkway coach Mitch Kaltsunas met with his batter and infield on the mound for a time-out chat to discuss the defensive strategy, Marrone spoke a few encouraging words to second-year all-star Gamache as he waited for play to resume. The Leominster and Parkway parents and fans, local and state-level league officials, and members of the media, all stood to see how this situation would unfold. On a personal note, I was sitting in the stands on the third-base side between the dugout and the concession stand. As Gamache was introduced as the batter, the noise from the crowed increased from a slight murmur to a roar as the focus returned to the field.

The tension in the air was thick with the realization of the stakes of the at-bat. Gamache added to that tension by working Farrell for a full count. With two outs, a 3-2 count, and the tying run 90 feet away, Gamache tapped the plate and looked back at Farrell while taking a couple of warm-up swings. Farrell peered past Gamache's gaze and looked for his catcher's sign. Gamache took the pitch and listened for the umpire to call "ball four!." The Leominster contingent, which had to number over a thousand fans that day, roared as Gamache scampered down to first-base. Runners on first and third, two outs, and Parkway maintaining a 4-3 lead.

There comes a moment in a tournament when coaching inevitably proves to be a difference maker in a game or in a situation. What transpired next did not show up in the box score; nor did it get any mention in newspaper coverage of the game. And unless you played for Jim Marrone, you probably would not even think of such a thing. With runners on first and third, down by a run, and with Parkway having the last at-bat as the game's home team, there is no doubt in my mind that Marrone was not thinking about the tie, but was thinking about the win. He immediately caught Parkway and everyone in the park not wearing a Leominster uniform by surprise by giving Gamache the steal sign, and giving the next batter, Mike Pignata, the take sign. The stunned Parkway catcher Joe Celeste jumped from his crouch and faked a throw to second-base, keeping Richard on third and putting the go-head run on second.

I've given this play and Marrone's hunch a lot of thought in retrospect. First, if successful, it places Gamache on second with the go-ahead run in scoring position. Second, by giving Pignata the take sign, he doesn't risk tiring Gamache should Pignata foul the pitch. Third, a straight steal would distract the pitcher, which in turn would increase the chance of Farrell balking, throwing a ball, or even better, throwing a wild pitch to bring in the tying run. And last, no one anticipated Marrone risking a season ending out at second base with the tying run at third. That said, with the benefit of hindsight, what I imagine is that Marrone was thinking that a successful steal created an opportunity to score two runs on one hit. And Pignata had been on fire offensively in the tournament.

As if the baseball gods scripted it themselves, Mike Pignata hammered the very next pitch down the left field line to score both Richard and Gamache, and Leominster shocked their opponents by taking a 5-4 lead into the bottom of the seventh inning. The hometown fans erupted in the stands, drowning out the honking cars surrounding the outfield fence.

And as fate would have it, Pignata himself shut Parkway down in order to close out the win, sending an exhilarated hometown crowd into a frenzy as the Leominster Babe Ruth stars now found themselves in the championship game after dropping their opening game, and battling back with four wins in three days.

Parkway	AB	R	H
Thomas, ss	3	0	0
Olsen, 3b	4	0	0
Perry, lf	3	0	0
Celeste, c	4	0	0
Rose, cf	3	1	1
Farrell, p	2	3	1
Conroy, 1b	1	0	0
Kelleher, 2b	1	0	1
Sullivan, rf	2	0	1
Totals	**23**	**4**	**4**

Leominster	AB	R	H
Richard, cf	2	2	0
Donnelly, 2b	4	1	1
Gamache, ss	2	2	2
Pignata, 3b-p	4	0	2
Burke, rf	3	0	1
Freda, 1b	2	0	0
Koch, c	3	0	1
Cantatore, lf	3	0	1
Leclair, p	2	0	0
Gasbarro, 3b	1	0	0
Totals	**26**	**5**	**8**

Pitcher	IP	H	R	ER	W	K
Leclair	5.2	4	4	4	4	1
Pignata (w)	1.1	0	0	0	1	1
Farrell (l)	7	3	5	4	5	2

Alas, Leominster's shot at the championship would have to wait one more night as the second game was rained out and postponed until the following day.[49]

Parkway vs. Leominster, Sunday, July 30, 1972
Massachusetts State Championship Game
Thinking back to the championship game, I, like most of the Leominster hometown fans, probably wondered if the championship game postponement helped or hurt Leominster's cause. Flying high off the stunning comeback win over Parkway in the semi-final, the locals certainly had the momentum and the crowd in their favor. And players such as Charlie Richard, Mike Pignata, Paul Gamache and Jim Donnelly were red hot at the plate. Finally, Parkway could not have been more vulnerable as they were following that loss.

However, giving Leominster's ace Rick Comeau an extra night's sleep and another day off from his last start could only help the team's cause. In any event, Leominster found itself in the enviable if not unbelievable position of defending its state championship, at home, and with their ace on the mound.

Marrone kept most of his lineup the same as in the semi-final, with one notable exception: moving left-handed hitting left-fielder John Cantatore up in the batting order to bat fifth and dropping Jay Burke to eight. This hunch, like so many others Marrone had made in this and the other all-star tournaments in 1971 and 1973 would pay off handsomely. The Leominster lineup and batting order then featured Charlie Richard in center-field and leading off, Jim Donnelly at second-base and batting second, Paul Gamache at shortstop and batting third, Mike Pignata at third-base and hitting clean-up, Cantatore in left and batting fifth, catcher Bob Koch batting sixth, Dick Freda at first-base and in the seventh slot, Jay Burke in right and batting eighth, and Rick Comeau on the hill and batting ninth.

Before the crowd of over one thousand had yet to settle into their afternoon seats, Parkway got off to a quick lead when shortstop Mike Thomas led the game off with a solid single to left. Thomas advanced to second when Parkway second-baseman Phil Olsen grounded into left-field through the hole at short. Parkway now had runners on first and second with no outs.

Parkway left-fielder and future Holy Cross basketball star Ronnie Perry hit into a fielder's choice forcing Olsen out at second, but advancing Thomas to third. First and third, one out.

Perry promptly stole second-base which now put both Parkway runners in scoring position. Still one out. Catcher Joe Celeste lined a solid single into left-center-field, driving in both runners for a quick 2-0 Parkway lead. Comeau bore down and retired the next two batters to escape any further damage.

Leominster would chip away at the two-run deficit in the bottom of the second inning. With one out, Bob Koch laced a double down the left-field line. After Dick Freda was retired for the second out of the inning, right-fielder Jay Burke lined a clutch single into right-field, scoring Koch with the first Leominster run.

After Comeau set Parkway down in the top of the third, Leominster got things rolling again in the bottom of the third. With one out, Jim Donnelly tapped a slow roller to third and hustled his way to first for the infield single. With Gamache at the plate, Donnelly bolted for second for the steal attempt and appeared out on the play. However, Parkway second-baseman Kevin Rose dropped the ball and Donnelly was declared safe. Gamache worked Parkway starter Mark Sullivan for a walk, putting runners on first and second with one out.

To no surprise to anyone in the Leominster dugout, Marrone gave his runners the steal sign and Donnelly and Gamache executed a perfect double-steal to put runners on second and third, still with only one out. Mike Pignata, yesterday's pitching and offensive hero, calmly took his practice swings, stepped into the box, stared down Sullivan, and lined the very first pitch down the left-field line scoring both Donnelly and Gamache for a 3-2 Leominster lead.

Leominster continued with its unrelenting pressure by scoring its final two runs in the bottom of the fourth inning. Right-fielder Jay Burke, who had been struggling offensively during the tournament, got hot at the right time. Anticipating a fast ball from Sullivan, Burke teed off on the first pitch and lined it over the left-field fence for a home-run, giving Leominster a 4-2 lead. Burke, having been dropped in the order to bat eighth, rewarded manager Marrone's hunch with 2 hits including the homer, a run scored and two RBI's.

But the rally was not yet over. After Comeau and center-fielder Charlie Richard both singled, Mike Pignata walked to load the bases, probably to the great relief of those on the Parkway side of the field. John Cantatore, who had been moved up in the order by Marrone for the day's game, fouled off a couple of pitches and worked Sullivan to a 3-2 count. Sullivan lost Cantatore on a ball just out of the strike zone and Cantatore trotted to first with the walk that forced in the fifth and final Leominster run. The score was 5-2 after four innings.

Leominster's defense and Comeau's gutsy performance on the mound held the powerful Parkway bats mostly silent the rest of the game. For the third straight game and when it mattered most, Leominster's defense played errorless ball. Comeau scattered eight hits, fanned eight and walked only one. And the play that ended the game was spectacular to say the least.

With one out in the seventh and final inning, Parkway shortstop Mike Thomas singled. Third-baseman Phil Olsen hit what appeared to be a drooping single to right-field, but Leominster second-baseman Donnelly tracked it down for the out, and turned to fire a strike to first-baseman Freda for the double-play and the final out of the tournament. The Leominster throng roared while the Leominster players rushed the infield to mob their teammates. For the second consecutive year, Leominster was Massachusetts Babe Ruth State Champions.[50] [51] [52]

Leominster	AB	R	H	RBI
Richard, cf	3	0	2	0
Donnelly, 2b	4	1	1	0
Gamache, ss	3	1	0	0
Pignata, 3b-p	3	0	1	2
Cantatore, lf	2	0	1	1
Koch, c	3	1	1	0
Freda, 1b	3	0	0	0
Burke, rf	3	1	2	2
Comeau, p	3	1	1	0
Totals	**27**	**5**	**9**	**5**
Parkway	**AB**	**R**	**H**	**RBI**
Thomas, ss	4	1	2	0
Olsen, 3b	4	0	2	0
Perry, lf	3	1	0	0
Celeste, c	3	0	2	2
Farrell, rf	3	0	1	0
Rose, c-2b	3	0	0	0
Kelleher, 2b	2	0	0	0
Knox, p	0	0	0	0
Sullivan, p-cf	3	0	0	0
Doherty, cf	0	0	0	0
Conroy, 1b	2	0	1	0
Nelligan, ph	1	0	0	0
Totals	**28**	**2**	**8**	**2**

Pitcher	IP	H	R	ER	W	K
Comeau (w)	7	8	2	2	1	8
Sullivan (l)	3.2	8	5	5	4	4
Knox	2.1	1	0	0	0	1

New England Regionals, Newport, Rhode Island
Leominster vs. Puerto Nuevo (Puerto Rico), Saturday, August 5, 1972
Leominster's reward for winning its second consecutive Massachusetts state championship was to open up the New England Regional Tournament against defending world champions Puerto Nuevo, Puerto Rico. With several days off since the state tournament, manager Jim Marrone's charges had a chance to mend the bumps and bruises earned from that hard-fought tourney. Ace Rick Comeau and the rest of the Leominster pitching corps also had the opportunity to rest their arms.

In a tight game that featured a tremendous pitcher's duel between Leominster starter Rick Comeau and Puerto Nuevo's Oscar Negron, the locals unfortunately found themselves on the losing end of a tight 1-0 game which placed them immediately in the regional tournament loser's bracket. Comeau and Negron gave up only two hits apiece; however the Puerto Nuevo squad made their hits count.

Leominster's starting lineup featured center-fielder Charlie Richard batting lead-off, second-baseman Jim Donnelly batting second, shortstop Paul Gamache hitting third and third-baseman Mike Pignata in the clean-up spot. John Cantatore got the start in left-field and batted fifth followed by catcher Bob Koch. First-baseman Dick Freda, right-fielder Jay Burke and pitcher Comeau rounded out the Leominster batting order.

Leominster threatened in the top of the second inning when John Cantatore dropped an opposite-field single into left-field. On his steal attempt, Cantatore slid safely into second-base and raced toward third when Cirino's throw sailed into center-field. However, center-fielder Ernesto Vasquez's perfect throw to third-base erased Cantatore from the base paths, ending the threat.

After breezing through the first three innings, Comeau walked first-baseman Ernesto Cruz on four pitches to open the bottom of the fourth inning. Cruz wasted no time and promptly stole second-base, putting himself in scoring position with no outs. Puerto Nuevo catcher

Henry Cirino lined to Charlie Richard in center-field for the first out, with Cruz holding at second-base. Right-fielder Carlos Carbassa then lined a single into right-field. Leominster right-fielder Burke charged the ball hard knowing that Cruz would have a jump, scooped up the ball, and rifled a strong throw to catcher Koch at home plate. Cruz narrowly beat the throw, sliding in with what turned out to be the only run of the game.

Burke reminisces, "The ball was a line drive in the right-center-field gap, I got a good jump and fielded the ball on one hop. It was a great game, the tension was high, and they earned that run. We knew at that point in the game that it was winnable. I knew I made a great throw, but unfortunately the runner beat the tag."

In the top of the fifth inning first-baseman Dick Freda picked up Leominster's second hit of the game but was thrown out trying to steal second. Other than the two hits, Leominster's only other baserunners were the result of three walks yielded by Negron. One of those walks posed Leominster's final threat in the seventh inning when Paul Gamache walked on four pitches. Mike Pignata attempted to advance Gamache with a bunt; however, Pignata's bunt was a pop-up to Negron coming off the mound. Gamache, running on the play, was doubled off first-base for the first two outs of the inning. Cantatore then worked Negron for a six-pitch walk but was stranded on a ground-out by Bob Koch.

Puerto Nuevo	**AB**	**R**	**H**	**RBI**
Concepcion, ss	3	0	0	0
Marcano, lf	3	0	0	0
Cruz, 1b	1	1	0	0
Cirino, c	2	0	0	0
Carbassa, rf	3	0	1	1
Vasquez, cf	2	0	0	0
Montana, 3b	2	0	0	0
Rivera, 2b	2	0	1	0
Negron, p	1	0	0	0
Totals	19	1	2	1

Leominster	AB	R	H	RBI
Richard, cf	3	0	0	0
Donnelly, 2b	2	0	0	0
Gamache, ss	2	0	0	0
Pignata, 3b	3	0	0	0
Cantatore, lf	2	0	1	0
Koch, c	3	0	0	0
Freda, 1b	2	0	1	0
Burke, rf	2	0	0	0
Comeau, p	2	0	0	0
Totals	**21**	**0**	**2**	**0**

Pitcher	IP	H	R	ER	W	K
Negron (w)	7	2	0	0	3	9
Comeau (l)	6	2	1	1	3	4

Leominster now found itself in the loser's bracket and would play again in two days versus the loser of Bath, ME vs. host Newport, RI.[53][54][55]

Bath (ME) vs. Leominster, Monday, August 7, 1972

With the sour taste of the loss to Puerto Rico still in their mouths, Leominster needed a victory to stay alive in the regional tournament. The benefit of playing in the winner's bracket is the occasional day off between games waiting for a new opponent from the loser's bracket. Leominster would need to find a way to keep their season alive by focusing on one game at a time and not be overwhelmed by the overall task at hand. Manager Jim Marrone was a master at keeping his team loose and in the moment.

The lineup for the tilt had center-fielder Charlie Richard in his traditional lead-off position in the order. Second-baseman Jim Donnelly batted second, followed by shortstop Paul Gamache. In the clean-up slot once again was third-baseman Mike Pignata with left-fielder John Cantatore batting fifth and catcher Bob Koch hitting sixth. Dick Freda at first-base, Jay Burke in right-field and Leclair completed the bottom third of the batting order.

Leominster	AB	R	H	RBI
Richard, cf	3	0	0	1
Szymkiewicz, cf	1	0	0	0
Donnelly, 2b	3	2	2	0
Jackson, 2b	1	1	0	0
Gamache, ss	3	1	1	2
Pignata, 3b	3	0	1	1
Gasbarro, 3b	0	0	0	0
Cantatore, lf	2	0	1	1
Koch, c	2	0	0	0
Carchidi, c	1	1	1	0
Freda, 1b	3	3	1	0
Burke, rf	3	2	1	0
Leclair, p	3	2	2	2
Totals	**28**	**12**	**10**	**7**

Bath (ME)	AB	R	H	RBI
D'Lass, ss	2	0	0	0
Wallace, ss	1	0	0	0
McGuire, cf	4	0	1	0
Black, p	3	1	0	0
Skillings, 2b	3	0	0	0
Dulik, 2b	1	0	0	0
Jacobs, c	3	0	1	0
Beade, rf	2	0	0	0
Underwood, 1b	3	0	1	0
Mulloy, 3b	1	0	0	0
Hersom, p	1	0	0	0
Clark, lf	2	0	0	0
Arbor, lf-p	0	0	0	0
Wallace, ph	1	0	0	0

Pitcher	IP	H	R	ER	W	K
Leclair (w)	7	3	1	0	4	8
Black, (l)	4	5	6	2	1	1
Hersom	1	2	4	3	3	1
Arbor	1	3	2	0	0	1

The grit and focus of the Leominster stars was on display that Monday evening as the locals slammed ten hits and rolled over Bath Maine 12-1. Mike Leclair, only 14 years-old in his second season of Babe Ruth baseball, was the hero of the game as he pitched a sparkling 3-hitter with eight strikeouts and no earned runs. Leclair also led the offensive attack with two extra-base hits, with two RBI's and two runs scored.

Nearly the entire Leominster squad saw action during this game with Donnelly (two singles), Gamache (triple, two RBI's), Pignata, Cantatore, Greg Carchidi, Freda, and Burke all joining the hit parade. Freda also scored three runs.[56][57]

Newport (RI) vs. Leominster, August 8, 1972

Fresh off the resounding win over Bath Maine on the day before, Leominster now faced the host team for the 1972 New England Regional Tournament. Leominster was favored to win this game with their ace Rick Comeau on the mound and with the Newport team not as tested as the local nine.

Manager Jim Marrone shuffled his usual starting batting order a bit with Charlie Richard leading off and playing center-field, Jim Donnelly at second and batting second, shortstop Paul Gamache batting third, third-baseman Mike Pignata hitting clean-up, John Cantatore batting fifth and in left-field, first-baseman Dick Freda batting sixth, right-fielder Jay Burke seventh, Comeau eighth, and catcher Bob Koch batting ninth.

Both teams went down scoreless in the first inning as both Comeau and Newport starting pitcher Mike Reagan dominated. After Newport went down in order in the top of the second, Leominster threatened when John Cantatore singled deep into the hole between short and third. Dick Freda followed with a single up the middle putting runners on first- and second-bases with no outs. Both runners advanced on a passed ball with Jay Burke at the plate. After Burke went down on strikes, Comeau hit a check-swing chopper to third-base, but Cantatore broke from third to home on contact and was thrown out at the plate for the second out of the inning. Burke and Freda ended up on second and third respectively on the play at the plate. Reagan escaped damage by striking out Bob Koch swinging.

Perhaps feeling the energy from their defensive performance from the previous inning, Newport put three runs on the board in the top of the third inning. What was unusual was that Newport scored all three runs as a result of four bunted singles.

Newport left-fielder Hugh Mally led off the third by working Comeau for a walk and advanced to second when Comeau's pick-off attempt at first sailed past Freda. Jay Burke's heady back-up of the play prevented Mally from attempting to take third.

Newport third-baseman Mickey DeCosta popped up his bunt attempt with Comeau sprinting off the mound to make the catch for the first out. Catcher Joe Neville then laid down a beautiful bunt to third-base with both Comeau and Pignata watching helplessly as the ball died in fair territory for a single. Mally ended up on third on the play, still with only one out.

One of the most exciting plays in baseball is the squeeze bunt. The strategy behind the play is for the batter to sacrifice himself with a bunt in order to score a run from third. A so-called "safety squeeze" calls for the runner on third-base to wait for the bunt to be put in play, and to break only when the fielder makes the play to first to get the batter out. The "suicide squeeze" involves the runner breaking for the plate during the pitch with the responsibility for the batter to bunt the ball in play and on the ground. The runner, with the head-start would usually beat any throw to the plate. If the batter fails to make contact, the runner is usually tagged out be the catcher or caught in a run-down between third-base and home-plate.

Such a bunt attempt is most frequently attempted with one out as the prevailing baseball logic is that attempting a squeeze bunt with no outs wastes an out, and with several other options to bring in the run from third. With two outs, an unsuccessful squeeze bunt ends the inning.

Now with runners on first and third with one out, Newport chose the suicide squeeze option and Mally broke for the plate on Comeau's pitch to home. Newport second-baseman successfully put the bunt in play toward Comeau who was coming off the mount. After fielding the ball cleanly, Comeau turned to make the play at first-base, but the runner was safe as Leominster first-baseman Dick Freda was charging on the play and second-baseman Jim Donnelly had not yet arrived at first-base to take the throw. Not only did Mally score, but Newport had runners on first and second with still only one out.

Newport shortstop Dan Corrigan again frustrated the Leominster defense with a perfectly placed bunt down the third-base line. With Neville running on the pitch, third-baseman Pignata was forced to cover third-base which left it to Comeau to come off the mound to field the ball. All runners advanced safely, and Newport now had the bases loaded with still only one out. First-baseman Bill Mathews then lined a solid single into center-field, scoring Neville and keeping the bases full.

After center-fielder Galvin struck out for the second out, Newport pitcher Mike Regan laid down the fifth bunt attempt and fourth for a hit, bringing Meehan home with the third run of the inning. Leominster trailed 3-0 as they came up to bat in the bottom of the third inning.

With one out in the Leominster third, Jim Donnelly singled and advanced to third on another Reagan wild pitch. Donnelly would not advance, however, as Gamache grounded to third and Pignata grounded to second to end the threat. Newport 3, Leominster 0 after three innings.

Cantatore slapped his second-base hit of the game with a single up the middle to lead off the fourth inning. Cantatore was erased at second on the front end of a fielder's choice with Dick Freda beating the throw to first. Freda advanced to second on when Jay Burke reached on an error. After Comeau fanned, Reagan picked Freda off first-base for the inning-ending out.

Leominster	AB	R	H	RBI
Richard, cf	3	0	0	0
Donnelly, 2b	2	0	1	0
Gamache, ss	3	0	0	0
Pignata, 3b	3	0	0	0
Cantatore, lf	3	0	2	0
Freda, 1b	3	0	1	0
Burke, rf	3	0	0	0
Comeau, p	3	0	0	0
Koch, c	2	0	0	0
Totals	25	0	4	0

Newport	AB	R	H	RBI
Meehan, 2b	3	1	1	1
Corrigan, ss	4	0	1	0
Mathews, 1b	4	0	1	1
Galvin, cf	4	0	1	0
Reagan, p	2	0	1	1
Palmer, rf	3	0	0	0
Mally, lf	1	1	0	0
DeCosta, 3b	3	0	0	0
Neville, c	3	1	2	0
Totals	27	3	7	3

Pitcher	IP	H	R	ER	W	K
Comeau (l)	7	7	3	3	4	11
Reagan (w)	7	4	0	0	2	7

Newport's Mike Reagan went the distance and faced only nine Leominster batters over the last three innings. Leominster's incredible all-star season run in pursuit of a World Series berth ended in that shut-out loss to host Newport.[58] [59]

I had attended all of the state tournament games in Leominster and the loss to Puerto Rico in the regionals. What struck me about this Leominster team was the way they immediately made it known that even though they were the host team in the state tournament, they belonged there. They could compete with any team, and they proved it by grinding it out in the loser's bracket. Rick Comeau did not have his best, but found a way to win the championship game with a gutsy pitching performance. Charlie Richard, Paul Gamache and Jim Donnelly somehow found ways to get on base when it mattered most. The defense was nearly flawless. The heroics of Mike Pignata when the game was on the line was quite an experience to witness. And finally, the magic touch of Jim Marrone was on display for all to see.

Section 4: True Grit - 1973 Babe Ruth All-Stars

The 1973 all-stars were selected as a result of a series of tryouts held late June of 1973. Holding tryouts for selecting an all-star team was not typical of the times. By the time the all-star tryouts were held, it was pretty clear who were the league's best hitters, fielders and pitchers from within such a relatively small sample size. At the time, Leominster Babe Ruth's Division 1 from which the all-stars were selected, was comprised of only 7 teams, each with 14 players to choose from – U-Trans, Tanzio, TAG, Solar Chemical, Elks, Werner's (from Lunenburg) and Sterling Lumber.

Coaches Jim Marrone, Steve Campobasso and Paul Harris were accompanied by several other league coaches who assisted with the tryouts. While the outfielders shagged fly balls from coach Harris, infielders took ground balls from coach Jack Koch of U-Trans. Following batting practice, we took to our designated positions for situational evaluations. This would typically involve a runner on a certain base, with a given number of outs and a coaching putting the ball in play. So for example, with a runner on second-base, a ball would be batted into the left-center field gap. The outfielder would field the ball and throw to the appropriate infielder either covering a base or acting as the cutoff man if the ball made it to the outfield fence. The tryout allowed players to demonstrate their mental acuity in game situations which was not measured in the box score or league statistics.

After two nights of tryouts, the coaches gathered and selected the 1973 team. To be honest, I did not expect to make the team as my overall batting average was good, but not great. However, I had a great tryout and believe I differentiated myself by hustling and taking advantage of the tryout format which rewarded making the right play in live situations. I was a left-handed hitter which was also an asset. I did, however, make the team which was a very proud moment for my family and me, especially given the expectation that we should do well in the upcoming all-star season.

John Crawley recalls the focus on fundamentals at tryouts. "At first day of the tryouts, Coach Marrone had us practicing base-stealing - taking a large lead and towards the pitcher to make it appear that our lead was smaller than it was, sliding back to first-base, focusing on the direction of the toe of the pitcher's front foot, and sliding on the wide side of the second-base bag" (J. Crawley, June 10, 2021).

Our team was stacked with talent. Not only did the team have the nucleus of the 1970 Leominster American Little League all-stars intact, but it was composed of the Leominster National and Northwest Little League all-stars as well. We also had returning state champions Mike Leclair, Mike Gasbarro and Jay Burke.

Player	Position
Bob Angelini (Elks)	2B, P
Mike Catalfamo (Elks)	1B
Pete Gamache (Elks)	C, IF, OF
Ted Rockwell (Elks)	CF, P
Mike Leclair (U-Trans)	P, OF
Mike Gasbarro (U-Trans)	SS, P
Mark Lefebvre (U-Trans)	LF
Jay Burke (Solar)	C, P
Ben Ruggles (Werner's)	IF, OF
John Crawley (TAG)	OF
Doug Girouard (TAG)	P
Dave Arsenault (TAG)	RF, P
Peter Robichaud (Tanzio)	2B, P
Jay Connors (Tanzio)	1B
Dave Bergeron (Tanzio)	3B

Coaches Jim Marrone, Steve Campobasso, Paul Harris, Doug Fellows, Bat boy, Jon (Connie) Hawkins

This team was a group of guys who could each play multiple positions, had a lot of experience playing in big games, and was fast. Lightning fast. Any one player on the team was capable of stealing bases and challenging opposing teams with aggressive base running.

The pitching staff was solid as we had four guys (Leclair, Burke, Arsenault and Rockwell) who each threw overpowering fastballs. Doug Girouard with his Luis Tiant-like windup and off-speed stuff completely baffled hitters after they faced one of the fire-balling starters.

Figure 42: 1973 Leominster Babe Ruth All-Stars (photo credit: Mark Lefebvre)

Front row: L-R: Jon Hawkins, bat boy, Doug Girouard, Pete Gamache, Jay Connors, Peter Robichaud, Coach Paul Harris, Bob Angelini
Middle row: L-R: Ben Ruggles, Mark Lefebvre, Mike Catalfamo, Dave Bergeron, Mike Gasbarro, Ted Rockwell, Jay Burke
Back row: L-R: Coach Jim Marrone, John Crawley, Dave Arsenault, Mike Leclair, Coach Steve Campobasso, Coach Doug Fellows

The team also had very experienced coaches who prepared the team to win, and who kept us loose with humor and good-natured ribbing. Coach Marrone coached the prior 1971 and 1972 state champions. Coach Harris helped coach the 1971 champions.

The coaching staff had high expectations. As a player, I thought back to the 1970 American Little League run, and the two consecutive state championship teams preceding me. I could not wait for the games to begin.

Chapter Thirteen: The Team

Bob Angelini
Bob Angelini grew up on Helena Street, a couple of blocks west of downtown Leominster, in the same neighborhood as Rich Kelly, Ted Rockwell, Steve Tata, and the Daigneault brothers. There he played whiffleball, basketball in front the Kelly's house, and baseball at Northwest School field. Bob starred for Foster Grant in the Leominster National Little League with future 1973 all-star teammate John Crawley.

Bob was the spark for our all-star team, batting lead-off and always getting his uniform dirty at second-base. Following Babe Ruth baseball, Bob had a storied career at Notre Dame High School in Fitchburg, starring in football, basketball and baseball. Bob was the point guard for the state champion Crusader basketball team that also featured Marty Caron and Jim "Soup" Campbell. Bob went on the play Division 1 baseball and football for Villanova. He is now retired and splits his time between Cape Cod and Florida (B. Angelini, July 17, 2021).

Doug Girouard
From the first time I played neighborhood pick-up baseball or whiffle-ball with Doug Girouard, I knew he would be a formidable pitcher. He was that unhittable even before he reached Little League.

Doug grew up on Dudley Street just down the street from my home on Elm Hill Avenue. He was a charter member of our so-called Lancaster Street gang that spent countless days playing street hockey in front of his house, or baseball and football at St. Leo's Cemetery with neighborhood pals Len Mallard, Tony and Joe Charielle, Bob Salvatore, John Cantatore, Rusty Tata and my brothers Mike and Billy. Doug and the rest of us would often trek to the Twelfth Street field to play on the American Little League fields with locals Steve Hamel, Rick Gallien and their neighborhood pals. Doug recalls Hamel being so much taller than the rest of us, and he would regularly clear the fences during our home-run derby contests.

As a pitcher for Holdet Vise in the Leominster American Little League, Doug was wizard on the mound. When he was not pitching, he played shortstop since he was also a great hitter and positional player. In 1970, he was a teammate of mine on the American Little League all-star team that made it to the state tournament in Oxford, MA. That Holdet Vise team was stacked with all-star teammates Kevin Buckley, Alan Quiet, and Paul Aubuchon. Holdet Vise would go on to win the 1970 American League championship defeating my team, Ranchers, even though Ranchers was loaded with all-stars Mike Leclair, Rick Gallien, Dennis Moquin, Elijah Rodriguez and me.

In 1970 Doug was drafted by Bob Boissoneau to play for TAG in the Leominster Babe Ruth League, joining future all-stars Dave Arsenault and John Crawley in that draft. In 1973 he earned his way on to the Babe Ruth all-stars as a pitcher.

Doug was a wizard on the mound. He offered a tantalizing curveball and slow change-up, which was a stark transition from the crew of fireballers Mike Leclair, Jay Burke, Dave Arsenault and Ted Rockwell. With a deceptive delivery and command over his entire repertoire of pitches, he left batters muttering on their way back to the dugout after helplessly flailing at his pitches. I don't think I ever made contact against

Doug. I'm gratefully he pitched on my team.

Doug shared recently that his biggest thrill was pitching against Puerto Rico in the 1973 New England Regionals in Lynn, MA. "I came into that game in the third inning in relief of Jay Burke and managed to shut down Puerto Rico for rest of the game," Doug shared. "I remember picking two runners off second base in that game. The Puerto Rico runners would take a weird stance coming off second base and would need to glance back at the bag to measure their distance. Bob Angelini and I had a pick-off routine with a silent count. Bob would break for second base on the count, and I would pivot and catch the runner flat-footed."

I also learned from Doug that he was slated to get the nod to pitch in the final game of 1973 Massachusetts State Championship game in Longmeadow. Mike Leclair had injured his leg in the semi-final and was getting treatment at a nearby hospital. With Leclair's status unknown after game 1 of the double-header, Girouard was warming up for the start. "I prayed that I would not have to start that game. I was rooting for Mike."

Following Babe Ruth ball, Doug played three years of varsity for LHS and the Leominster Post 151 American Legion teams. He was a favorite of coach Emile Johnson, both as a starter and relief pitcher. Doug still lives in Leominster (D. Girouard, July 31, 2022).

Ted Rockwell
Ted Rockwell spent his youth growing up on Orchard Street in a neighborhood rich with athletic talent. He played for Tilco in the Leominster National Little League as a pitcher and outfielder, leading Tilco to the Leominster Little League City championship over North Leominster Little League champs, Federals, and American Little League's winners Holdet Vise.

Ted is a lifelong Leominster resident and former Executive Officer of Northern Products Inc. He is now retired and spends much of his free time with his grandchildren and golfing (T. Rockwell, August 17, 2021)

Ted was one of the few Leominster Little League baseball players who had a city-wide reputation across the other two Little Leagues. While pitching for the National Little League All-Stars in 1970 he was dominant on the mound as evident by his near no-hitter over the Bordertown All-Stars with 15 strikeouts out of a possible 18 batters.

Ted played youth hockey for Anwelt of the Fitchburg Youth Hockey League junior division in 1970, and later for Fitchburg Penguins in the Bantam Division of the Midland Youth Hockey League. Home games were played at the George R. Wallace Jr. Civic Center in Fitchburg.

He attended Applewild School in Fitchburg playing soccer and baseball. In high school Ted started as a sophomore at Notre Dame of Fitchburg before transferring to Leominster High School in 1974 for his junior and senior years. During his time at Notre Dame, the Crusaders won the North Central Massachusetts Hockey League and District 3 championships.

As a senior at Leominster High School, Ted batted .438 and knocked in 45 runs batting clean-up for the Blue Devils. On the mound he had a 10-1 record with an ERA under 2.00.

Ted was inducted into the LHS Athletics Hall of Fame in 2017, and his athletic accomplishments are legendary:

- Worcester County All Star Senior and Junior years (baseball)
- 1976 Team MVP (baseball)
- College – Holy Cross – Baseball – CAC All New England Senior year
- Hop Riopel Award – (Holy Cross baseball MVP)
- Cape Cod Baseball League – All Star Team – 1 of only 17 players selected
- Signed with NY Mets and played 2 seasons in the minor leagues
- LHS Soccer Senior Year – Tri-Captain – Mass All State Team
- 3 Year Team Unbeaten Streak of 42 games (soccer)
- LHS Hockey Tri-Captain – Senior Year Team - school record of 17-0-1

Figure 43: Ted Rockwell Leominster Athletic HoF Induction
(l-r) Rick Daigneault, Ted Rockwell, Emile Johnson, Mark Gasbarro (photo credit: Leominster Athletic HoF Gallery)

Dave Arsenault

Dave Arsenault was one of my best friends during the early 1970's, was my teammate on the 1970 American Little League All-Stars, and again on the 1973 Babe Ruth All-Star state championship team. In Little League, Dave pitched and played outfield for Whitton's Insurance. At the Babe Ruth level Dave played for TAG and was their ace on the mound. Dave was extraordinarily talented in both football and baseball, but it was his mischievousness as a friend that brought the two of us together.

During this time period, the Arsenault's had moved to Hickory Road off upper Pleasant Street. In 1972 we had moved to Glenwood Drive near "Dead-Man's Curve" on upper Union Street. Although our streets were several miles apart by car, our houses were only about 300 yards apart through the woods between us. It was not usual to make that quick trip through the woods several times a day during our teenage years, often times camping out in the woods or in the pop-up trailer that Dave's parents Harry and Nancy Arsenault kept open in their driveway. Our families would go on outings together and Dave's brother Jay was a great friend of my brother Billy.

Prior to moving to Hickory Road, Dave's family lived up on French Hill off Mechanic Street, and he attended St. Cecilia's Grammar School. He would spend much of his free time playing baseball at the Twelfth Street Field and at the Spruce Street School playground.

At Leominster High School Dave would star as a fearless and hard-hitting defensive end on both the 1973 and 1974 Central and Western Massachusetts Super Bowl Championship football teams. The 1974 team from Dave's senior year went undefeated including a shocking 17-7 upset over Massachusetts powerhouse Brockton High. Dave also starred as a right-fielder and pitched for LHS baseball teams as well as the 1975 and 1976 American Legion baseball teams.

After graduating from Leominster High, Dave attended Choate Academy in Connecticut for one year before attending Tufts University where he graduated in 1980 with degrees in Psychology and Biology.

Sadly, we lost Dave who passed in 2008 at the age of 50 after an illness. I will always remember his love for life and his competitiveness on the field. I think back fondly of all the things we did together as kids and the impish "hey check this out" whenever something captured his imagination.[60]

John Crawley

John Crawley recently shared with me that he felt he did not belong on the 1973 Babe Ruth all-star team. Just as I had also experienced at the all-star tryouts, John looked around at the talent on the field in June 1973 and thought to himself, why am I even here?

"Mark, I'm not gonna lie," John shared. "I never felt I should have been on that team. Subbing for you in the outfield brought absolute panic on those few occasions when I was asked to so. All I'd ever played was catcher. I was willing to do whatever the team needed, but seriously questioned my ability to help that team."

John is selling himself short. If not for John's contributions in the 1973 state tournament, we would not have made it to the championship game. John chipped in two hits and knocked in what turned out to be the winning run in our 19-17 win over Wakefield that sent us to the semifinals against Burncoat of Worcester.

John and I have spoken several times over the past two years regarding our experiences. "That Babe Ruth all-star team planted the seeds for high school success throughout north central Massachusetts," he marveled. "Every single player from those 1971-1973 teams went on to success in numerous high school teams from the area. My opinion is that all of those teams were filled with incredible young and talented athletes. Simply look around, I cannot think of one that was not an all-star in baseball, football, basketball or soccer at the high school levels in Leominster, Lunenburg, at Saint Bernard's, and Notre Dame, and with many going on to play sports at the college level."

"I saw Coach Marrone some years later at the Leominster Knights of Columbus," recalls Crawley. "I believe I had to be in my 30's at the time. We had a really nice talk, reminiscing about the old days, and the coach shared how much he loved that '73 team and the players on it. I asked him 'why did you pick me for the team knowing you had already two great catchers in Jay Burke and Peter Gamache, and knowing I hadn't played the outfield, and that I couldn't hit a lick?' Coach Marrone responded that he got a lot of flak for picking me but emphasized how happy and vindicated he was with my role in the Wakefield game. He said he picked me because he knew I'd do whatever he asked on the field and that was what he was looking for in reserves. He then told me those were the same characteristics that later led to football successes and my college scholarship. Coach noted two games and scores from my Central Connecticut days, shocking me that he had actually followed my college football career. It seemed to me that while many of us had lost touch with coach Marrone, he never let the connection with any of us lapse."

John grew up near Rockwell's Pond, first on Cottage Street, and then moved to Pond Street while in the 6th grade. His neighborhood friends included Timmy, Jeff and Doug Decarolis with whom he played whiffle-ball and street hockey on Pond Street. He played for Foster Grant in the Leominster National Little League with future BRL all-star teammate Bob Angelini. He was drafted to play for TAG in the Leominster Babe Ruth League and cited his admiration for fellow TAG teammates Dave Arsenault, Doug Girouard, and Tony Charielle.

During the summer, John participated in the Leominster Recreation Summer League for Bennett School playground, playing basketball, softball, and street hockey with future Leominster High School stars Kevin Buckley, Dave Arsenault, and Fran Thomas. John eventually became a summer a camp counselor himself.

John attended Bennett elementary for two years until Fall Brook School was built. He then transferred and forged his long and lasting friendships with Steve Ringer, Charlie Kirouac and Kevin Buckley.

Crawley was a basketball court rat. Some of his favorite memories include playing basketball at the courts at Bennett School. The court was eventually named for Tommy Miller who started the summer league at Bennett. John recalls, "Tommy owned the house adjacent to Bennett School. The Bangrazi's lived across the street. Tommy would tell me, 'The porch will always have a basketball and the door is open. Remember to return it as others are dependent on that ball being there.' There were some great players there including Johnny Ippolito, Benny Bangrazi, Mike O'Neill, Tony DiNardo, Bill Haverty, Gerry Flynn, and Tom Miller. Us 14-year and 15-year-olds had to wait until a team needed an extra player when another left. We'd watch and wait until we got our turn. The older kids would send me across the street to Lane's Market for refreshments and snacks. 'Remember to get one for yourself' was the incentive."

After Babe Ruth baseball, John focused his athletic attention on football and basketball at LHS. Following his senior season of football, John was named to the North Worcester County Sportswriters Association All-Star Football Team. He went on to play college ball at Central Connecticut.

John is retired as an attorney after a long career at Hewlett-Packard, and now teaches business law at Fitchburg State College. He credits his coaches and older players on the field and the court for instilling the work ethic that he has carried with him throughout his adult life. John, his wife Lisa, and their family live in Winchendon (J. Crawley, December 19, 2021).

Peter Robichaud
Peter Robichaud considered it a great day when he, his older brother Paul, and neighborhood friends Ron Saudelli, brothers Danny and David Champagne, Mike and Mark Gasbarro, and other lower Willard Street/Lancaster Street kids would head down to the Babe Ruth Field for a game of pick-up baseball. And if they were lucky, the underground sprinkler system would not turn on while the game was in progress. But there was no guarantee. I would sometimes join the group when visiting my cousins who lived across the street from the Robichaud's.

Pete was the middle son and second oldest child over Richard "Robie" and Marilyn Robichaud. The family lived at the end of Sunset Drive across the street from the Arel family. My family and I frequented the neighborhood for barbecue outings with my cousins Linda, Nancy, Patty and Sheila, and their parents Fran and Rachel Arel. The afternoons and evenings on Sunset Drive in the summer were magical. We'd swim at my cousins or at any of the myriad of pools in the neighborhood including that of the Robichaud's. Older brother Paul was a gifted guitarist and there were frequent garage performances on hot and muggy summer nights. It was a great place to grow up.

The Sunset Drive/Willard Street gang, like countless other

neighborhoods, would rotate their pick-up games with the professional seasons. In the fall they would play football on the outfield at the Babe Ruth field, and street and ice hockey during the winter.

"There was always a game to be played," Pete reminisced recently. "We were always on the go, riding our bikes down to the Babe Ruth field, or down to Monster Land with our bikes."

Pete was a clutch contributor to the 1973 all-star team. For example, he replaced the injured Bob Angelini at second-base for the game against Greenfield that would vault us into the state tournament. Pete batted second and contributed two hits and scored two runs. And he was flawless in the field that day as well.

During the regular season he played for Bob Lamothe on the Tanzio squad as a pitcher and an infielder. Tanzio was stacked that 1973 season, as was U-Trans, the team I played for during the regular season. Pete and I spoke recently about the league championship series that culminated that 1973 season when Robichaud almost single-handedly won the championship for Tanzio.

U-Trans and Tanzio Park finished in a tie when the final out of the regular season was recorded. Normally, the league stages a 2-round best-of-three series for the top four finishers. However, the season ran late into the late summer due to the all-stars advancing to the New England Regionals. Therefore, the league decided to hold a single best-of-five tournament between our two teams.

We (U-Trans) took the opening game 4-0 behind the dominating no-hit pitching of ace Mike Leclair. Robichaud pitched Tanzio to a 7-4 victory in game 2 and contributed a triple to his own cause. Don Stebbins pitched and Pete Robichaud batted Tanzio to a 7-2 victory in game 3, giving Tanzio a 2 games to 1 lead over U-Trans. U-Trans evened the series at 2-2 with a 6-4 nail-biter behind the arm of Mike Leclair and the bats of Mike Gasbarro and Leclair. Mike Gasbarro fired a no-hitter in the deciding game giving U-Trans a 3 games to 2 margin of victory for the league championship series.

"We played a lot of baseball that summer," mused Pete during our talk recently. "Between playing a ten-game season at May A. Gallagher Junior High, a 15-game regular season at Babe Ruth, 15 all-star games and this playoff series of 5 games, that's 45+ games."

By the time this series commenced, Pete and I and the rest of the Leominster High School football team were secluded at our pre-season football camp at Fort Devens. LHS coach Leon "Huck" Hannigan was not too pleased to see two of his sophomore players ask for permission to leave camp to play baseball. Fortunately for us, coach was ultimately supportive and allowed for us to make the trip back and forth. As a result and right on the heels of the completion of the Babe Ruth playoffs, Pete and I showed up back at the Devens barracks still in our baseball uniforms. We snuck in to quickly change our clothes and join our football teammates just before lights-out. As I closed my eyes in my bunk that night, I drifted off in exhaustion over that long, long summer of baseball.

Pete was a gifted football player. He had big hands and a strong arm and could throw a spiral 50 yards down field. As a sophomore, he made varsity and started as a hard-hitting safety and punter by his junior year. Unfortunately, he broke his leg badly early in his senior football season against Nashua, and not only missed out on the rest of that season, but was also forced to remain home during rehabilitation, and therefore home schooled by a tutor. Sad to say, he never made it back on the diamond to continue playing for Emily Johnson's baseball squad for his senior year.

Pete lives in the Leominster area with his wife Jeannine. They have two adult sons (P. Robichaud, March 23, 2022).

Ben Ruggles
Ben Ruggles played youth basketball in the Lunenburg Junior League for Eyles Electric, and also played for the Lunenburg Bengals in Pop Warner football. For baseball he played for Lunenburg Little League all-stars and

in 1970 pitched in a losing cause against the Leominster American Little League all-stars which featured future Leominster BRL all-star teammates Mike Leclair, Mark Lefebvre, Jay Burke and Mike Gasbarro.

Following Babe Ruth, Ben starred in football and baseball at Lunenburg High School, graduated in 1976, and attended UConn where he earned a degree in Recreation. While at UConn, Ben was a member of the football team and baseball teams. As a member of the Huskies baseball team, he played in the College World Series in 1979.

Sadly, Ben passed in 2019 after a courageous battle with cancer.[61]

Peter Gamache

As a kid, Pete played for Dupont in the National Little League at Northwest Field. Around this time, Pete's family moved to upper Union Street on a hill overlooking Fall Brook Elementary School. During the 1973 Babe Ruth all-star season his family graciously hosted a pool party for the 1973 team before we headed to Longmeadow for the state tournament.

In Babe Ruth, Pete played for Coach Jim Marrone on the Elks team and made the 1973 all-star team as a 14-year-old. Pete was a fierce competitor who was always a coach's favorite. During the 1973 New England regional tournament, I roomed with Pete in Lynn.

Following Babe Ruth, Pete was a star athlete at St. Bernard's High School in Fitchburg, playing both baseball and basketball. He currently lives in Gardner with his wife Madeline (P. Gamache, April 30, 2021).

Dave Bergeron

Dave Bergeron recalls playing home run derby behind Carter Junior High School as a kid growing up on View Street near the high school. "My brother Mike and would join neighborhood friends Joey and Rocco Siciliano, Dan and Mike (Seatrain) Curley, and Dave Duffy, and we would rain home-runs over the playground fence until they posed a threat to neighborhood homes. We would then ride our bikes and take our baseballs, bats, and gloves to Northwest School field to join scores of other kids for pick-up games."

Dave played on Kingman in the Leominster National Little League with future Babe Ruth League all-stars, Jay Connors and Steve Shaw. As a ninth grader he played baseball and football at Carter Junior High School. Following Little League, Dave was drafted by Bob Lamothe to play on the Tanzio Park team in Babe Ruth where he would play third-base. He would later be joined by brother Mike on that same team. Mike played on the 1974 all-star team that lost in the state finals in Falmouth, narrowly missing the opportunity to extend Leominster's run of Massachusetts state championships to four consecutive years. Dave coached his brother on that all-star team.

Figure 44: Dave Bergeron (photo credit: Dave Bergeron)

Typical of the level of family and community support of kids across the city of Leominster, Dave's dad Fran Bergeron was a long-time treasurer of the Leominster Babe Ruth League; and Dave's grandfather Fred Bergeron received the 1983 Fan of the Year appreciation award from the league.

Following Babe Ruth, Dave played Leominster High School varsity baseball. He studied mechanical engineering at Worcester Polytechnic Institute, where I would often see him on campus during our time there (D. Bergeron, May 28, 2022).

Mike Catalfamo
Mike grew up on Weber Street near Saint Ann's church and attended Lancaster Street elementary school. I first met Mike in the fourth or fifth grade after he moved to the neighborhood, and I remember Mike being a quiet and very polite kid.

Mike played for Elks in the Leominster Babe Ruth League and made the all-stars as a left-hand batting and throwing first-baseman. At Leominster High School, Mike played varsity soccer and baseball.

Jay Connors
Jay Connors played for Kingman in the Leominster National LL with future Tanzio and Leominster BRL all-star teammate Dave Bergeron. Jay made the Babe Ruth all-stars as a clutch-hitting first-baseman who provide a sure target for his fellow infielders. At Leominster High School Jay played both soccer and baseball for the Blue Devils.

Mike Leclair
Mike Leclair and I spent most of the summer of 1970 together as best friends and teammates for Ranchers of the Leominster American Little League. Our friendship extended deep into the summer, cemented by the amazing ride of our Little League All-Star team which made it all the way

to the Massachusetts State Tournament in Oxford that August. Mike was the superstar of that team, going 5-0 as a starting pitcher and terrorizing opposing pitchers with his bat.

At that time, Mike lived on Manchester Street with his mom, Janette, and his younger brother Danny. His dad was a police officer for the Leominster Police Department. Sleepovers were popular during that time, and we spent several days together going to practice, games, and playing at each other's houses in between.

Our American Little League all-star team was loaded and included several members of the 1972 and 1973 Babe Ruth state championship teams. In addition to Mike Leclair and me, Mike Gasbarro, Doug Girouard, Jay Burke and Dave Arsenault made that 1970 Little League all-star team.

Mike was drafted first overall in the 1970 Babe Ruth League draft, being snapped up by coach Donnie Bigelow of U-Trans. Mike Gasbarro and I would also be drafted by U-Trans in later rounds. Mike excelled as a 13-year-old rookie the following summer, both as a pitcher as well as an outfielder, which earned him Rookie of the Year honors for 1971.

Leclair carried this success into high school when he posted a sterling 5-0 record as a sophomore at Leominster High. He continued his success for the next two years playing for coach Emile Johnson for both high school and American Legion teams.

Mike is currently enjoying his retirement, playing golf and fishing in the Leominster area. When I caught up with him to interview him for this book, he shared that he recently golfed with Joe and Eddie Cataldo. He remembered fondly our summers together and the successes he had as a youngster in Leominster (M. Leclair, May 12, 2021).

Mike Gasbarro
The sun was setting over the tree tops as 12-year-old Mike Gasbarro pedaled his Schwinn 5-speed stingray through the Monster Land woods

located at the end of Old Mill Road in southeastern Leominster. Ever mindful of the roots and rocks that dotted the beaten path, Mike learned from many spills to keep his eyes on the pathway while simultaneously peddling with all his might to make his parents' curfew.

Mike recalls that Bel-Air Heights was a great neighborhood with lots of kids his age which provided many opportunities for pick-up games. He and his siblings would often head over to South End Market for penny candy and soda. The neighborhood kids would organize baseball, football, and basketball games with other nearby neighborhoods according to the seasons. His neighborhood team was named the Bel-Air Bombers and they played against the South End Lions and Litchfield Panthers. Games were played at Fall Brook School and without adult supervision. In the winter he and his friends would play ice hockey up at Lake Samoset where he swam and fished during the summer months.

Like many 11- and 12-year-olds of that era, Mike recalls going to the Lancaster Street field to watch Babe Ruth baseball games and dream of one day playing there. He and scores of other boys chased foul balls and returned them to the field thinking they were heroes. Because of his proximity to the fabled Monster Land forested area, Mike and his friends would ride their bikes on the paths worn down by generations of kids that preceded him.

When Mike was younger, his family lived on Longwood Avenue behind Archie's Shell Station and The Lazy A restaurant until he was 8-years old. The Lazy A eventually was sold and renamed to Gondola Restaurant right around the same time that my dad, Archie Lefebvre, sold the Shell station. The Gasbarro's then moved to the corner of Mechanic and Ninth streets which was a short bike ride to 12th Street American Little League. It was at the 12th Street field that Mike, and his younger brother Mark would develop their passion for baseball.

While attending Fall Brook Elementary School, Mike played Little League for Holdet Vise and made the American Little League all-stars as my teammate in 1970. Holdet Vise would win the American Little League championship that same season.

"Looking back, at that time my life centered around baseball," Mike shared recently. He added, "great coaches and great tradition. At fifteen, I played for U-Trans, and we won the league championship. I was on top of the world that summer." Among his numerous and notable accomplishments that summer of 1973, Mike pitched a no-hitter in the opening game of that season's best-of-three league championship series against rival Tanzio Park. Mike Leclair and I were teammates of Mike's on that championship U-Trans team.

At Leominster High School, Mike played baseball and soccer. After graduating from LHS in 1975, Mike served in the US Coast Guard. He is enjoying his retirement and splits this time between Leominster and Myrtle Beach, South Carolina (M. Gasbarro, April 27, 2021).

Jay Burke

Jay Burke remembers playing off-the-wall behind Spruce Street School with some of the boys from Leominster's French Hill section of the city, named for the community of French-Canadian immigrant families who relocated to the community during the rise of Leominster's renown plastics industry. Off-the-wall was game with automatic baseball rules that involved bouncing a tennis or rubber ball off the wall of a building which was fielded by the team on defense. If the defensive team did not field the ball cleanly it was a single. If the ball crossed a pre-determined boundary it was a double. If the ball went over the head of the outfield, it was deemed a home-run. Rules could vary and often times we would use a super-ball rather than a tennis ball. As Jay grew older, his playground of choice shifted to Saxton Trade Field up off Mill Street, and the Ronnie Bachand Little League field on 12th street. Jay also loved to play street hockey behind Spruce Street School with Sheehan brothers, Guy Gagnon, the Richards brothers, and Rick Gallien.

"We were perhaps the only Irish family living on French Hill at the time," he recalls. "We lived on Fourth Street which is about a mile out of downtown Leominster heading east on Mechanic Street." His dad, George, was a construction worker and his mom, Jane, a nurse at Leominster Hospital.

Jay was used to standing out in a crowd. Ever since his early playground days behind Spruce Street School, Jay would tower over his friends. This phenomenon continued as he migrated up through Little League, Pop Warner football, and Babe Ruth Baseball. I faced Jay in what was my first at-bat for Ranchers in the American Little League in April of 1970. Jay was on the mound for Crossman's and as I walked up to the plate I thought he was so tall, and the mound was so close to the plate that he would literally hand the ball to his catcher. Nonetheless, I made contact and shot a ground ball up the middle and into centerfield for my first Little League Majors hit. In addition to baseball, Jay played football for the Dolphins in the Leominster Pop Warner football league and played hoops in the St. Ann's Parochial Basketball League. He went on to play football and basketball at Gallagher Junior High.

When not on the mound, Jay could be found behind the plate as an all-star catcher and was my teammate on the 1970 American Little League all-star team that advanced to the Massachusetts Little League state tournament in Oxford. He was drafted by Solar Chemical by coach Ray Racine and made the Babe Ruth all-stars at both 14- and 15-years old. Looking back, Jay claims that his three years playing Babe Ruth were the best years of his youth, and he especially enjoyed playing for coach Jim Marrone who Jay claimed was like a second father to him.

Following Babe Ruth, Jay played Leominster High School and Leominster Post 151 American Legion baseball leading up to a great collegiate experience playing for the Lancers at Worcester State College. He currently lives with his family on the Massachusetts south shore (J. Burke, April 21, 2021).

Mark Lefebvre

My experience growing up on Elm Hill Ave and the greater Lancaster Street area is well documented earlier in this book, as are my later teenage years on Glenwood Drive and upper Union Street.

In 1970 I played for Ranchers in the American Little League for only one year in the majors. I had a late start in organized baseball, and spent my first two seasons of eligibility in 1968 and 1969 in the American minor league playing for Leominster Credit Union with two of my younger brothers, Mike and Billy. My maternal grand-parents, Gus and Susie Lanciani had convinced my parents that we should be playing Little League. Both "Ma and Pa" as they were affectionately known, were avid baseball and basketball fans and always showed up at our games.

I recall my very first at-bat for Ranchers which was against Crossman's with their ace Jay Burke on the mound. Jay was already approaching six feet in height as a 12-year-old, and he loomed even larger on the mound. I was batting lead-off and can remember watching Jay warm up in the first inning and that the game ball was new and still very white.

Any doubt that I could play against these seasoned Little Leaguers was gone as I hit the first strike up the middle and past Burke into center-field for my very first Little League hit in the Majors. Following that initiation, my nerves were calmed, and I spent that summer enjoying every inning and every at-bat of that season. I earned a spot on the all-star team, and we advanced to the Massachusetts state tournament in Oxford later that summer.

Following the amazing Babe Ruth all-star run in 1973, I had quickly turned my attention to Leominster High School football camp at Fort Devens. I had only one year of organized football under my belt having played at Gallagher Junior High School for my ninth-grade year. There had to be at least 75 kids at camp late that August of 1973, and I distinctly remember the weather being very hot and humid. Despite the weather, double-sessions were held, we ate meals in the mess hall, and slept in bunks in the barracks.

Figure 45: The author, 1973 Picture Day (photo courtesy: Mark Lefebvre)

That football camp was my first experience participating in athletics at the high school level. It was a real eye-opener for me as the coaches, especially head coach Huck Hannigan, and assistant coaches John Dubzinski, Pete Beaulieu, Roger Mercier, and Mike Vaillette, were no-nonsense personalities. If you screwed up, you ran. Each practice ended with wind-sprints. Every practice, every drill, every snap had the expectation of performance and winning. I ate it up.

In the following spring, the LHS baseball team was loaded with several returning upperclassmen outfielders including Charlie Richard, Dick Freda, Dave Malatos, and Dave Arsenault, as well as incoming sophomore Mike Leclair. As a result I was a victim of numbers and played junior varsity for coach Dick LaBelle who I absolutely loved as a coach. The long reach of varsity coach Emile Johnson was felt even at the JV level, so coach LaBelle served as a buffer during my sophomore year. I did very well my sophomore year and earned a call-up to varsity late in the season after the JV schedule expired.

During my junior and senior years at LHS I played varsity and American Legion baseball for coach Johnson. With the exception of my final year at the Legion level, I was not a standout player. Perhaps knowing that my days of playing organized baseball were numbered, I was dialed-in during that final year of Legion. I played every inning of every game in either left- or right-field depending on who was pitching between Ted Rockwell, Mike Leclair or Dave Arsenault. I batted third for most of the season, had a .311 batting average and scored a ton of runs with Leclair, Rockwell and Arsenault batting behind me, and for the first time in my entire organized baseball career, I started to hit for power with a couple of home runs and several other extra-base hits. Looking back wistfully, I now believe my success that last year was due to the lack of pressure I put on myself to try to make it to the next level. I was playing for the sheer joy of baseball that last summer.

I played with and against many gifted baseball player from central Massachusetts including Rick Comeau who was drafted by the Texas Rangers, Ted Rockwell who was drafted by the Mets, and future Major League Baseball all-stars Ron Darling (St. Johns, Shrewsbury Legion) and Rich Gedman (St. Peters, Grafton Hill American Legion of Worcester).

After graduating from Leominster High in 1976, I attended Worcester Polytechnic Institute where I graduated with a degree in Electrical Engineering. In my last at-bat as a sophomore on the WPI baseball team, I struck out.

I spent the next 37 years working in the technology industry with five years of service at Teradyne of Boston, eleven years at Digital Equipment Corporation and the last twenty-two years of my career as a marketing and sales executive at IBM. I retired from high-tech in 2017 and have been working as a consultant in the field of addiction prevention and recovery.

I currently live in the Seacoast of New Hampshire with my wife Vivian of 38 years, and our two adult children, Joey and Selena.

Chapter Fourteen: The Games

Leominster vs. Athol, Saturday, July 7, 1973
The 1973 Leominster Babe Ruth League all-stars were certainly considered the favorite to advance through the district sectional rounds and to make a run at defending Leominster's status as state champions. Getting off on the right foot, on Saturday, July 7, 1973, Leominster opened up at home with a 3-1 win against the Athol all-stars at the Lancaster Street home field behind the strong pitching performance by Leominster ace Mike Leclair. There is no recap on record for this game.[62]

Holden vs. Leominster, Sunday, July 8, 1973
There was little time to rest following the 3-1 win over Athol as the locals hit the diamond again the very next day against the all-stars from Holden. Jay Burke picked up the win as Leominster convincingly defeated Holden 8-3. There is no recap on record for this game. At 2-0 in the single-elimination play-in to the state tournament, Leominster advanced to face rival Fitchburg with the district championship at stake.[63]

Fitchburg, vs. Leominster, Wednesday, July 11, 1973
With a couple of days of rest, Leominster eagerly faced their rivals from Fitchburg at the Lancaster Street Field in Leominster. Coach Marrone started second-baseman Bob Angelini in the lead-off spot, followed by hard-hitting third-baseman Dave Bergeron in the second slot. First-baseman Jay Connors batted third, and pitcher Mike Leclair batted clean-up. Jay Burke, started behind the plate and batted fifth, followed by center-fielder Ted Rockwell sixth, and right-fielder Dave Arsenault in the seventh spot. Left-fielder Mark Lefebvre batted eighth and shortstop Mike Gasbarro completed the line-up, batting ninth.

Mike Leclair, already with one win under his belt vs. Athol, took the hill against Fitchburg and went the distance with a sparkling 2-hit shutout, striking out six and walking only two Fitchburg batters. Fitchburg starter Chris Cummings held Leominster to one run and two hits heading into the sixth inning before being replaced by Bob Sullivan following a lead-off single to Leominster catcher Jay Burke.

The locals scored the first run of the game in the bottom of the third when third-baseman Dave Bergeron walked and promptly stole second-base. After first-baseman Jay Connors struck-out, Leclair hit a shot to shortstop that was misplayed and resulted in a wild throw to first, allowing Bergeron to scamper in to score all the way from second.

Leominster threatened again in the fourth inning when center-fielder Ted Rockwell opened with a solid single to left-center and promptly stole second-base. Right-fielder Dave Arsenault sacrificed Rockwell to third, but was stranded after left-fielder Mark Lefebvre flew out to short right field, and shortstop Mike Gasbarro flew out to deep center-field to end the inning.

In the fifth, second-baseman Bob Angelini reached on an error and was sacrificed to second-base by Bergeron. Cummings bore down and retired the next two batters on ground outs to squelch the threat.

In the sixth, Burke led off with a sharp single to left which led to Cummings being replaced by Sullivan with one on and no outs. Rockwell drew a walk putting men on first and second with no outs. Arsenault lofted a pop-up to short left field which fell between the Fitchburg shortstop and left-fielder. Jay Thomas, playing short for Fitchburg quickly picked the ball up and fired a strike to third-base to force Burke for the first out. Lefebvre then singled to center to load the bases. Gasbarro popped another looper into short left-field, forcing Rockwell out at the plate. With 2 outs and Angelini at bat, Arsenault scored the second Leominster run on a wild pitch from Sullivan. Angelini ultimately walked which again loaded the bases. Dave Bergeron then walked scoring Lefebvre from third making the score 3-0. Finally, Connors rapped a single to right-field scoring Gasbarro with the final Leominster run.

Fitchburg did not go quietly, however. In the seventh and final inning, pinch-hitter Paul Cioffi led off with a walk.

Leominster	AB	R	H	RBI
Angelini, 2b	3	0	1	0
Bergeron, 3b	0	1	0	1
Connors, 1b	3	0	1	1
Leclair, p	4	0	0	0
Burke, c	3	0	1	0
Rockwell, cf	2	0	1	0
Arsenault, rf	1	1	0	0
Lefebvre, lf	3	1	1	0
Gasbarro, ss	3	1	0	0
Totals	**22**	**4**	**5**	**2**

Fitchburg	AB	R	H	RBI
Clifford, lf	3	0	0	0
Alario, cf	3	0	0	0
Cummings, p-3b	2	0	1	0
Keane, rf-c	3	0	0	0
Cioffi, ph	0	0	0	0
Sullivan, ss-p	2	0	0	0
LaFreniere, 1b	3	0	0	0
Borone, 2b	2	0	1	0
Blanchette, c	1	0	0	0
Thomas, ss	1	0	0	0
Dame, 3b	2	0	0	0
Totals	**22**	**0**	**2**	**0**

Pitcher	IP	H	R	ER	W	K
Cummings L	5	3	1	0	3	2
Sullivan	1	2	3	3	3	0
Leclair W	7	2	0	0	2	6

After Fitchburg's Tony LaFreniere struck out, second-baseman Tony Zanghi lined a rope to Angelini at second, who doubled Cioffi off at first, ending the game. Final score Leominster 4, Fitchburg 0. Next up for Leominster will be South Hadley in the sectional semi-finals at U-Mass Amherst.[64][65]

Leominster vs. South Hadley, Saturday, July 14, 1973
The game-time temperature registered 95 degrees as the Leominster all-stars faced South Hadley in the sectional semi-finals held at Strople Field in Longmeadow. Ted Rockwell, operating on six days rest took the hill for the locals. With a win, Leominster would advance to the sectional finals.

Due to the oppressive heat and humidity, Coach Jim Marrone planned to use the entire lineup in an effort to keep fresh legs and arms in the game. With Rockwell on the mound, Mike Leclair got the nod in center-field, flanked by Mark Lefebvre in left and Dave Arsenault in right. Jay Connors started at first-base, Bob Angelini at second, Mike Gasbarro at shortstop and Dave Bergeron at third. Jay Burke completed the starting line-up behind the plate as catcher.

Leominster struck first with a run in the top of the 3rd inning. With two outs, second-baseman Angelini lined a single into left field. Bergeron followed that with a double in the left-field gap bringing Angelini home all the way from first-base. The game would remain 1-0 into the sixth when Leominster erupted for five more runs.

Gasbarro tripled off the left-center-field fence, a blast that came within a few feet of leaving the park for a home run. Angelini reached on an infield error which brought Gasbarro home with the second run of the game. With the hit-and-run on, Angelini advanced the third-base on a single to right field by Bergeron. After Bergeron stole second-base which resulted in Leominster having runners on second- and third-bases with no outs, South Hadley starter Gary Grant was lifted for southpaw Dan Hawkyard.

Leominster first-baseman Connors worked Hawkyard for a walk that loaded the bases. Mike Leclair grounded to short which forced Angelini at the plate for the first out. Burke also grounded to short, forcing Bergeron at the plate for out number two. Rockwell then also grounded to short but with no one covering second-base, shortstop Roger Moreau rushed his throw to first which sailed wide, scoring both Connors and Leclair and making the score 4-0, Leominster. Burke ended up on third and Rockwell on second as a result of the throwing error. Dave Arsenault was walked intentionally which brought Mark Lefebvre to the plate with the bases loaded and two outs. Lefebvre made South Hadley pay by lining a shot into the right-center-field gap which brought in the final two Leominster runs. After Gasbarro flied to right field for the final out, Leominster took the field in the bottom half of the sixth with a commanding 6-0 lead.

South Hadley	AB	R	H	RBI
Peitras, 2b	4	0	1	0
Brown, cf - ss	4	0	0	0
Dubue. 1b	3	0	2	0
Turgeron, lf	1	0	0	1
Griffin, c	4	1	1	0
Bigelow, rf	1	0	0	0
McDonald, rf	1	0	1	1
Vieu, 3b	3	0	1	0
Moreau, ss	1	0	0	0
Moriarty, cf	1	0	0	0
Grant, p	2	0	0	0
Hawkyard, p	0	0	0	0
Christopher, p	1	1	1	0
Totals	26	2	7	2

Leominster	AB	R	H	RBI
Angelini, 2b	2	1	1	0
Robichaud, 2b	0	0	0	0
Bergeron, 3b	3	0	2	1
Ruggles, 3b	1	0	0	0
Connors, 1b	2	1	0	0
Catalfamo, 1b	1	0	0	0
Leclair, cf	4	1	0	0
Burke, c	3	1	1	0
Gamache, c	0	0	0	0
Rockwell, p	3	1	1	0
Girouard, p	0	0	0	0
Arsenault, rf	2	0	0	0
Lefebvre, lf	3	0	1	2
Crawley, lf	0	0	0	0
Gasbarro, ss	3	1	1	0
Totals	27	6	7	3

Pitcher	IP	H	R	ER	W	K
Rockwell, W	6.2	7	2	2	6	4
Girouard	.1	0	0	0	0	0
Grant, L	5.2	6	2	2	0	1
Hawkyard	.1	1	4	1	2	0
Christopher	1	0	0	0	1	0

South Hadley scored their first run in the sixth when Gary Grant singled and scored on a double by right-fielder Andy McDonald. In the bottom of the seventh, Dave Christopher who had come on to pitch for South Hadley in the top half of the seventh, doubled with one out. Second-baseman Walt Peitras singled with Christopher holding at third-base. After Rockwell struck out center-fielder Keith Brown for the second out, two consecutive walks brought Christopher home with the second South Hadley run. Doug Girouard was brought in to relieve Rockwell and retired John Griffin to end the game. Final score, Leominster 6, South

Hadley 2.

The win advanced Leominster to the district finals to face Greenfield at UMass Amherst. However, a key starter was sidelined with an injury.[66][67][68]

Greenfield vs. Leominster 8, Wednesday, July 18, 1973
With a trip to the Massachusetts state tournament on the line, Leominster faced off against Greenfield on Wednesday, July 18 at the University of Massachusetts Earl Lorden Field in Amherst. Greenfield was a formidable opponent having romped over Pittsfield 8-0 to arrive at the sectional final.

Leominster had their veteran ace Mike Leclair rested and on the hill. With second-baseman Bob Angelini out with an injured ankle, coach Jim Marrone shook up the lineup with Pete Robichaud getting the start at second-base and batting lead-off. Left-fielder Mark Lefebvre was moved up in the order to bat third as Marrone wanted a left-handed hitter in the meat of the order and due to Lefebvre's recent clutch hitting with runners aboard. As usual, Marrone's magic paid off as Leominster erupted for eight runs through a combination of timely hitting and aggressive running on the base paths.

After falling behind 1-0 in the first inning, the locals roared back with a four-run outburst in the bottom of the second. Lead-off batter and center-fielder Ted Rockwell singled to left-center. With right-fielder Dave Arsenault at the plate, Rockwell stole second-base. Arsenault walked, putting runners on first and second with no outs. After third-basemen Mike Gasbarro went down on strikes, first-basemen Jay Connors slapped a single up the middle, sending Rockwell home with the tying run and Arsenault to third. After Connors stole second, Pete Robichaud delivered the first of his two hits on the day, scoring Arsenault with the go-ahead run. With Connors on third, Robichaud stole second.

With first-base vacant, Bergeron was intentionally walked to load the bases and create a force out opportunity around the infield. With two outs and for the second game in a row, Lefebvre again made an opponent pay for the intentional walk by singling to center-field, sending both Connors and Robichaud in to score the third and fourth runs of the inning. After 2 innings, Leominster led 4-1.

Leominster struck again in the bottom of the third with three more runs. Ted Rockwell once again got things started with a walk and promptly stole his second base of the game. With one out, Rockwell scored on an infield error increasing Leominster's lead to 5-1. With Gasbarro on second-base as a result of the throwing error, Connors struck out for the second out of the inning. Robichaud walked and both he and Gasbarro advanced on a wild pitch. Dave Bergeron walked to load the bases and Greenfield starting pitcher Mike Maloney was relieved by Tom Winseck. Mark Lefebvre greeted Winseck with a first pitch single over the shortstop's leap to bring in Gasbarro and Robichaud for a 7-1 Leominster lead.

Figure 46: The author about to take a lead from third-base (photo credit: Ken Albridge for the Leominster Enterprise)

Leominster	AB	R	H	RBI
Robichaud, 2b	2	2	2	1
Ruggles, 2b	0	1	0	0
Bergeron, 3b	2	0	0	0
Lefebvre, lf	2	0	2	4
Crawley, lf	0	0	0	0
Leclair, p	4	0	0	0
Burke, c	3	0	0	0
Gamache, c	0	0	0	0
Rockwell, cf	3	2	1	0
Arsenault, rf	3	1	1	0
Gasbarro, ss	4	1	0	0
Connors, 1b	2	1	1	1
Catalfamo, 1b	2	0	0	0
Totals	27	8	7	6

Greenfield	AB	R	H	RBI
York, cf	2	0	0	0
Lawrence, cf	0	1	0	0
Hanley, lf	4	0	1	0
Maloney, p-2b	2	0	0	0
Rice, 2b	1	0	0	0
Welenc, ss	4	1	2	0
Mowry, c	2	0	0	0
Duprye, 1b	3	0	1	1
Kostanski, rf	3	0	0	0
Vivier, 3b	1	0	0	1
Dziekonski, 2b	1	0	0	0
Winseck, p	2	0	0	0
Totals	25	2	4	2

Pitcher	IP	H	R	ER	W	K
Maloney L	2.1	5	7	4	6	5
Winseck	3.2	2	1	0	3	1
Leclair W	7	4	2	2	8	7

Figure 47: Mark Lefebvre, Mike Leclair and Pete Robichaud accept Section 1 Championship Award (photo credit: Ken Albridge)

Three walks and a Greenfield error provided Leominster with another run as Leominster entered the seventh inning with an 8-1 lead. Greenfield threatened in the seventh with a bases-loaded walk which tightened the deficit to 8-2. Leclair once again went the distance, fanning Greenfield right-fielder John Kostanski with the bases loaded to end the game, sending Leominster to the state tournament for an unprecedented third consecutive year. [69] [70]

Longmeadow vs. Leominster, Tuesday, July 24, 1973
Massachusetts State Tournament

The opening game of the 1973 Massachusetts State Tournament saw defending state champs, Leominster face the host team from Longmeadow on Tuesday, July 24, 1973, and at the same Strople field where Leominster defeated South Hadley just 10 days earlier. Manager Jim

Marrone rolled out a lineup that had the returning Bob Angelini at second-base and batting leadoff, and Dave Bergeron at third-base and hitting in the second slot.

Figure 48: 1973 Massachusetts Babe Ruth State Tournament Guide (photo credit: Mark Lefebvre)

Mark Lefebvre remained in the third slot and in left-field, center-fielder Mike Leclair batting clean-up, and catcher Jay Burke batting fifth. Starting pitcher Ted Rockwell, right-fielder Dave Arsenault, short-stop Mike Gasbarro and first-baseman Jay Connors rounded out the starting line-up.

Although Leominster was heavily favored, Longmeadow patiently took advantage of Leominster's pitching and fielding miscues to stun the locals 7-6 to the delight of their hometown fans. Leominster held a 6-1 lead entering the top of the fifth inning only to see that lead evaporate when Longmeadow scored 5 runs to tie the game, all without the benefit of a hit.

Figure 49: 1973 Longmeadow Babe Ruth All-Stars (photo credit: Mark Lefebvre)
Front row: James Peys, Anthony Ricco, Scott Williams, James Durocher, Edward Dwyer, Dennis Markell, David Bryer, bat boy Steven Duclos center.
Back row: Coach Peter Sarant, Stephen O'Connor, Steven Hurwitz, Jeff Seaman, Jack Sadler, Jeff Folkins, Eric Michelman, Coach Ron Durocher.

Leominster got their offense rolling in the bottom of the first inning when second-basemen, Bob Angelini lined a single into right-center field to lead off. Angelini advanced to second on a hit-and-run fielder's choice with third-basemen Dave Bergeron out at first. With Angelini still nursing an injured ankle, coach Jim Marrone replaced him with Peter Robichaud. With Robichaud at second-base, left-fielder Mark Lefebvre popped out to the catcher for the second out. Mike Leclair, playing center-field with Ted Rockwell on the mound, drove a double deep over the Longmeadow center-fielder's head to score Robichaud with the first run of the game. Jay Burke reached on an infield error scoring Leclair for a 2-0 lead.

Leominster extended their lead with two more runs in the top of the second inning. Right-fielder Dave Arsenault and shortstop Mike

Gasbarro both walked to open the inning putting men on first and second with no outs. After first-baseman Jay Connors was retired, Robichaud knocked in Arsenault with a single making the score 3-0. Gasbarro eventually came home on a throwing error which increased the Leominster lead to 4-0.

Longmeadow struck for a single run in the bottom half of the third when lead-off batter and first-basemen Frank Maddux worked Rockwell for a walk. Third-basemen Ed Dwyer singled putting runners on first and second with no outs. Center-fielder Steve O'Connor singled to score Maddux cutting the Leominster lead to 4-1.

Leominster added two more runs in the fourth when Arsenault opened the frame with a double. Gasbarro reached on an error and advanced to second on the play putting runners on second and third with no outs. After Jay Connors fanned for the first out, Robichaud doubled to bring home both Arsenault and Gasbarro, increasing Leominster lead to 6-1.

Pinch-hitter Tony Ricco opened up the Longmeadow half of the fourth inning with a walk and ended up on third following two wild pitches. After Dwyer walked putting men on first and third with no outs, Rockwell balked bringing in Ricco and advancing Dwyer to second. Apparently shaken, Rockwell walked the next three batters in a row bringing in the third Longmeadow run. Another wild pitch brought in the fourth run and Longmeadow suddenly found themselves back in the game. With runners on second and third with two outs, right-fielder Jeff Folkins hit what appeared to be an inning-ending infield out, but which found its way through the infield for a two-run error and the score was tied 6-6 after four innings.

Longmeadow took the lead in the bottom of the fifth when left-fielder Steve Hurwitz reached on another Leominster infield error and ended up at second-base on the play. Folkins plated Hurwitz with a single to right-center giving Longmeadow their first lead of the game at 7-6.

Leominster	AB	R	H	RBI
Angelini, 2b	1	0	1	0
Robichaud, 2b	3	1	2	3
Bergeron, 3b	2	0	0	0
Lefebvre, lf	4	0	0	0
Leclair, cf	4	1	1	1
Burke, c	2	0	0	0
Gamache, c	1	0	0	0
Rockwell, p	2	0	0	0
Girouard, p	0	0	0	0
Arsenault., rf	2	2	1	0
Gasbarro, ss	3	1	0	0
Connors, 1b	3	0	0	0
Totals	27	6	5	4

Longmeadow	AB	R	H	RBI
Dwyer, 3b	3	1	1	0
Durocher, 2b	2	1	0	0
O'Connor, cf	3	1	1	0
Hurwitz, lf	2	2	0	1
Folkins, rf	3	0	1	2
Seaman, p	4	0	1	0
Lincoln, ss	1	0	0	0
Ricco, ss	2	1	0	0
Peys, c	3	0	0	0
Maddox 1b	1	1	0	0
Totals	24	7	4	3

Pitcher	IP	H	R	ER	W	K
Rockwell	3.2	2	6	6	9	6
Girouard (l)	2.1	2	1	0	2	4
Seaman (w)	7	5	6	3	4	7

Leominster left-fielder Mark Lefebvre prevented any further damage by hustling to cut off a double to the left-center field gap which kept Folkins from scoring all the way from first. Leominster reliever Doug Girouard fanned Ricco to end the inning, but the damage was done. Leominster put up one more threat in the seventh inning when Dave Bergeron opened the inning with a walk and promptly stole second-base. Lefebvre hit a long fly to deep center-field which was hauled in by O'Connor. With one out and Bergeron on second-base, Leclair looped a soft fly into short left-center field which looked like it would drop in for a game-tying single. However, O'Connor made a stunning sliding catch and doubled off Bergeron who was running on the play to end the game. Final score, 7-6, Longmeadow.

Now in the loser's bracket for the second year in a row, Leominster would face an uphill battle to advance in the tournament.[71][72]

Leominster vs. Wakefield, Thursday, July 26, 1973
Following the shocking opening loss to host Longmeadow, Leominster found itself playing in the loser's bracket and facing elimination in their next game against Wakefield. During the off-day on Wednesday, the Leominster team gathered for a morning practice shaken, but not defeated.

Figure 50: 1973 Wakefield Babe Ruth All-Stars (photo credit: Mark Lefebvre)
Front row: Steve Luciano, Mike Gonella, Mike DeMarco, Mike Boyages, Bob Curtin, Joe Ferraro, Jim Zahareas, Joe Trotta.
Back row: Manager Bill Buitenhuys, Jim Bresnahan, Larry Collins, Jim Melanson, Steve Evangelista, Roger Lapham, Tom Ring, Pete Mooney, bat boy Bill Buitenhuys, Coach Kirk Moran.

I can distinctly remember coach Jim Marrone gathering us in a circle to give us a bit of a pep talk and to loosen the team up from the tension of the predicament. Coach Marrone waited for the banter to subside and said something to the effect of, "well fellas, we got 'em right where we want 'em. Are we going to roll over?" After the team responded with a resounding "NO!," we sprinted out to our positions and proceeded with practice still believing we could beat anyone in this tournament.

Leominster ace, Mike Leclair, got the nod against Wakefield with over a week's rest, with Jay Burke as his battery mate. Jay Connors started at first-base, Bob Angelini at second, Mike Gasbarro at short, and Dave Bergeron at third. The outfield was patrolled by Mark Lefebvre in left, Ted Rockwell in center and Dave Arsenault in right.

Leominster wasted no time in getting on the board with a four-run outburst in the first while sending nine batters to the plate. Angelini led off with a walk and scored all the way from first on a triple by Bergeron. After Bergeron was awarded home plate as a result of runner interference, Mark Lefebvre walked, but was picked off first on a slick move by Wakefield starting lefty, Jim Melanson. After Leclair flew out to deep center-field, Jay Burke walked and scored on Ted Rockwell's double to left-center. Rockwell then scored on a base hit by Dave Arsenault. Wakefield went down in order in their half of the first giving 4-0 Leominster after one inning.

Leominster put two more runs on the board in the top of the second inning when Angelini reached on an error and scored on a double by Bergeron. With one out, Leclair drove in Bergeron with a long double off the 350-foot marker on the left-center fence.

In the top half of the third, Leominster made it 8-0 with Arsenault and Bergeron connecting for key hits. Arsenault extended the lead with an RBI double that scored Ted Rockwell who had reached on a single. After 4 innings Leominster appeared to be on their way to a rout with a 9-0 lead.

Wakefield	AB	R	H	RBI
Mooney, 2b	4	0	0	0
Curtin, cf	3	1	0	0
Bresnahan, lf	3	1	1	1
Lapham, c	3	1	1	2
Trotta, 3b	4	2	2	0
DeMarco, rf	3	2	1	3
Farraro, ss	1	0	0	0
Zahareas, ss	2	0	0	0
Boyages, 2b	3	1	0	0
Melanson, p	0	0	0	0
Evangelista, p	0	0	0	0
Luciano, p	1	0	0	0
Gonnella, p	1	0	0	0
Collins, ph	1	1	1	0
Totals	**29**	**9**	**6**	**6**

Leominster	AB	R	H	RBI
Angelini, 2b	1	2	0	0
Ruggles, 2b-ss	2	0	1	0
Bergeron, 3b	4	3	3	4
Lefebvre, lf	2	0	0	0
Crawley, ph-lf	2	0	2	2
Leclair, p	4	0	2	1
Burke, c	2	1	0	0
Gamache, c	1	0	0	0
Rockwell, cf	5	2	2	1
Arsenault., rf	4	1	4	2
Catalfamo, 1b	2	0	0	0
Connors, 1b	1	0	0	0
Gasbarro, ss-p	2	2	0	0
Totals	**32**	**11**	**14**	**10**

Pitcher	IP	H	R	ER	W	K
Leclair, (w)	5	2	2	1	1	9
Gasbarro	2	4	7	6	4	4
Melanson (l)	.2	3	4	1	3	0
Evangelista	.2	2	2	1	1	2
Luciano	3	7	5	3	2	1
Gannella	2.2	2	0	0	2	2

Leominster scored what would become the margin of victory with two more runs in the fifth inning. After reaching on an error, Gasbarro stole second and reached third on a single by Angelini. After stealing second, Angelini was picked off by the Wakefield pitcher Steve Luciano. Bergeron walked and stole second, putting two runners in scoring position with one out. John Crawley stepped up to the plate as a pinch-hitter for Lefebvre and drilled a single into left field scoring both Gasbarro and Bergeron for an 11-0 lead after five innings.

Wakefield's bats would awaken in the bottom half of the fifth with two runs. After five innings Coach Jim Marrone opted to lift Leclair to save his arm for a possible start should Leominster advance into the finals and called on shortstop Mike Gasbarro to pitch the sixth. Gasbarro proved his mettle retiring Wakefield pinch-hitter Jim Zahareas with the bases loaded in the sixth. Gasbarro would not be so lucky in the seventh inning when Wakefield would plate seven more runs to reduce Leominster's lead to two runs. After giving up a three-run homer to Wakefield right-fielder Mike DeMarco, Gasbarro bore down and struck out Zahareas and retired second-basemen Mike Boyages on a pop-up to first to end the game, and setting up a tilt against Barnstable later that same afternoon.

Dave Arsenault and Dave Bergeron led the Leominster hit parade with four hits (double, three singles) and three hits (single, double, triple), respectively. Mike Leclair picked up the win increasing his 1973 all-star record to 4-0.[73][74]

Leominster vs. Barnstable, Friday, July 27, 1973
With just one day of rest, Leominster's reward for Thursday's 11-9 victory over Wakefield was to face a double-header the very next day in order to stave off elimination. The locals' first opponent of the day was Barnstable, and all of coach Marrone's magic would be required in this sloppy, but thrilling extra-inning contest.

Figure 51: 1973 Barnstable Babe Ruth All-Stars (photo credit: Mark Lefebvre)
Front row: Donald Murray, Keith Drinkwater, Fred Sullivan, Mark Miller-Jones, Ron Burlingame, John Johnson, Tim Storer, Joh Rosario, Daniel Hoxie.
Back row: Manager Dick Teel, Coach Bill Mullin, Fred Dooley, Jeff Bacon, Dean Stanley, Kevin Davis, league president Ellis Johnson, Coach George Karath.

Leominster jumped out to a 10-3 lead by the middle of the fourth inning as Barnstable was bitten by the deadly combination of walks and errors. Catcher Jay Burke and shortstop Mike Gasbarro provided the only hits during the Leominster scoring spree.

In the bottom of the fourth, Barnstable sent fifteen batters to the plate as Leominster fell apart, yielding eleven runs on five hits, six walks and five errors. After four innings, Barnstable held a formidable 14-10 lead.

Leominster cut the deficit in half in the top of the sixth when third baseman Mike Bergeron opened with a single and advanced to second-base when Burke walked. Left-fielder Mike Leclair drove Bergeron in with a single. Both center-fielder Ted Rockwell and right-fielder Dave Arsenault walked to force in the second run of the inning making the score 14-12 after five-and-a-half innings.

Undaunted, Barnstable scored three more runs in their half of the sixth on three walks and base hits by pitcher Keith Drinkwater and right-fielder Fred Dooley. After six innings, Barnstable had a commanding 17-12 lead, and Leominster was down to their last three outs in order to avoid elimination.

Coach Marrone gathered the team in the dugout and reminded us to be patient as Barnstable had gone deep into its pitching staff, and admonished us to not help our opponent by swinging at bad pitches. The advice paid off as no less than the first four batters - Angelini, Bergeron, Burke and Leclair all walked to force in a run and load the bases. Rockwell and Arsenault went down on strikes leaving Leominster's season on the line with one out remaining.

Miraculously, Pete Robichaud was hit by a pitch which cut the deficit to 17-14 with the bases still loaded. First-basemen Jay Connors, subbing for starter Mike Catalfamo, drove in two more runs with a clutch single making the score 17-16. A wild pitch brought in Robichaud, and the score was tied 17-17 at the end of seven innings.

After a scoreless eighth inning, Leominster took the lead in the top half of the ninth inning when Ted Rockwell singled, stole second and scored on a two-out error on a chopper to short by Jay Connors. After stealing second, Connors scored on a single by Mike Gasbarro.

Leominster led 19-17 with Barnstable coming to bat in the bottom of the ninth. However, Jay Burke slammed the door shut on Barnstable in the bottom of the ninth to preserve the win. Facing elimination, Leominster let all the horses out of the barn with Bob Angelini, Dave

Arsenault, Doug Girouard, Pete Robichaud and the games eventual winning pitcher, Jay Burke, all pitching for the winners. Burke was largely credited with saving the day with a 3-inning scoreless, one-hit performance to close out the game.

Barnstable	AB	R	H	RBI
Dumont, lf	3	1	0	0
Rosario, c	6	3	2	1
Miller-Jones, ss-p	5	3	3	0
Burlingame, cf	3	3	1	2
Stanley, p-1b	3	1	0	1
Murray, rf-2b	4	2	2	2
Johnson, 1b-p	4	1	0	1
Drinkwater, p-2b	4	2	1	1
Bacon, 3b	1	0	0	0
Dooley, 3b	3	1	1	1
Totals	**36**	**17**	**10**	**9**

Leominster	AB	R	H	RBI
Angelini, p-2b	5	2	0	0
Bergeron, 3b	6	4	1	0
Burke, c-p	4	3	1	1
Leclair, lf-cf	4	3	3	2
Rockwell, cf-p	5	1	2	2
Arsenault, rf-p	4	1	1	2
Ruggles, 2b-rf	2	1	1	0
Girouard, p-lf	1	0	0	0
Lefebvre, lf	1	1	0	0
Robichaud, p	0	1	0	0
Gamache, c	1	0	0	0
Crawley, ph	1	0	0	0
Catafalmo, 1b	3	0	0	0
Connors, 1b	2	0	1	2
Gasbarro, ss	4	2	2	2
Totals	**43**	**19**	**12**	**11**

Pitcher	IP	H	R	ER	W	K
Angelini	0	1	1	0	2	0
Arsenault	2	1	2	0	5	4
Girouard	1	3	7	2	3	1
Rockwell	2	2	6	4	5	3
Robichaud	1	2	1	0	1	0
Burke (w)	3	1	0	0	1	4
Stanley	3	3	6	2	2	0
Johnson	3	5	6	0	5	4
Miller Jones	1	2	5	5	5	3
Drinkwater (l)	2	2	2	0	0	0

Both Leominster and Barnstable were obviously fatigued from the grind of playing in the losers' bracket, and it showed on the scorecard. Leominster pitchers allowed seventeen runs on ten hits, and gave up seventeen walks.

Leominster's defense committed six errors. Barnstable pitchers combined for nineteen runs, twelve hits, and twelve walks. Barnstable's defense committed nine errors including six wild pitches.[75][76]

Leominster vs. Longmeadow, Friday July 27, 1973

On the heels of the exhausting 19-17 marathon win over Barnstable earlier that day, Leominster coach Jim Marrone was hoping for a less dramatic result in the nightcap against host Longmeadow, the scrappy team that handed the Leominster squad their only defeat in the tournament. Mike Leclair got the nod from Marrone without any rest from the Wakefield game the day before. The rest of the lineup included Bob Angelini at second-base and batting lead-off, Dave Bergeron at third, Pete Gamache behind the plate and batting third, Ted Rockwell batting clean-up and starting in center-field, Mike Leclair on the mound, Dave Arsenault in right-field, Mark Lefebvre in left-field, Mike Catalfamo at first and Mike Gasbarro at shortstop.

Leominster scored the only run it would need in the second as

Mike Catalfamo opened the frame with a single to left-field and stole second. With two outs, Bob Angelini brought him in with a sharp single to left.

Leominster added an insurance run in the fifth inning when Dave Bergeron was hit by a pitch. After Gamache flew out to left-field, Leclair chopped a ground ball to third-base which forced Longmeadow third-basemen Ed Dwyer to rush his throw to first which sailed wide, scoring Bergeron with Leominster's second run.

Longmeadow	AB	R	H	RBI
Dwyer, 3b	2	0	0	0
Durocher, 2b	3	0	0	0
Markell, ph	1	0	0	0
Sadler, 1b	3	0	1	0
Hurwitz, lf	2	0	0	0
Seaman, rf	3	0	1	0
O'Connor, cf	2	0	0	0
Ricco, ss	3	0	1	0
Michelmann, c	3	0	0	0
Folkins, p	2	0	1	0
Totals	**24**	**0**	**4**	**0**
Leominster	**AB**	**R**	**H**	**RBI**
Angelini, 2b	4	0	2	1
Bergeron, 3b	3	1	0	0
Gamache, c	3	0	0	0
Rockwell, cf	2	0	0	0
Leclair, p	2	0	0	0
Arsenault., rf	3	0	0	0
Lefebvre, lf	3	0	0	0
Catalfamo, 1b	3	1	1	0
Gasbarro, ss	3	0	0	0
Totals	**26**	**2**	**3**	**1**

Pitcher	IP	H	R	ER	W	K
Folkins (l)	7	3	2	1	2	8
Leclair (w)	7	4	0	0	4	4

With Leominster leading 2-0 in the sixth, Longmeadow threatened when left-fielder Steve Hurwitz walked with one out, bringing up right-fielder Jeff Seaman who in turn singled to right. Leominster right-fielder Dave Arsenault charged hard on the play, scooped up the bounce and fired a strike to Bergeron who put the tag on Hurwitz for the out. Leominster escaped the threat and Leclair retired the bottom of the Longmeadow order in the seventh to pick up his second win in two days.

Standing between Leominster and their third consecutive state title was Burncoat of Worcester who was undefeated in the tournament. Leominster would need to win twice the next day in order to take home the championship.

Burncoat (Worcester) vs. Leominster, Saturday July 28, 1973

Figure 52: 1973 Burncoat (Worcester) All-Stars

Front row: Mark Consolmagno, Joe Kittridge, Marty Hastings, bat boy Chris Swift, Sal DiStefano, Bill Riley, Lou Gosslin.
Back row: Coach Sal DiStefano, Paul Quist, Pat Remington, Joe MacLean, Mike Quinn, Manager Mike Simmarano, Frank Palermo, Wade Boviard, Mike McGrath, Mike Eressy, Coach Al Bonofiglio.

Leominster faced Burncoat of Worcester in what would be their fourth game in less than 72 hours. A win would send the locals to the state championship game later that day to defend their title.

Jay Burke got the nod from coach Jim Marrone. Towering over six feet tall, Burke warmed up on the Leominster side of the diamond with catcher Pete Gamache. The line-up for Leominster included Bob-Angelini at second-base and batting in his usual lead-off spot, Dave Bergeron at third-base, Gamache catching and batting third, Mike Leclair in left-field, Burke on the mound, Ted Rockwell in center-field, Dave Arsenault in right, Mike Catalfamo at first and Mike Gasbarro at short.

Not wasting any time, the aggressive Angelini led off the bottom half of the first inning with a double down the left-field line. With one out, Burncoat starting pitcher Pat Remington walked the next three Leominster batters to force in a run, giving Leominster a 1-0 lead.

Leominster padded their lead with a four-run outburst in the bottom of the third. Leclair singled to open the inning and advanced to second on a base hit by Burke. Rockwell followed with another base hit scoring Leclair from second-base. With two runners on, Dave Arsenault launched a towering shot over the left-field fence for a 3-run homer and a 5-0 Leominster lead. Burncoat left-fielder Bill Riley's extraordinary effort resulted in him flipping over the fence, falling just short of making the catch.

In the fourth inning, Dave Bergeron led off with a bunt single catching the Burncoat infield off-guard. However, Bergeron was cut down at second-base as he tried to advance on an errant throw to first. After Pete Gamache flew out to center, Mark Lefebvre, batting for Leclair after the Leominster ace injured his groin running out a ground ball, singled and stole second. Jay Burke walked to put men on first and second with two outs. With Ted Rockwell at the plate, Lefebvre and Burke pulled off a surprise double-steal which advanced them to second and third. Rockwell then lined a single to left-center scoring Lefebvre; however, Burke was nailed at the plate on a perfect relay to the plate by Burncoat third-baseman Mike Eressy. Leominster led 6-0 after four innings.

Leominster	AB	R	H	RBI
Angelini, 2b	4	1	2	0
Bergeron, 3b	3	0	1	0
Gamache, c	3	0	1	0
Leclair, lf	1	1	1	0
Lefebvre, lf	2	1	2	0
Burke, p	2	1	1	1
Rockwell, cf	3	1	2	2
Arsenault, rf	3	1	2	3
Catalfamo, 1b	3	0	0	0
Gasbarro, ss	3	0	0	0
Totals	**27**	**6**	**12**	**6**

Burncoat	AB	R	H	RBI
Hastings, cf	3	0	0	0
Consolmagno, ph	1	0	0	0
DiStefano, 2b	2	0	0	0
Riley, lf	3	0	1	0
Quinn, 1b	3	0	2	0
Palermo, rf	3	0	0	0
Eressy, 3b	2	0	0	0
Remington, p	3	0	0	0
Gosslin, ss	3	0	1	0
Bovaird, c	1	0	0	0
Kittridge, ph	1	0	0	0
Totals	**25**	**0**	**4**	**0**

Pitcher	IP	H	R	ER	W	K
Remington (l)	6	12	6	6	4	8
Burke (w)	7	4	0	0	3	6

Burke was immense on the mound for Leominster giving up only four hits and three walks. He struck out six Burncoat batters. The momentum from this game was clearly in Leominster's favor as they had now won four games in a row to force a championship showdown with Burncoat.

Coach Marrone now turned his attention to Mike Leclair's groin injury since Leclair was slated to start the championship game, which would be his third start in three days. Unbeknownst to the players and the fans, Leclair was taken to the local hospital for whirlpool treatment for his injured groin. It remained to be seen how effective Leclair would be in the championship game. [77] [78]

Burncoat vs. Leominster, Saturday July 28, 1973
Massachusetts State Championship Game

After slugging it out for four games in two days in the loser's bracket, Leominster now stood at the brink of winning its 3rd consecutive state championship. Mike Leclair's status for the title game was in question right up to warm-ups after suffering a groin injury in previous game. However, Leclair and coach Paul Harris returned to Strople Field following whirlpool treatment with the news that Leclair was good to go. Knowing that we had our ace ready to take the mound against Burncoat, the team shifted its focus on the game ahead.

Since Jay Burke pitched three innings in the prior game, coach Marrone elected to start Pete Gamache at catcher and save Burke for mound duty should Leclair be negatively impacted by his groin injury. The rest of the starting lineup included Bob Angelini at second-base, Dave Bergeron at third, Ted Rockwell in center-field, Dave Arsenault in right, Mark Lefebvre in left, Mike Catalfamo at first-base and Mike Gasbarro at short.

Bill Riley, Burncoat's ace got the nod and opened the bottom of the first-inning by striking out Angelini and Bergeron. After Pete

Gamache worked Riley for a walk, Leclair towered a double to deep left-field scoring Gamache with the game's first run. After yielding that run in the first, Riley settled down and retired the next 7 Leominster batters in a row.

Leominster would strike again in the fourth when Dave Arsenault opened with a single and advanced to second when Mark Lefebvre grounded out to first. Mike Catalfamo lofted a bloop single down the right field line which brought in Arsenault with what would be the deciding run.

Burncoat scored its only run in the top of the sixth when Leclair walked Burncoat center-fielder Bob Swift. With a lengthy lead off first-base, Swift drew a pick-off attempt which was misplayed by Catalfamo. Right-fielder Arsenault scooped up the errant throw and made the throw to third in an attempt to nail Swift. However, Arsenault's throw was off the mark which resulted in Swift scoring all the way from first for an unearned run.

The score after six innings remained 2-1 in Leominster's favor with Burncoat coming up to bat in the top of the seventh. Leominster was three outs from winning the Massachusetts State Championship. Burncoat catcher Mike Quinn led off the seventh inning with a sharp grounder towards the gap between short and third. Bergeron dove to his left to snag the ball, rose to his feet and fired a dart to first, nailing Quinn by two steps. One down.

Right fielder Frank Palermo grounded out to second-basemen Angelini for the second out of the inning. With two outs, Burncoat third-basemen Mike Eressy singled, placing the tying run on first-base with two outs in the seventh. Coach Marrone called time and walked to the mound to confer with Leclair.[79] [80]

"Please God, let him hit it to me," I thought as I bent over to pick up a pinch of left field grass and to check the wind for the third time in as

many minutes. The timeout called by coach Jim Marrone and the trip to the mound to talk with Mike Leclair seemed interminable. Catcher Pete Gamache stood by Leclair's side with his catcher's mask in his mitt. Sweat was beading from Gamache's chin in the late afternoon humidity of the day. Gamache and Leclair listened intently as Marrone gave the Leominster battery a chance to catch their breaths. My heart was pounding as I internalized the enormity of the moment.

There were two outs in the seventh inning, and we were leading 2-1 over Burncoat of Worcester with the potential tying run on first-base. Another out and we'd be Massachusetts Babe Ruth State Champions, a feat achieved by Leominster in each of the prior two seasons. I did not know it at the time, but until then, no other Massachusetts town had ever won three consecutive state championships.

It wasn't that I felt that I was the only player on the field capable of making that third put-out. I wanted to be the hero. I wanted to fulfill every kid's dream of either knocking in the winning run in a walk-off, or making the final put-out on the field. Ted Rockwell was to my left in center field. Dave Arsenault in right. Dave Bergeron, who made a dazzling play to his left earlier in the inning to rob a Burncoat batter of a potential extra base hit was at third-base. Mike Gasbarro at short. Bob Angelini at second and Mike Catalfamo at first.

My mind drifted to the journey we took to get to this moment. In some regards it started in the summer of 1970 when I and several of my current teammates, were eliminated in the Massachusetts Little League State Championship tournament just three years prior while playing for the Leominster American Little League all-stars. And here we were again with a chance for redemption.

Back to the moment. We were sharp. We were focused. And we were very talented. Yet we were mentally and physically exhausted. We had needed to win five games just to advance to this tournament. And since we lost our tournament opener to Longmeadow, we were dropped to the losers' bracket which in turn required us to crawl back to play this, our fifth game in the last three days.

The stands at Strople Field were packed with fans, coaches and players from the other teams, and league officials. The lights were turned on to neutralize the late afternoon shadows. I could see my parents on the first-base side of the grandstands. They and the rest of the Leominster following were standing and clapping.

As coach Marrone jogged back to the dugout, I surveyed the situation. Two outs with a man on first. Joe McLean, Burncoat's right-hand-hitting first-baseman, stepped into the box. Leclair, pitching from the stretch, peered in for the sign from Gamache. I crouched into a ready stance on the balls of my feet, waiting for the pitch. From the set, Leclair fired a fastball to the mitt. I pivoted as I heard the crack of the bat....

Figure 53: Mobbing Mike Leclair (photo credit: Cynthia Lefebvre)
Ted Rockwell (center) and the author (right) joining the celebration

After the final out we mobbed Mike Leclair on the infield. The scene was surreal, yet the feeling was exhilarating to say the least. Our parents and siblings joined us as we eventually worked our way to the first-base dugout. We had done the improbable -- winning the Massachusetts state championship after losing the opening game and grinding our way through the loser's bracket. For the first time in Massachusetts Babe Ruth history, a single city had won the state championship for the third year in a row. I can't ever recall a feeling so rewarding and so thrilling in my life. What it cemented for me was the reward for effort, teamwork and resilience. I would take this lesson with me for the rest of my life.

Thinking back to the entirety of the 1973 all-star season, it is even more remarkable today to think of the contributions that Mike Leclair made in leading the us to our third straight Massachusetts state title. Leclair's pitching line for the state tournament was a ridiculous three games started, a 3-0 record, two complete games, nineteen innings pitched, and a 0.37 ERA. He yielded only nine hits, struck out eighteen, and walked six. And he did this in three days with no rest in between starts. In addition to his pitching heroics, Leclair batted .444 in the state tournament with five runs scored and four RBIs.

Leominster	AB	R	H	RBI
Angelini, 2b	3	0	0	0
Bergeron, 3b	3	0	0	0
Gamache, c	2	1	1	0
Leclair, p	3	0	1	1
Rockwell, cf	2	0	1	0
Arsenault, rf	2	1	1	0
Lefebvre, lf	3	0	0	0
Catalfamo, 1b	2	0	2	1
Gasbarro, ss	1	0	0	0
Totals	**21**	**2**	**6**	**2**

Burncoat	AB	R	H	RBI
Hastings, cf	2	0	1	0
Swift, lf	0	1	0	0
DiStefano, 2b	3	0	0	0
Riley, p	3	0	0	0
Quinn, c	3	0	0	0
Palermo, rf	3	0	0	0
Eressy, 3b	3	0	2	0
McLean, 1b	2	0	0	0
Gosslin, ss	2	0	0	0
Totals	**21**	**1**	**3**	**0**

Pitcher	IP	H	R	ER	W	K
Riley (l)	6	6	2	2	3	2
Leclair (w)	7	3	1	0	1	5

His pitching line for the entire Massachusetts All-Star season was equally stellar with six games started, a 6-0 record, five complete games, a 0.53 ERA, yielded only fourteen hits in six games, struck out thirty-one batters and walked sixteen.

I recalled the comment that Coach Marrone made at practice the morning after losing our first game to Longmeadow, "we got 'em right where we want 'em." In hindsight, I still wonder if this was his way of keeping the team loose or was it a premonition? Regardless, it is now on to Lynn, MA and the 1973 New England Regionals.

Town Celebration

It had been a long week since the 1973 Massachusetts State Champions left Longmeadow and entered the Comb City to a welcoming escort of Leominster police cruisers and fire trucks. I soaked in the scene against the backdrop of my own memories of cheering the 1971 and 1972 teams making their way through the streets of Leominster. It was during those moments when I fantasized that perhaps one day I might be sitting on a similar bus of champions.

The entire scene was surreal for the scrawny kid from the Lancaster Street and Fall Brook gangs, who made it to the local big-time representing his home town. It was then, on that bus, that I felt an immense sense of pride as a teammate of these great ball-players. As we exited Route 2 eastbound onto North Main Street, I felt a connection to my city and to those heroes who played in the years prior. It was not lost on me as we traveled east on Route 2 from Amherst that we defeated Athol and Fitchburg on the way to the championship. And that the route we took home on this bus, brought us through both communities on our way to Leominster, city of champions. We turned south onto North Main Street with the city of Fitchburg in our rear view.

It wasn't more than a couple of days of rest before we shifted our attention to the upcoming New England Regional Tournament to be played at the Manning Bowl in Lynn, Massachusetts. It was difficult to ignore the fact that Puerto Nuevo again stood in the way of a coveted New England Regional championship and a trip to Manchester, New Hampshire where the 1973 Babe Ruth World Series was being held later in August.

We could not afford to dwell on an eventual game with the stars from Puerto Rico as we were scheduled to open against the boys from Portland, Maine in the opener on Sunday, August 5. We practiced several times that week leading up to the tournament. As was his typical style, coach Marrone kept us loose by cracking jokes before practice. However, the talk during practice was all business. Marrone, with two prior years' worth of experience under his belt, explained what to expect. He also reminded us of the great city we were representing and to carry ourselves accordingly.

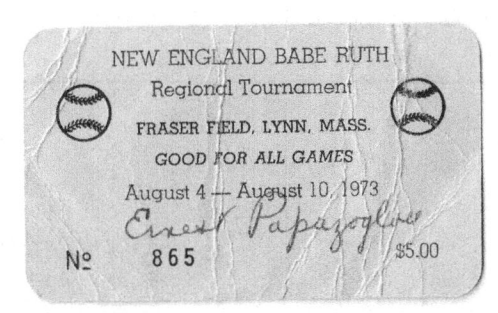

Figure 54: (l) Window sticker; (r) 1970 State Tournament pass (photo credits: Dave Bergeron)

Figure 55: Worcester Telegram cartoon send-off to the New England Regionals (photo credit: Worcester Telegram)

(Author's note: this cartoon was from the Worcester Telegram and created by the legendary sports cartoonist Phil Bissell who is perhaps most famously known as the creator of the original "Pat the Patriot" logo for the New England Patriots.)

By the end of the week we were champing at the bit in anticipation of the tournament. At the last practice before heading off to Lynn we posed for a team photo at the Babe Ruth Field.

Figure 56: 1970 Massachusetts Babe Ruth State Champions (photo credit: Mark Lefebvre)

Front row: Bob Angelini, Doug Girouard, Pete Robichaud, bat boy Jon "Connie Hawkins," John Crawley, Mike Leclair, Mark Lefebvre, Dave Bergeron, Jay Burke
Back row: manager Jim Marrone, Ben Ruggles, Pete Gamache, Mike Leclair, Mike Catalfamo, Dave Arsenault, Ted Rockwell, Jay Connors, Coach Paul Harris, Coach Steve Campobasso

My own enthusiasm for the upcoming regional tournament was suddenly tempered by a freak injury to my right hand while fishing in Lunenburg with my friend Brian McNally (see Dedication). We were fishing for catfish or "horned pout" as they are sometimes referred to locally. As those who have fished these delicacies know, they are

220

dangerous to handle as they have spines on their back as well as to the sides of their mouth. There is a technique to holding them which involves approaching them from the back with forked fingers to grip the side fins in a manner that allows the spines to be rendered harmless.

That summer afternoon, Brian and I were dropped at a local pond by his father with the agreement that he would pick us up in a couple of hours. Like many ventures to that pond, Brian and I were catching smaller catfish for about an hour or so when I hooked a very large pout that was so big that my hand was not big enough to apply the proper and safe technique for handling the fish. As a result I ended up getting "stung" by the spine on its back. To make matters worse, the spine broke off and was embedded through my middle fingernail and protruded out the bottom of that finger. Needless to say, I was in agony. We did not have cell phones in those days, so we needed to wait for Brian's father to return which was interminable given the pain I was experiencing. As soon as Mr. McNally arrived he rushed me to Leominster Hospital where the nail was removed in order to remove the stinger.

The reader will notice in the team photo above that I am hiding my right hand and middle finger which was stitched, splinted and bandaged. Needless to say, coach Marrone and my teammates were not amused, and at the time I truly felt I let the team down.

New England Regional Tournament, Lynn, Massachusetts
Leominster vs. Portland (Maine), Sunday, August 5, 1973

The city of Lynn did a fantastic job preparing for the New England Regional Tournament, opening their doors to the players who stayed with local families, hosting a series of social events allowing the players and coaches the opportunity to decompress, and preparing Fraser Field for the action. Fraser Field features permanent covered stands behind home plate which extended up the baselines to first and third-base, respectively.

It was Sunday morning, August 5, and we were playing in the tournament opener against Portland, Maine. Portland's ace, Jeff Gardiner, was a tall right-hander who was known for his blazing fastball. For our part, Coach Marrone was countering with our ace, Mike Leclair. Our lineup for the opener featured Bob Angelini at second-base, Dave Bergeron at third, Jay Burke catching, Leclair on the mound, Ted Rockwell in center-field, Dave Arsenault in right-field, Mike Catalfamo at first, Peter Robichaud in left-field taking my normal spot, and Mike Gasbarro at shortstop.

Leominster wasted no time in getting on the scoreboard in the top of the first inning. Bob Angelini opened the game with a four-pitch walk to start things off. Dave Bergeron was hit by the very next pitch, and we had men on first and second with no outs. As expected, Angelini and Bergeron pulled off a double-steal on the very first pitch putting both runners in scoring position with only six pitches being thrown by Gardiner. This obviously rattled the Portland ace as he uncorked a wild pitch while facing Jay Burke, scoring Angelini and advancing Bergeron to third. After Burke fouled out and Leclair grounded out, Ted Rockwell hit a fly ball to center which was muffed by the centerfield, sending Bergeron home with the second Leominster run. Dave Arsenault struck out to end the inning. Leominster led 2-0 without the aid of a hit, and with Portland coming up to bat.

As it turned out, Mike Leclair took the hill for Leominster with all the runs he would need and cruised through six shut-out innings while scattering only four hits and walking three to that point. Leominster, however, still did not have a hit entering the top of the sixth inning.

Jay Burke led off the sixth with a walk, but was forced out when Leclair hit into a fielder's choice. With Leclair on first, Ted Rockwell hit a hard grounder to third which was misplayed by Portland third-basemen Bob Antoine putting Leominster runners on first and second with one out. Dave Arsenault attempted to advance the runners with a sacrifice bunt;

however his attempt landed in front of the mound. Gardiner elected to try to force Leclair at third, but his throw arrived too late. Bases were now loaded, still with one out. Leclair drew a tantalizingly big lead off third-base which prompted Gardiner to balk in his attempt at a pick-off. Leclair trotted home with the run giving Leominster a 3-0 lead after five-and-half innings.

Coach Marrone sent me out to my usual left-field position in the bottom of the seventh inning, trusting that I could help protect our lead despite my not yet being fully recovered from the injury to my finger injury. I had since had the splint removed, but the stitches remained. I privately hoped I would not be required to make a throw.

Down to their last three outs, Portland would finally solve Leclair in the bottom of the seventh. First-basemen John Foley opened up the inning with a pop single just over the head of Leominster second-baseman Bob Angelini. On a hit-and-run, Portland second-basemen Jack Morse chopped a grounder to the mound forcing Leclair to take the easy out at first, with Foley advancing to second with one out. Bob Antoine reached first-base without a throw on a slow roller to shortstop. Leominster shortstop Mike Gasbarro wisely held on to the ball to prevent Foley from going any further than third. With one out, and with men on first and third, Portland center-fielder Carrol Shephard stepped into the box. Portland then attempted a delayed double steal which was snuffed when Jay Burke fired a dart to Angelini at second-base to catch Antoine on his attempted theft. Foley remained at third and Portland was down to their final out. Shephard hit a grounder to Leominster third-basemen Bergeron for what should have been the final out of the game; however, first-baseman Mike Catalfamo could not squeeze the throw from Bergeron which allowed Foley to score.

Portland continued the threat when Gardiner singled to right-center and Portland left-fielder Gary Wilmont walked, loading the bases. With two outs, bases loaded and Leominster clinging to a 3-1 lead, Portland shortstop Bruce hit a flyball to right field that brought the Portland dugout to its feet. However, the rally was not to be as Dave Arsenault calmly gloved the ball and ended the threat.

Portland (ME)	AB	R	H	RBI
Antoine, 3b	4	0	1	0
Shephard, cf	4	0	0	0
Gardiner, p	3	0	2	0
Allen, lf	2	0	1	0
Maria, lf	0	0	0	0
Carey, ss	3	0	1	0
Redmond, c	3	0	0	0
Dean, rf	2	0	0	0
Finks, ph	1	0	0	0
Wilmont, rf	0	0	0	0
Foley, 1b	3	1	2	0
Morse, 2b	2	0	0	0
Totals	**27**	**1**	**7**	**0**

Leominster	AB	R	H	RBI
Angelini, 2b	3	1	0	0
Bergeron, 3b	4	1	0	0
Burke, c	2	0	0	0
Leclair, p	3	1	0	0
Rockwell, cf	3	0	0	0
Arsenault., rf	2	0	0	0
Catalfamo, 1b	3	0	0	0
Robichaud, lf	3	0	0	0
Lefebvre, lf	0	0	0	0
Gasbarro, ss	2	0	0	0
Totals	**25**	**3**	**0**	**0**

Pitcher	IP	H	R	ER	W	K
Leclair (w)	7	7	1	0	4	3
Gardiner (l)	7	0	3	0	4	6

We took the opener 3-1 despite being no-hit in a powerful and gutsy performance from Portland's Jeff Gardiner. Gardiner deserved better, but Coach Marrone had us prepared to play "small ball" in order to eke out a win. Coach Marrone was a big proponent of aggressive baseball. And he selected this all-star team with the players who had the speed to steal bases or force the opposition to make the defensive plays.

I believe that Marrone's foresight and perhaps his experience from the previous two championship seasons, were the reasons we were able to steal this game.

By virtue of this win we entered the winner's bracket and were finally slated to play our nemesis from Puerto Nuevo, Puerto Rico.[81] [82]

Leominster vs. Puerto Nuevo (PR), Monday, August 6, 1973
For the fourth time in three consecutive years, the Leominster Babe Ruth All-Star team faced the all-stars from Puerto Nuevo, Puerto Rico. Puerto Nuevo is located on the north coast of Puerto Rico, in Vega Baja, about a 45-minute drive west of San Juan. More than 30 baseball stars from the Vega Baja region have been drafted by Major League teams including Juan Gonzalez (Texas), Luis Aguayo (Philadelphia), Ricky Otero (NY Mets), Luis Quintana (San Francisco), Ramon Castro (Florida), and Hector Valle (LA Angels). Future Philadelphia Phillies star Luis Aguayo played third-base that day for Puerto Nuevo.

Puerto Nuevo was the defending New England Regional champions, and won the Babe Ruth World Series in 1971 after eliminating Leominster on that year's New England Regional tournament.

Still nursing my injured finger, I was forced again to watch the game from the sidelines which was a huge disappointment for me. I watched each of the 1971 and 1972 all-star losses to Puerto Nuevo, and had been eagerly awaiting an opportunity to play against one of the top Babe Ruth teams in the world.

Jay Burke got the nod to start our second game in two days since

Mike Leclair had pitched the opener versus Portland, Maine. Burke, along with Leclair and Mike Gasbarro, had the experience of playing in the 1972 tournament in Newport. The rest of the line-up included Bob Angelini leading off and playing second-base, third-baseman Dave Bergeron batted second followed by first-baseman Jay Connors. Leclair was in left-field and batted clean-up. Burke batted fifth, followed by center-fielder Ted Rockwell sixth. Right-fielder Dave Arsenault batted seventh, catcher Pete Gamache eight and shortstop Mike Gasbarro rounded out the line-up batting ninth.

We knew that we would need to play flawless baseball in order to beat Puerto Nuevo. As manager Jim Marrone walked back and forth from the top of the dugout, he encouraged us to just play our game and to avoid forcing a play that was not there. When at bat, he directed us to make Puerto Nuevo's starting pitcher Juan Agosto work, perhaps taking a pitch or two depending on the count.

Puerto Nuevo was the home team and therefore took the field first. Leominster bats remained quiet, and could not score despite a couple of walks off Puerto Nuevo starter Juan Agosto. In the bottom half of the first, however, Puerto Nuevo erupted for four unearned runs. Center-fielder Abner Ortiz led off with a single on a chopper up the middle that eluded shortstop Mike Gasbarro and second-baseman Bob Angelini. Taking a long lead at first, Ortiz broke for second-base on a steal attempt which may have rattled Leominster pitcher Jay Burke who threw a wild pitch that caromed off the backstop. By the time Leominster catcher Pete Gamache caught up to the ball Ortiz made it to third-base standing.

Burke then walked the next batter, second-baseman Walter Maldonado, putting runners on first and third. Burke, who typically had pinpoint control, unloaded another wild pitch which scored Ortiz and sent Maldonado to third. Puerto Nuevo left-fielder Huan Madera then grounded to Angelini at second who fielded the ball cleanly and made a strong throw to home as Maldonado was running on contact. However, the throw was late, Maldonado scored, and Madera was safe at first.

Burke settled down and the next batter, right-fielder Al Monge hit a grounder that forced Madera at second for the first out. Puerto Nuevo shortstop Ed Hernandez popped out to third-base for the second out of the inning. However, Puerto Nuevo scored their third run when Monge scored on a single by first-baseman Ben De La Rosa. When De La Rosa attempted a steal of second, catcher Gamache's throw was high and De La Rosa scampered home with the fourth running of the inning. At the end of one, we trailed 4-0.

As a testament to their grit, Leominster responded with four runs of their own in a bizarre inning that saw starter Agosta balk three times. Jay Burke walked to open the inning and was awarded second-base on Agosta's first balk. Center-fielder Ted Rockwell also walked and both runners advanced on Agosta's second balk. On the bench the Leominster dugout was raucous with runners on second and third with no outs. However, Leominster right-fielder Dave Arsenault popped out the third, keeping Burke and Rockwell at third and second respectively. Pete Gamache then walked which loaded the bases with only one out. Agosta, who as a left-handed pitcher had an unorthodox motion from the stretch, again balked which send Burke home with the first Leominster run.

Mike Gasbarro walked which re-loaded the bases, still with only one out. Rockwell, now at third, scored when Agosta issued another walk to Angelini, his fifth walk of the inning and seventh in the game. Puerto Nuevo manager Jerry Cruz then lifted Agosta for Felix Lopez who took the mound with bases still loaded.

Dave Bergeron launched a fly ball to center-field which scored Gamache and sent Gasbarro to third. Gasbarro scored when first-baseman Jay Connors singled through the gap between short and third, tying the score at 4-4. This was Leominster's first hit in the tournament. The rally stalled, however, as Mike Leclair grounded out to end the inning. It is noteworthy that there were 8 unearned runs scored thus far in this game after only one and a half innings.

Puerto Nuevo answered again in the bottom of the second inning when they scored what would be the deciding and final runs of the game. Burke dug himself in a hole when he walked both Ortiz and Maldonado to lead off the inning. Juan Madera then hit a solid single to left-field, but Mike Leclair charged hard, scooped the ball and fired a strike to catcher Pete Gamache, nailing Ortiz at the plate. Madera and Maldonado advanced to second and third on the play. Al Monge then plated both runs with a line drive signal to center-field. Ted Rockwell's throw to the plate short-hopped Gamache who made a great play to block the ball; however, Monge advanced all the way to third on the play. Burke struck out Ed Hernandez for the second out of the inning. With Monge on third, Puerto Nuevo third-basemen Luis Aguayo singled past the diving Bergeron at third for an RBI as Monge scored on the play. Burke struck out De La Rosa to end the inning. After two innings, Puerto Nuevo led 7-4 which ended up being the final score.

Puerto Nuevo (PR)	AB	R	H	RBI
Ortiz, cf	3	1	1	0
Maldonado, 2b	2	2	0	0
Madera, lf	3	1	2	0
Monge, rf	3	2	1	1
Hernandez, ss	4	0	1	0
Aguayo, 3b	4	1	1	2
De La Rosa, 1b	1	0	1	0
Conception, c	0	0	0	0
Agosto, p	1	0	0	0
Lopez, p	2	0	2	0
Totals	**23**	**7**	**9**	**3**

Leominster	AB	R	H	RBI
Angelini, 2b	2	0	0	1
Bergeron, 3b	3	0	1	1
Connors, 1b	1	0	1	1
Catalfamo, 1b	2	0	0	0
Leclair, lf	3	0	0	0
Burke, p	2	1	0	0
Rockwell, cf	2	1	0	0
Ruggles, cf	1	0	0	0
Arsenault, rf	3	0	0	0
Gamache, c	0	1	0	0
Girouard, p	2	0	0	0
Gasbarro, ss	1	1	0	0
Crawley, lf	0	0	0	0
Totals	**22**	**4**	**2**	**3**

Pitcher	IP	H	R	ER	W	K
Agosto	1.1	0	4	0	6	1
Lopez (W)	5.2	2	0	0	0	2
Burke (L)	2	5	7	2	4	2
Girouard	4	4	0	0	4	1

Lopez, who managed to shut down Leominster's offense the rest of the way and yielding only one hit over the final five innings, picked up the win. Doug Girouard came in to relieve Burke in the top of the third and shut down the Puerto Nuevo offense, scattering only four hits the rest of the way.

As a result of the loss, Leominster dropped to the loser's bracket and awaited the winner of Portland, Maine vs. Barre, Vermont.[83] [84]

Figure 57: (l) Puerto Nuevo third-baseman Luis Aguayo beats the throw third, with Leominster's Dave Bergeron awaiting the throw; (r) Luis Aguayo with the Phillies; (photo credits: Dave Bergeron)

Leominster vs. Portland (ME), Wednesday, August 8, 1973

Facing elimination from the New England Regional Tournament, Leominster once again faced the all-stars from Portland, Maine, the very same squad that the local nine had defeated in the opening game of the tournament despite being no-hit by Portland's Jeff Gardiner.

John Dixon got the assignment that Wednesday evening for Portland, facing Leominster ace Mike Leclair who was pitching on three days' rest. Manager Jim Marrone decided to shake the batting lineup a bit with the hopes of jump starting the lethargic Leominster offense. Second-baseman Bob Angelini remained in his usual lead-off spot followed by shortstop Mike Gasbarro. Third-baseman and solid hitting Dave Bergeron batted third and with my injured finger finally healed enough to play, I returned to the lineup in left-field and batted clean-up. Leclair batted fifth, catcher Jay Burke sixth, center-fielder Ted Rockwell batted seventh, right-fielder Dave Arsenault hit eighth, and left-handed hitting first-baseman Mike Catalfamo batted ninth.

After a scoreless first inning for both team, Leominster would strike first in the bottom of the second. Both Ted Rockwell and Dave Arsenault reached on separate errors which put runners on first and second with two outs. Ben Ruggles, who had entered the game to replace an injured Mike Gasbarro hit a long double in the right-center-field gap, driving in both Rockwell and Arsenault. Leominster took a 2-0 lead after two innings.

The lead did last long as Portland would strike for four runs in the top of the third. Right-fielder Jack Morse led off the inning with a walk, advanced to second on a terrific sacrifice bunt by Dixon, and then to third on a fielder's choice. Morse scored on a wild pitch by Leclair. Leclair did not help himself by walking shortstop Bruce Carey as the next Portland batter, left-fielder Mike Allen dropped a single into right field advancing Carey to third. First-baseman John Foley then drilled a single into left-field scoring Carey with the second Portland run of the inning. With Portland runners on first and third, third-baseman Bob Antoine doubled over the head of Arsenault in right-field scoring both Allen and Foley giving Portland a 4-2 lead.

Portland would strike again in the fourth when catcher Jack Redman led off with a walk and was forced out at second on a fielder's choice off the bat of Morse. Dixon then hit a hard grounder off the glove of second-baseman Angelini which allowed Morse to reach third. When right-fielder Dave Arsenault caught up with the ricochet, his attempt to nail Morse at third sailed high and Morse scampered home with the fifth Portland run. Dixon hustled to third-base on the play. However, Leclair avoided further damage as Gardiner flied out to left-field and Carey grounded out. The score after three-and-a-half was Portland 5, Leominster 2.

After Leominster went scoreless in the fourth and fifth innings, Redman led off the Portland sixth inning with a single to right field. Pinch hitter Jim Dean walked to put runners on first and second. Dixon helped his own cause by laying down a bunt to third, but Bergeron's attempt to force Dean at second-base was just a bit late. Redman scored on the play but Leominster catcher Jay Burke alertly thew Dean attempting to advance to third. Leclair than retired Gardiner on a fly ball and Carey on strikes.

After Leominster again went down in the bottom of the sixth inning without a threat, Portland scored its seventh and final run in the top of the seventh inning. With two outs, Portland third-baseman Bob Anthoine beat out an infield hit and ended up at third-base on consecutive wild pitches by Leclair. Following a walk by center-fielder Carroll Shephard, Anthoine scored on a perfectly executed double steal.

Down to its last three outs, Leominster failed to score in the bottom of the seventh giving Portland a solid 7-2 victory, thus avenging the opening game loss. Leominster's incredible all-star run that began with tryouts in late June, and competition in early July, had come to a sudden and unceremonious end.[85][86]

So what happened? First, we did not hit. For a team that pummeled opposing pitchers and terrorized opposing defenses for over a month, our bats went silent. During the New England Regional tournament we managed only seven hits in three games, with Ben Ruggles' double against Portland being the only extra-base hit.

For a team that committed precious few errors over the district and state tournaments, we committed ten errors in three games for this tournament. And finally, we struggled on the mound. Even Mike Leclair, who carried the team up until this point, who started seven all-star games, completed all seven with a perfect 7-0 record, had a ridiculous ERA below 0.50, and who had averaged less than three walks per game, could not find the plate during this elimination game.

Portland (ME)	AB	R	H
Gardiner, 3b	3	0	0
Carey, ss	3	1	0
Allen, lf	4	1	1
Foley, 1b	4	1	1
Anthoine, 3b	3	1	2
Shepard, cf	3	0	0
Redman, c	3	1	1
Morse, rf	1	2	0
Dean, ph	0	0	0
Wilmont, pr	0	0	0
Maria, rf	0	0	0
Dixon, p	2	0	1
Totals	**26**	**7**	**6**
Leominster	**AB**	**R**	**H**
Angelini, 2b	3	0	1
Gasbarro, ss	1	0	0
Bergeron, 3b	2	0	0
Lefebvre, lf	3	0	0
Leclair, p	3	0	1
Burke, c	3	0	0
Gamache, c	0	0	0
Rockwell, cf	3	1	2
Arsenault, rf	3	1	0
Ruggles, ss	3	0	1
Catalfamo, 1b	2	0	0
Connors, 1b	1	0	0
Totals	**27**	**2**	**5**

Pitcher	IP	H	R	ER	W	K
Dixon (w)	7	5	2	0	1	4
Leclair (l)	7	6	7	3	7	4

Looking back after 50 years of distance and time, I honestly don't recall feeling sad following our exit from the tournament. We had a great run of sixteen games, of which we won all except for three. We won an unprecedented third consecutive Massachusetts State Championships. This achievement would not be repeated until 1999-2001 when Leominster again won three consecutive state championships, thus cementing the city of Leominster's reputation as one of the most successful Babe Ruth programs in Massachusetts state history.

I forged relationships with a great group of guys from other Leominster Babe Ruth teams, many of whom I would have as teammates at Leominster High School and Leominster American Legion Post 151 programs. I was coached by some of the finest, most knowledgeable and generous men in Jim Marrone, Paul Harris, Steve Campobasso and Doug Fellows. The city of Leominster rallied around us and supported every game.

Perhaps most importantly, our parents essentially set aside any plans they made for summer vacations as a result of our success. They transported us to and from practices, traveled considerable distances for games leading up to the tournaments, and booked motel reservations for extended overnight tournaments. My parents and grandparents showed up to every game. Each of them have since passed, yet their cheers of encouragement echo through my mind today as I think back to that magical summer.

Not lost on me was the fact that many of our siblings were kept in tow for all of these activities. I was fortunate in that my younger brothers were baseball junkies themselves. Today both of my surviving brothers recall that summer as something special.

I recently asked my brother Tony, six years my junior, about his recollections from that summer following the 1973 all-star team. "That year I was nine years old, and I was mesmerized," he recalled. "I could not believe the incredible talent on that team, and it was if I were watching Major League Baseball playoffs, hanging on every pitch, hit, or defensive play. I knew the name of every player and position without a program. The enthusiasm from the families and supporters was deafening in the stands. One of the best sporting events I have witnessed in my life" (T. Lefebvre, August 25, 2021). Tony would go on to play for the 1980 Leominster Babe Ruth All-Stars that hosted the New England Tournament that year. He would become a standout catcher for Leominster High School that nearly won the Massachusetts High School state tournament several years later.

My brother Mike was also a catcher and played for TAG. He would consistently be in the top ten batters in the league his final year. He too was mesmerized that summer and recalls the civic pride he and so many others experienced that summer.

My late brother Billy was perhaps the most athletically gifted of all of us, being a standout baseball and football player. Sadly, we lost Billy in 1979 after a 3-year battle with cancer, shortly after graduating from LHS and playing for that remarkable 1979 undefeated and nationally ranked football team.

Puerto Nuevo advanced to the 1973 Babe Ruth World Series which was held in Manchester, NH. John Crawley and I attended most of the games which resulted in Monterrey, Mexico winning the world title.

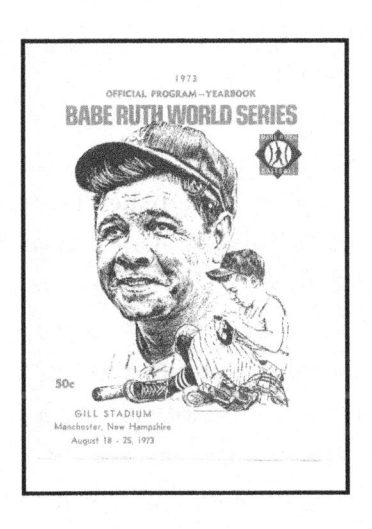

Figure 58: 1973 Babe Ruth World Series Program (photo credit: Mark Lefebvre)

Chapter Fifteen: Not So Sour Grapes

On August 10, 1973, the *Fitchburg Sentinel*'s Chip Donahoo wrote a column decrying the placement of Puerto Rico in the New England Regionals. Donahoo wrote that if not for Puerto Rico, Leominster might have advanced to the Babe Ruth All-Star World Series three years in a row. He argued that Puerto Rico should have competed against Florida or other southern states who enjoy a longer season and play ball year-round, whereas in New England, we're lucky to have 3-4 months of baseball before the return to school in September.[87]

For the most part, I agree with Donahoo; however, I doubt that my 1973 team would have advanced since we also lost to Portland, Maine in the loser's bracket. And we only managed seven hits in three New England tournament games. But to Donahoo's point, a number of scenarios could have prevailed in our favor in 1973 if not for the 7-4 loss to Puerto Rico in our second game of the tournament.

What is certain to me, however, is that the 1971 team would have advanced to the Babe Ruth All-Star World Series given they lost to Puerto Nuevo not once, but twice including the finals. Those two losses were the only losses for that 1971 team.

The 1972 Leominster squad also lost to Puerto Rico in the New England Regionals in Newport, RI, by score of 1-0 with the winning run scored on a very close play at home plate. Therefore, one could make a case that the 1972's could have also advanced to the World Series if not for Puerto Rico playing in in the New England tournament.

So why was Puerto Rico placed in the New England Regional Tournament? There were two working theories at that time and in my research for this book I was never able to confirm the rationale. The first theory is based on the fact that there were six New England state champions and a host team, for a total of seven. Puerto Rico was added to round out the tournament to eight teams. The second is based on a story that Puerto Rico was booted from the Southeastern and Mid-Atlantic regions due to eligibility violations. Again, I was not able to confirm either theory.

Regardless, a case could be made that at least one (1971) and possibly two (1972) Leominster teams were essentially cheated out of a chance to represent New England in the 1971 and 1972 Babe Ruth All-Star World Series. Which does not tarnish the accomplishments of Puerto Rico, and certainly not the success of the Leominster teams. But it does cause one to pause and wonder what would have transpired if Puerto Rico's trip to the World Series was not through New England.

Chapter Sixteen: So Agonizingly Close - 1974 All-Stars

Leominster's incredible run of three consecutive Massachusetts Babe Ruth Baseball state championships came agonizingly close to a four-year streak by virtue of the success of the 1974 all-star squad. Managed by legendary Tanzio Park skipper Bob Lamothe, the locals won the districts and sectional; however, they were eliminated by Somerville in the state tournament held in Falmouth.

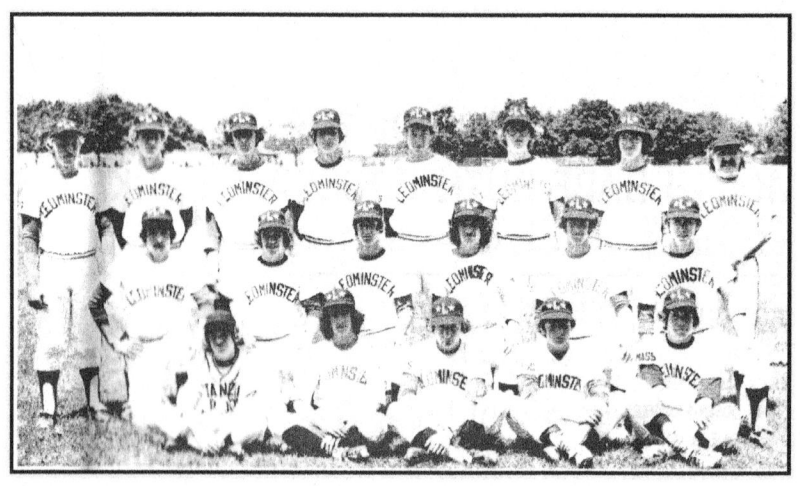

Figure 59: 1974 Leominster Babe Ruth All-Stars (photo credit: Mike Bergeron)

Front row: Batboy Mike Leger, Dave Altobelli, Rick Corliss, Paul Amadio, Steve Shaw
Second row: Rick Daigneault, Rick Gallien, Pete Gamache, Tony Charielle, Jim Normandin, Mike Bergeron
Back row: Coach Paul Harris, Mark Gasbarro, Don Stebbins, Brian McNally, John Moynihan, John Donnelly, Coach Dave Bergeron, Manager Bob Lamothe

After working their way out of the loser's bracket Leominster advanced to face Somerville to whom they lost 1-0 earlier in the tournament despite a gutsy 2-hit pitching performance from Rick

Daigneault. In order to claim their fourth consecutive title, however, Leominster would need to defeat Somerville twice.

Trailing 5-4 in the seventh inning of that final game, and down to their last three outs, Leominster pitcher Brian McNally led off with a walk. Left-fielder Pete Gamache's ground ball was mishandled and skirted into the outfield to put runners at second and third with no outs. Somerville pitcher Bob McNeil retired the next two hitters which left Leominster down to its last out. Catcher Jim Normandin was hit by a pitch which loaded the bases for shortstop Rick Gallien. With the runners moving on contact with two outs, Gallien hit a shot to the hole at shortstop which was fielded cleanly by Jim McCune. McCune's throw to first nipped the speedy Gallien by a half-step, ending the game and ending Leominster's historic stretch of consecutive Massachusetts state championships.[88][89]

For a city accustomed to winning, there was a moment of realization that the incredible winning streak was snapped. That said, Leominster's place on the pantheon of great baseball cities within the Commonwealth was cemented. There would be more championships on the horizon.

Section 5: Changes in the Game

Chapter Seventeen: Leominster Babe Ruth's Success

Since that 1973 season, Leominster Babe Ruth baseball has evolved like nearly every institution from our youth. And there were several other local teams over the years that have won Massachusetts state titles along the way. All told as of this writing, twenty-eight Leominster Babe Ruth teams have won state championship. These include:

Age 13: 1981, 1984, 1987, 1994, 1995, 2001, 2002, 2009.
Age 14: 2001, 2002, 2007, 2009, 2012
Age 13-15: 1952, 1971, 1972, 1973, 1979, 1984, 1986, 1987, 1990, 1999, 2000, 2001, 2006, 2010, 2011

This list, as impressive as it is, fails to tell the whole story regarding Leominster's success. Consider that in 2001 all three (13- 14- and 15-year-olds) Leominster teams won their respective state titles. Also consider that in one season, those three teams of fifteen players, nine coaches, and three bat boys, practiced and played their way to the state tournament, against the top talent across the state, AND ultimately emerged champions. I can only image the excitement in Leominster that summer.

Not to be outdone, the 2002 14-year-old's went on to win the New England Regional Tournament and represent Leominster in the Babe Ruth World Series. And perhaps the most successful Leominster Babe Ruth team of them all, the 1984 team not only represented Leominster in the Babe Ruth World Series, but came within one game of winning the World Series championship in Niles, Michigan.

Mike Pavilaitis, 1970 graduate of the Leominster Babe Ruth League, was the manager for that 1984 team. When I reached out to Pavilaitis, he joked that his claim to fame was the fact that he made the last out in Leominster's 1970 Babe Ruth All-Star run, ending that season and setting the stage for the three-year run of state championship run of 1971-1973.

As a youngster, Mike played for Rancher's in the Leominster American Little League up at the Twelfth Street Field. Mike credits his dad Al as a major influence, teaching him not only the fundamentals of the game, but also instilling in him a great love for the game of baseball. Under his dad's tutelage, Mike enjoyed success as a player, but also absorbed the intangibles that would later lead to his success as a coach.

Pavilaitis first coached at the Little League level for East Side Oil. My brother Tony had the opportunity to play for Mike on that East Side Oil team. "I had him as a coach when I played for East Side Oil," Tony recalls. "Mike was the best coach I ever had - no nonsense, great instruction, practiced hard. He also coached against me when I played for TAG in Babe Ruth. Mike was well respected by many, and I can't say enough good things about him" (T. Lefebvre, August 25, 2021).

I was not surprised to learn from Mike that he also credits managers Jim Marrone of those three championship teams from the 1970's, and coach Emile Johnson of Leominster High School and Leominster American Legion baseball teams as examples on how to manage a successful baseball team.

"With regards to Coach Marrone, I learned his recipe for winning was two-fold," said Pavilaitis. "First, because his teams were built for speed, any lead-off hitter who reached first-base would steal second on the very first pitch, and based on the count, would then steal third" (M. Pavilaitis, March 1, 2022).

For baseball junkies like me, it is obvious that this strategy completely changes the dynamic of an inning. The pitcher is frazzled as he now has a runner on third-base with no outs. The catcher is on high alert because he not only needs to manage his pitcher, but he also needs to protect the plate against a passed ball. And the infield now needs to play in and protect against a run at the plate as a result of an infield ground ball. In order to beat Leominster, the opposition could not afford to put the lead-off runner on.

The second lesson Pavilaitis learned from Marrone was how to run his practices. "Every element of practice, from infield/outfield practice to batting practice, was situational," recalled Pavilaitis. "We would break up the team into 3 groups of five batters who would collectively bat until the defense made 9 outs."

What this accomplished was to address and execute in-game situations live during batting practice. And it kept the team on their toes and attentive for the whole practice, which is not always easy to do in baseball. Pavilaitis also mentioned that this approach to practice was also reinforced during his years in high school playing for Coach Johnson.

Pavilaitis apparently put these techniques to good use during his own coaching tenure when he coached the 1984 Leominster Babe Ruth all-star team that went on to come within one game of winning the Babe Ruth World Series, losing to Tallahassee FL in the championship game. My step-brother Matt Aubuchon played third-base for that team and according to Pavilaitis, Matt hit the longest homerun he had ever seen in youth baseball, which towered over the center-field scoreboard. Matt recalls, "the center-field fence was 360 feet from home plate and the fence was 20 feet high. There was a runner on base, and I was working the pitcher for a fastball. I have vague recollections of the count being in my favor. I waited for the pitch I wanted and obviously made solid contact. I guess since the ball cleared the center-field fence and the scoreboard by quite a distance, it must have traveled over 400 feet." Further researched revealed that the official measurement for that titanic blast was 462 feet. Against Babe Ruth World Series pitching.

Matt chuckles when he recalls his days playing for Coach Pavilaitis. "Coach Pav would have the team line up on the top of the dugout crouched on one knee to watch the opposing team take practice before a game. He'd point out the opposing team's strengths and weaknesses, explaining to the team our strategy to exploit those mistakes during the game" (M. Aubuchon, March 9, 2022).

Matt made the 1984 World Series Tournament All-Star team with teammates Dave White, Joe Sawyer and Pete Charpentier. That's four Leominster players picked as the top 11 for the entire tournament. Leominster pitcher Kevin Labbe threw a no-hitter against Staten Island, NY in the World Series. This team was stacked. "Signing autographs for youngsters at the tournament was something I'll never forget," Matt reminisces.

Matt went on to play four years of varsity baseball at LHS, and his 1986 team won the first state championships for Emile Johnson and the Blue Devil baseball team. Matt played third-base and was elected team captain his senior year. He also played three years of LHS varsity football as a running back.

Figure 60: 1984 Babe Ruth World Series, Tournament All-Star Bat (photo credit: Matt Aubuchon)

Figure 61: 1984 New England Regional Champions - Leominster Babe Ruth All-Stars (photo credit: Matt Aubuchon)

Front row: Guy Thomas, Tony Pirro, Kevin Labbe, Dave White, Danny Baron, Matt Aubuchon, Mike Membrino
Back row: Coach Ray Racine; Manager Mike Pavilaitis; Ronnie Lamothe, Billy McNiff, Eric Hytenen, Joe Sawyer, Jamie Bernard, Peter Charpentier, Teddy Steele, Rob Gagne, Coach Pin Cannavino

Eleven years my junior, Matt is also a product of neighborhood pick-up baseball. He and his friends would bike to a make-shift diamond behind Duke's Welding on Central Street and play ball until dark, day after day. He also came through a similar pathway as his predecessors, playing for Banner Mold in the American Little League. He was drafted to play for Star Toyota (formerly U-Trans) for Pavilaitis. Matt considers the summer of 1984 and his Leominster Babe Ruth Baseball all-star journey the greatest athletic experience of his life. And he credits Mike Pavilaitis as the greatest coach he's ever had. 1984 was indeed a special year for Leominster youth sports.

From *Sports Illustrated*'s Vault Archives:

No Room for a Parade
  Leominster, Mass., a city of 34,000 about 35 miles west of Boston, is suddenly a hotbed of baseball talent. Four of its youth teams—from Little League, Lassie League for girls, 13-year-old and 14-and-15-year-old Babe Ruth leagues—were Massachusetts state champions this year, and all but the Little League team went on to win northeast regional competition and advance to World Series play. None of the Leominster teams won the whole ball of wax, but the 14-and-15 Babe Ruther's went all the way to the national finals before losing to Tallahassee, Fla.
  Leominster, previously known mostly for the odd way its name is pronounced (Leominster is approximately how the locals say it), is proud of its young heroes and heroines, but no special celebration is being planned. Benjamin Ruggles, director of the recreation department, says that ordinarily the city would lay on at least a police escort, but a police department spokesman says even that modest attention is unlikely. "Right now our downtown is completely destroyed," he explains. "They're doing urban-renewal work. There isn't a street that's passable." [90]

Chapter Eighteen: Leominster Babe Ruth Baseball Today

The modern-day champion of Leominster Babe Ruth and Leominster American Legion baseball is Jeff Dedeian. Jeff has been coaching baseball since 1997 and has been president of the Leominster Babe Ruth League since 2006. In June of 2021 I caught up with Jeff to discuss the evolution of Leominster Babe Ruth over the years. It is not a happy story.

Jeff is a burly guy and looks like he's very comfortable around ballparks. We met on a warm and sunny weekday afternoon. While sitting in my truck in the parking lot watching Jeff mow the upper field, I surmised that Jeff spent a lot of weekday afternoons at the fields as both upper and lower fields were in pristine condition. The infield gravel was raked smooth. The mound was as groomed as a PGA bunker. When I shook his hand I could feel the callouses of a working man. Jeff was no stranger to physical labor. He was equally adept at handling a rake as he was a fungo bat.

I showed up early to our scheduled meeting at the McLaughlin Field clubhouse that early summer day. It was sunny and pleasant, and while watching Jeff mow the field from the first-base bleachers, I closed my eyes and took in the smell of the fresh-cut grass and the droning engine of the mower.

The lights stood proud as sentries around the perimeter of that field, the signs that heralded local businesses gave the outfield a cozy feel, not unlike the arms of the community embracing a precious child. With my eyes closed I could imagine the ghosts of seasons past taking their customary places on the field. Mike Pignata at third-base. Dave Arsenault in right-field. Ben Ruggles at the plate. Bobby Koch behind the plate throwing his catcher's mask aside as he wheeled about to the backstop to catch a foul pop-up. Umpire Deico Pignata picking up his cigar from the grass behind home plate to coax a smoke between innings. First-baseman Bryan Beaudette throwing practice grounders to the infield. Joe DePasquale and Paul D'Onfro lobbing fly balls to each in the outfield. And manager Jim Marrone holding court with infield umpire Egidio Charielle at the top of the first-base dugout chatting up his coaches.

Then league president and volunteer-in-chief John McLaughlin would be passing a tambourine up and down the bleachers for nightly donations. The smell of popcorn and hotdogs wafted from the concession stand that was staffed by parents and other volunteers. These were the ghosts of seasons past who had spent countless hours doing what they loved. The image of that daydream remains cemented in my mind to this day.

The idyllic scene was interrupted by a sudden reality. None of these heroes of my childhood, the players before me, my teammates, my coaches, the umpires and league officials were here today. The significance of their absence was a premonition of what Jeff was about to share with me regarding the current state of Babe Ruth Baseball in Leominster and the region.

"Over the last ten or so years, everything started to fold," explained Jeff as I sat across the table from him in the McLaughlin Field clubhouse. "Not enough players. Not enough coaches. Not enough volunteers" (J. Dedian, June 2, 2021).

In addition being a coach, Dedeian became league president in 2007. He proudly shared that multiple Leominster all-star teams made the trip to the Babe Ruth World Series during the 1980's. Since that period, interest in the league began to wane.

By 2014 only three teams remained in the league and Dedeian was forced to ask thirty players to fill the fifteen roster spots on the all-star team. Vacations, part-time jobs, and social commitments became more important for kids of that age. Today there remain only two Leominster-based Babe Ruth teams. All-Star selections are also a thing of the past as there are not enough players.

At the height of its popularity, the 1970's era Leominster Babe Ruth League was comprised of thirteen teams of 13–15-year-olds with seven teams (Solar Chemical, U-Trans, Tanzio, TAG, Werner's, Elks and Sterling Lumber) playing in Division 1, and six (Modern Tool, Leominster News, AFL-CIO, ACWA, Russo Construction, and Moose) playing Division 2. The league was fertile source of players to feed local and regional high schools and American Legion baseball teams. Today lacrosse and to a lesser extent, spring football, subtract from the player pool for baseball. Further compounding the challenge for town leagues is the advent of Cal Ripken baseball and AAU club teams for highly skilled players. AAU baseball is the primary feeder system today for high school and Legion ball.

Figure 62: Jeff Dedeian, June 2021 (photo credit: Mark Lefebvre)

Childhood friend Joe Charielle has continued his involvement with youth sports over the decades since hanging up his spikes. As a kid, Joe played for Whitten's Comets in the Leominster American Little League, Solar Chemical in the Leominster Babe Ruth League, and pitched for Leominster High School. After graduating from LHS, Joe pitched for NCAA Division 1 Hofstra University. In the early 1980's, Joe umpired and officiated countless Babe Ruth, high school and Legion games. I asked him about his experiences, the games he officiated, and the players who stood out.

Figure 63: McLaughlin Field, June 2021 (photo credit: Mark Lefebvre)

"Joe Killelea, who if I recall correctly, struck out something like thirteen out of the first fifteen players as a freshman at Notre Dame High School. I worked the plate that game and I barely worked up a sweat," recalls Charielle. "Also, Brian McNally of Lunenburg. I was working behind the plate for one of his high school games, and could not believe the command he had over several pitches including his fastball, curve, and change-up. It was highly unusual to see a player at 17-years-old who could completely own the plate like McNally did that game" (J. Charielle, March 18, 2022).

What was once Leominster Babe Ruth Baseball now operates as Central Massachusetts Baseball, and is composed of teams from Leominster, Fitchburg, Ashby, Townsend, Pepperell, Ashburnham, Westminster and Winchendon. There are no all-stars. The teams play only league games. There is no concession stand. The electronic scoreboard remains dark. There is no newspaper coverage. There are simply not enough volunteers. It's all gone.

Chapter Nineteen: Changes Reflected in the Community

Leominster Little League has not been immune to the challenge of attracting players and parent volunteers. The Leominster National Little League disbanded in 2021 after 60 years of operation citing lack of players and volunteers. On January 3, 2022, the Leominster American Little League and North Leominster Little League organizations announced a merger under the umbrella of the Leominster Little League.[91]

Former Leominster High School baseball star and former LHS baseball coach Don Freda is wistful about his youth and the importance of neighborhoods, playgrounds and the friends who helped shape him as an adult, as a father, and as a coach. "It makes me wonder how it happened that all our sandlots and playgrounds and fields have disappeared. Suburban expansion has replaced precious spots where young baseball players could ride bikes to play every day with their friends, without parental interference, and take other road trips to play. Now it seems to me that the game is left to those elite players who can afford to play year-round in AAU tournaments, get instruction throughout the winter at batting cages, access modern high-tech software to learn about their own progress on a radar gun, measure launch angles and bat speed, and how to get in college via baseball" (Do. Freda, February 1, 2022).

1972 Babe Ruth all-star Greg Carchidi agrees with this notion as well, and feels that travel and so-called elite teams such as AAU and even the focus on building strong all-star teams has had a long-term detrimental effect on youth baseball in particular and youth sports in general. "Town sports by and large no longer exist as these so-called elite programs are exclusive when they should be inclusive. What we see today with leagues such as the Leominster Babe Ruth League struggling to field teams is a direct result of these elite programs" (G. Carchidi, February 1, 2022).

Figure 64: Leominster High School Coach Don Freda in 2015 (photo credit: Don Freda)

    Many parents get caught up in these elite programs thinking that if their child plays at the highest levels of competition, that a college athletic scholarship is within reach. The long-term result of elite and club teams is that there are less programs, less volunteers and therefore, less opportunities for the majority of kids to participate in these sports at the town level.

    After coaching and serving in local and district capacities for Cal Ripken Baseball in the Blackstone Valley area south of Worcester, Joe Charielle shared similar thoughts about the demise of the game of youth baseball. "Elite teams, club teams, and AAU teams take players away from their towns leagues and high school teams. As a result, the notion of a three-sport star in high school is largely extinct due to parents and coaches encouraging athletes to focus on one sport," said Charielle (J. Charielle, March 18, 2022).

This is not a local phenomenon. According to *The Atlantic*, ("American Meritocracy is Killing Youth Sports," November 2018), the share of children ages 6-12 who play a team sport on a regular basis declined from 41.5% in 2011 to 37% in 2017. Youth baseball experienced a 20% drop during that period.[92]

While many of us are quick to blame the decline on other competing distractions such as video games, television and smart-phones, research points to a class-war between haves and have-nots as the culprit. And town and recreational sports have paid the price with significant declines in local participation.

Among wealthy families, participation in youth sports is actually rising whereas families in lower income brackets have seen participation decline. "Kids' sports have seen an explosion of travel-team culture, where rich parents are writing a $3,000 check to get their kids on super teams often two counties, or two states away," said Tim Farrey, executive director of Aspen's Sports & Society Program. "When these kids move to the travel team, you pull bodies out of the local town's recreation league, and it sends a message [to those] who didn't get onto that track that they don't really have a future in the sport."

Dedeian has been the Leominster American Legion Post 151 coach since 2012 which now plays home games at McLaughlin Field on Lancaster Street, and not Doyle Field. There is no newspaper coverage of the games whereas in the mid-1970's games were covered by the *Leominster Enterprise*, *Fitchburg Sentinel*, and *Worcester Telegram*. Dedeian needs to conduct outreach to area high schools to attract players for the Legion squad. Baseball is no longer a regional priority despite the rich history of the Little League, Babe Ruth, Leominster High School, and Leominster American Legion teams, players and championships. Today baseball in Leominster only matters to those who are playing, and perhaps their families.

Conclusion: A Place in Time

Looking back, I'm filled with a sense of gratitude for the role that community played in my childhood. I can close my eyes and vividly recall the many times I would sit on the stoop of our backyard on Elm Hill Avenue looking out past my grandfather Gus Lanciani's vegetable garden up above Litchfield Street, and to the Charielle's house up on the hill. I would stare past our swimming pool, bask in the sunlight and just listen. And thinking of how great my world was at that time.

This is a visceral sensation that is still very present with me today as I sit here in my mid-60's tapping on a keyboard. I can literally hear the church bells from St. Ann's church, signaling the start of Sunday mass. I can hear the cacophony of birds calling to each other above the din of the occasional street traffic on Litchfield Street. I can smell my grandmother Susie's irises in vivid splendor, shades of violet that defy description. My recollection is of a place and time that I believe cannot and will not soon be replicated in today's culture. It was lightning in a bottle. I was born at the right time. Time stood still during those three magical summers of 1971, 1972 and 1973.

Okay, I'll say it. It was sure better when I was a kid. I say it even though I promised myself as a kid that I would never repeat the words that the elders in my circle of family and friends would say. I would roll my eyes and dismiss the comment out of hand as just that of an out-of-touch curmudgeon incapable of keeping up with the times. Do you know what? I've become *that* person. But hear me out.

What it comes down for me are relationships and experiences. Relationships that were founded on connection to real people in real time. Experiences that were based on being mindful and by being present in the moment. Juxtapose that against relationships and experiences today that are often virtual and established through a 4" x 6" screen on a hand-held device, and through the portal of a social media application.

Our children and grandchildren are bombarded with messages through advertisements, live news 24x7, app notifications, and junk mail sent by mindless bots and personalized to their individual interests through sophisticated algorithms. "Alexa, who won last night's Red Sox game?" has replaced a walk to the corner store to buy a paper to catch up on last night's games. "Okay Google, play the Beatles Abbey Road" has eliminated the need for trip to the record store to browse for music. If such a record store still exists. Yes, all of this is convenient, but where is the human interaction?

Coaches Jim Marrone and Emile Johnson were my primary non-parental mentors, both of whom have had a profound effect on me. They believed in me. They challenged me, and took the time to be teachers and role models for me. I felt validated and important. I was part of a community. And I was heard.

I remember a bus ride back from a game at St. Peter's of Worcester during my senior year at LHS. We were driving south on Route 12 on a section of Park Avenue that brought us to a traffic light with Worcester Polytechnic Institute on our right. Coach Johnson stood up from his customary front seat on the bus and declared out loud, "boys, this is where Mark Lefebvre will be studying engineering this fall. Good luck there, Mark."

Now, I can't tell you the score or if we even won against St. Peter's that day. But those words, and the fact that coach Johnson knew where I was going to college, has stuck with me after over 46 years.

My non-profit work today involves addiction prevention and recovery. I help build community coalitions that come together in a coordinated fashion to address substance use disorders. Our non-profit organization provides education and training to build individual, family, and community resilience against childhood trauma and addiction in our communities. We work with communities to increase resilience against addiction and social upheaval through the creation of positive childhood experiences and fostering healthy adult relationships for our kids. I'll repeat that for emphasis - *positive childhood experiences and healthy adult relationships for our kids.* Sound familiar?

It's stunning for me to see how much money and effort are being invested today in re-building our communities - the very things that folks my age may have taken for granted from our childhood. What was once organic is now being manufactured through after-school programs, clubs, play dates and youth organizations. Research has shown that social programming, whether organized or unstructured, provide positive childhood experiences to off-set the impact of adverse childhood experiences.

Teachers, coaches, and other non-parental mentors play in important role in our kids developing healthy relationships. Youth sports, clubs and social affiliations, which during my childhood were ubiquitous, are now being re-established across our communities to again connect our kids to healthy developmental relationships.

Looking back, I also recall vividly the role youth sports played in galvanizing the Leominster community, and in providing structure and adult role models through volunteer coaches. However, it was the unstructured play where we found the freedom to learn through our experiences. My friends, teammates and I were fortunate to have the freedom to gather in neighborhood fields, parking lots, and playgrounds to participate in ad-hoc pick-up games without adult supervision. It was there where we learned to be independent. We participated in the democratic process of picking teams, setting ground-rules, settling scores.

Today, the neighborhood playground or schoolyard is no longer the default gathering place for kids to develop social skills such as cooperation, negotiation, teamwork, competitive spirit, success (pride) and failure (humility). School playgrounds were a safe haven for us to become independent from our parents. For me, it was Lancaster Street School and St. Leo's Cemetery. For others it was Pierce, Bennett, Lincoln, George Street, Northwest, Fall Brook, or Priest Street. For organized sports we attended try-outs and earned our way onto teams that played on the courts and gymnasiums at the YMCA, St. Ann's, St. Cecilia's, St. Marks, St. Leo's, Gallagher and Carter Junior High Schools. We joined others for tryouts at Ronnie Bachand Field (American Little League), Northwest School (National Little League), Bernice Avenue (North Leominster Little League), or the Lassie League complex on Bassett Street.

Youth sports as I experienced in the late 1960's and early 1970's has been forever changed as a result of a combination of forces. My tired saw about the so-called good ole days aside, this is not an argument about whether circumstances today are better or worse. It is just a different reality. Today there are club teams that decimate and redistribute the local town talent pool to regional or state-level teams that compete in tournaments and require travel and financial commitment. Parents, with well-meaning rationale, place their child in the most competitive environment that affords the best opportunity for their kid to play at the prep school or collegiate level. I know. I was one of those parents.

But the impact to town sports is undeniable. Communities such as Leominster can no longer field a league of 12-14 teams across two divisions like it did in the late 1960's and 1970's. This saddens me for a number of reasons but not solely for nostalgic reasons. Like many of us, I sometimes yearn for the simplicity of my childhood, where my obligations were restricted to making it to whatever location my friends were gathered, and in time for when the team sides would be chosen. Choosing sides at the ball-field for me was a sacred ritual that required the negotiation skills of a statesman and the talent assessment skills of an NFL general manager. At least it did in the moment. It is not a stretch to state that many of my people skills were developed during those unstructured competitions on the fields, lots and schoolyards of my youth.

When it comes to organized sports, my wistfulness stems from thinking about the lost opportunities for kids to learn and develop important character traits that for me, were essential to my success in high school, college, in my professional life, and as a parent. And these skills were equally important when confronted with life's inevitable times of difficulty, loss, uncertainty and setbacks.

My experience in 1973 with the Leominster Babe Ruth all-stars was nothing less than magical. First, the effort to make the team in the first place was a personal challenge. I needed to find a way for the coaches to notice me during the tryouts. I was not a star player. I rarely hit for power, but I would find a way to get on base. I didn't have the strongest arm, but I could hit the cut-off man without failure. I wasn't fleet of foot, but I knew how to steal a base on the pitcher rather than on the catcher. I hustled and tried to be the first one to line up for a drill. I learned at a very young age to correlate results to effort.

Once on the team, I learned about commitment and sacrifice. I learned to show up for practice on time. I did what the coaches asked. I became a better teammate and put the goals of the team ahead of my own interests. When the coaches asked me to sit for a pinch-hitter or pinch-runner, I did so with the trust that the coaches had a plan. And that plan invariably led to success.

I learned about respect for authority and understood the relationship between player and coach. As a fan of the 1971 and 1972 teams that preceded my 1973 team, I watched in awe over what they were able to achieve, and redoubled my commitment to improve my own game.

I learned at the age of fifteen the lesson of humility. When we lost, I looked inward on where perhaps I could have done something differently that may improve our chances in the next game. I learned not to blame others for our failures or negative outcomes.

After losing the opening game in the 1973 state Babe Ruth

tournament, I learned how to persevere. Yes, we were now faced with having to grind it out in the losers bracket, knowing that another loss would end our all-star run. But we pressed on, patiently taking one game, one inning, one at-bat, one pitch at a time.

As a representative of our town all-star team, I learned about honor. My actions both in and out of uniform reflected on the city of Leominster, our league, my parents and my teammates. Our community cared deeply about our successes. They held banquets and lavished awards and ceremonies to recognize our achievements.

Looking back with pride on our accomplishments and how it affected the community that rallied behind us, I can appreciate the factors that allowed me to be part of this special experience. Hence the lesson of gratitude for those who supported us along the way - the parents, the neighbors, the businesses, volunteers and officials that shared in the glory of that place in time.

Is this experience unique to me? Of course not. My former teammates and the group of players before and the years after me each have experienced their own journeys of growth from teenagers to adults. There are perhaps countless other examples of communities coming together to rally around a cause, whether it be sports-related or some other activity or series of events that deliver all of the life lessons I experienced in my youth while growing up in my community.

But as a parent who has been involved in youth sports and in my work building community coalitions, I know first-hand the difficulties facing society today as a result of the lack of community connection for today's kids. Now as an older adult with adult children, I think often of the multitude of ways that my experiences in youth sports helped shape me as an adult, a father and a member of my community.

Figure 65: Relics from the Past (photo credit: Mark Lefebvre)

From left to right – 1968 Punt, Pass and Kick Silver Trophy, 1970 American Little League All-Star Trophy, 1970 Little League All-Star State Tournament Trophy, 1973 Massachusetts Babe Ruth State Championship Trophy (awarded by the Boston Red Sox).

To be clear, I am not passing judgment on which so-called era is better than others. The current situation regarding youth, community, and baseball is a by-product of the current times. It is no better or worse. It is just different.

So as I open my eyes from this vivid daydream, I am thankful for being born and raised in that place, and at that time. I am grateful to have had the experiences that may never again be replicated, which afforded me the opportunity to be the person I am today, here and now in THIS place in time.

In Memoriam

Dave Arsenault
Bryan Beaudette
Bob Boissoneau
Steve Campobasso
Joe DePasquale
Paul D'Onfro
Bob Koch
Jim Marrone
Mike Pignata
Ben Ruggles

Acknowledgments

This project would not have been possible without the encouragement, support and generous contributions from the players of the 1971, 1972 and 1973 teams.

The game summaries in this book are presented in third-person persona except in situations where I was present and had a personal recollection of the game. In these situations I use a first-person perspective. Where there were box scores provided by newspaper outlets, I've included them here in the book.

I've attempted to reach each of the surviving players to include their memories and perspectives for this book. For those with whom I've had the pleasure of re-connecting, your accounts are included. For those with whom I've not had an opportunity to reach, I've tried to include as much as research provided. I apologize in advance for any omissions. Where recollections around specific events were not clear, I used my best judgment and my own recollections from these events.

The contents of this book are largely based on newspaper records, interviews, historical research, and my own personal recollections. Although I've strived for historical accuracy of these events some fifty years ago, some of the historical records such as newspaper coverage of the games are at times inaccurate. And also at times, recollections of the same events by multiple individuals varied to some degree. Game summaries were not always accurate and in some cases the *Fitchburg Sentinel* and *Leominster Enterprise* had different coverage and statistics from the same game. This was no fault of anyone as editors at the newspapers relied on hand-written scorecards and line-ups. I've tried my best to preserve historical integrity. I apologize for any errors or omissions.

To my family, Vivian, Joey, Selena, parents Archie and Cynthia Lefebvre, brothers, Tony, Mike, Billy, and Patricia Aubuchon Lefebvre, thank you for your patience and encouragement. This project would not have been possible without you.

I am grateful for the generous time and resources each of the following people have granted to me in my quest to write this book. Perhaps the most personally rewarding outcome for me was the opportunity to reconnect with so many players, teammates and friends, To all of you, this book is YOUR story.

Bob Angelini
Matt Aubuchon
Dave Bergeron
Jay Burke
Greg Carchidi
Joe Charielle
John Crawley
Jim Donnelly
Dick Freda
Peter Gamache
Doug Girouard
Emile Johnson
Mike Leclair
Tony Lefebvre
Pete Lieneck
Terry McNally
Mike Pavilaitis
Peter Robichaud
Bob Salvatore
Scott Szymkiewicz

Fran & Rachel Arel
Patricia Aubuchon-Lefebvre
Mike Bergeron
John Cantatore
Joe Cataldo
Rick Comeau
Jeff Dedeian
Gordon Edes
Paul Gamache
Mike Gasbarro
Steve Jackson
Rich Kelly
Mike Lefebvre
John Lieneck
Steve McCumber
Ron Patry
Ray Racine, Jr.
Ted Rockwell
Dan Shaughnessy
Steve Tata

To Mary Marotta from the Leominster Historical Society
To Diane Sanabria from the Leominster Public Library

To Fran Thomas for so eloquently saying in three pages what it took for me over 350 pages to say.

To Mark Bodanza for the encouragement before I ever put pen to paper and throughout the journey of writing this book.

To Don Freda for providing access to his memoirs and the treasure trove of content for this book.

To my coaches throughout my youth, thank you for your time and for the life lessons that have helped me both on and off the field.

Don Bigelow	Doug Fellows
Peter Iacobone	Jack Koch
Paul Paquette	Don Freda
Paul Aubuchon, Sr.	Dick LaBelle
Dick Gallien	Ron Patry
Jim Marrone	Egidio Charielle
Paul Harris	Emile Johnson
Steve Campobasso	Archie Lefebvre

About the Author

Mark Lefebvre is a consultant for Pinetree Institute, a non-profit organization that assists communities in Maine and New Hampshire build their capacity to address Substance Use Disorder (SUD) in the community. He and his wife Vivian are co-founders of Safe Harbor Recovery Center in Portsmouth, NH. He also serves on two non-profit boards that provide mental health and substance use disorder services to teens and families.

Mark is a radio DJ and host of *Scurvy Dog Radio* on WSCA Portsmouth Community Radio, fulfilling a childhood dream of playing records on the airways. He has been with WSCA as a DJ, music director, and board member for over 10 years.

Mark enjoys fishing and hunting the northern wilderness of Maine with his son Joey. He enjoys sharing musical tastes with his daughter Selena. And he enjoys kayaking, hiking, and attending live punk rock shows with his wife Vivian.

Mark lives in the Seacoast of New Hampshire with his family and their rescue lab Layla.

A Place in Time: Youth, Community & Baseball is the author's first book. The author can be reached at marklefebvre9@gmail.com .

Notes

Author's note: Adherence to APA conventions for most of the newspaper articles were not possible as many of the sources for game summaries were from personal clippings and scrapbooks.

---

[1] *Fitchburg Sentinel*, March 24, 1972, page 11.
[2] Fitchburg Sentinel, August 23, 1972.
[3] Leominster Recreation Department home page, https://www.leominster-ma.gov/205/Recreation .
[4] *Fitchburg Sentinel*, September 10, 1968, p7.
[5] www.maxpreps.com, November 13, 2020.
[6] *Leominster Enterprise*, August 17, 1971.
[7] Various *Fitchburg Sentinel* and *Leominster Enterprise* archives.
[8] Ibid.
[9] *Fitchburg Sentinel*, March 14, 1970, p. 6.
[10] *Babe Ruth Baseball 2022 Media Guide.*
[11] *Fitchburg Sentinel and Leominster Daily Enterprise* July 20, 2001.
[12] Sentinel & Enterprise Legacy Page, November 26, 2003,(https://www.legacy.com/us/obituaries/fitchburg/name/james-marrone-obituary?id=27385303).
[13] *Sentinel & Enterprise* Legacy Page, November 18, 2017, (https://www.legacy.com/us/obituaries/fitchburg/name/joseph-depasquale-obituary?id=11337881).
[14] *Sentinel & Enterprise Legacy Page,* April 20, 2009,(https://www.legacy.com/us/obituaries/fitchburg/name/bryan-beaudette-obituary?id=24268064).
[15] *Telegram Legacy Page*, July 14, 2018,(https://www.legacy.com/us/obituaries/telegram/name/paul-d-onfro-obituary?id=9655652).
[16] *Leominster Enterprise*, July 10, 1971.
[17] *Leominster Enterprise*, July 12, 1971, page 5.
[18] *Fitchburg Sentinel*, July 12, 1971, page 6.
[19] *Fitchburg Sentinel,* July 13, 1971, page 8.
[20] *Fitchburg Sentinel,* July 15, 1971, page 22.
[21] *Leominster Enterprise*, July 15, 1971, page 6.
[22] *Leominster Enterprise*, July 21, 1971, page 6.
[23] *Fitchburg Sentinel*, July 21, 1971, page 7.
[24] *Worcester Telegram*, July 25, 1971.
[25] *Fitchburg Sentinel*, July 26, 1971.
[26] *Fitchburg Sentinel*, July 29, 1971, page 10.

[27] *Leominster Enterprise,* July 29, 1971.
[28] *Fitchburg Sentinel,* July 30, 1971, page 6.
[29] *Leominster Enterprise,* July 30, 1971, page 6.
[30] *Fitchburg Sentinel,* August 2, 1971, page 6.
[31] *Fitchburg Sentinel,* August 9, 1971, page 6.
[32] *Fitchburg Sentinel,* August 10, 1971, page 6.
[33] *Fitchburg Sentinel,* August 11, 1971, page 10.
[34] *Fitchburg Sentinel,* August 12, 1971, page 12.
[35] *Leominster Enterprise,* August 12, 1971, page 6.
[36] *Nashua Telegraph,* August 13, 1971, page 14.
[37] *Nashua Telegraph,* August 14, 1971, page 13.
[38] *Fitchburg Sentinel,* August 14, 1971, page 6.
[39] *Worcester Telegram,* August 14, 1971.
[40] *Leominster Enterprise,* August 14, 1971, page 8.
[41] *Sentinel & Enterprise* Legacy Page, June 2, 2019, https://www.legacy.com/us/obituaries/fitchburg/name/michael-pignata-obituary?id=8829733.
[42] *Fitchburg Sentinel,* July 26, 1972, page 20.
[43] *Leominster Enterprise,* July 26, 1972.
[44] *Fitchburg Sentinel,* July 28, 1972, page 6.
[45] *Leominster Enterprise,* July 28, 1972, page 5.
[46] *Fitchburg Sentinel,* July 29, 1972, page 8.
[47] Ibid.
[48] *Worcester Telegram,* July 29, 1972.
[49] *Worcester Telegram,* July 30, 1972.
[50] *Fitchburg Sentinel,* July 31, 1972, page 8.
[51] *Leominster Enterprise,* July 31, 1972, page 7.
[52] *Worcester Telegram,* July 31, 1972.
[53] *Fitchburg Sentinel,* August 7, 1972, page 14.
[54] *Worcester Telegram,* August 7, 1972.
[55] *Leominster Enterprise,* August 7, 1972, page 6.
[56] *Leominster Enterprise,* August 8, 1972, page 6.
[57] *Fitchburg Sentinel,* August 8, 1972, page 6.
[58] *Fitchburg Sentinel,* August 9, 1972, page 8.
[59] *Leominster Enterprise,* August 9, 1972, page 6.
[60] *Sentinel & Enterprise* Legacy Page, April 15, 2008, https://www.legacy.com/us/obituaries/fitchburg/name/david-arsenault-obituary?id=24978717..

[61] *Sentinel & Enterprise* Legacy Page, December 26, 2019, https://www.legacy.com/us/obituaries/fitchburg/name/benjamin-ruggles-obituary?id=8508746.
[62] *Fitchburg Sentinel*, July 11, 1973, page 10.
[63] Ibid.
[64] *Fitchburg Sentinel*, July 12, 1973, page 10
[65] *Leominster Enterprise*, July 12, 1973.
[66] *Fitchburg Sentinel,* July 15, 1973.
[67] *Leominster Enterprise*, July 16, 1973
[68] *Fitchburg Sentinel,* July 16, 1973, page 5.
[69] *Fitchburg Sentinel*, July 19, 1973, page 6.
[70] *Leominster Enterprise*, July 19, 1973
[71] *Fitchburg Sentinel,* July 25, 1973, page 5.
[72] *Leominster Enterprise*, July 25, 1973.
[73] *Fitchburg Sentinel,* July 27, 1973, page 4.
[74] *Leominster Enterprise,* July 27, 1973.
[75] *Fitchburg Sentinel,* July 28, 1973, page 6.
[76] *Leominster Enterprise,* July 28, 1973.
[77] *Fitchburg Sentinel*, July 30, 1973, page 4.
[78] *Leominster Enterprise*, July 30, 1973.
[79] *Fitchburg Sentinel,* July 30, 1973, page 4.
[80] *Leominster Enterprise*, July 30, 1973.
[81] *Fitchburg Sentinel,* August 6, 1973, page 4.
[82] *Leominster Enterprise,* August 6, 1973.
[83] *Fitchburg Sentinel,* August 7, 1973, page 6.
[84] *Leominster Enterprise,* August 7, 1973.
[85] *Fitchburg Sentinel,* August 9, 1973, page 8.
[86] *Leominster Enterprise,* August 9, 1973.
[87] *Fitchburg Sentinel*, August 10, 1973, page 6.
[88] *Worcester Telegram,* July 27, 1974.
[89] *Fitchburg Sentinel,* July 28, 1974.
[90] SI Staff, (1984, September). No Room For A Parade. *Sports Illustrated*, Retrieved from https://vault.si.com/vault/1984/09/10/scorecard.
[91] Dore, D. (2022, January 3). North Leominster, Leominster American Little League programs announce plans to merge. *Leominster Champion*. https://www.leominsterchamp.com/story/news/local/2022/01/03/north-leominster-little-league-leominster-american-merger-plans/9075965002/.
[92] Thompson, D. (2018, November). American Meritocracy is Killing Youth Sports. *The Atlantic*. https://www.theatlantic.com/ideas/archive/2018/11/income-inequality-explains-decline-youth-sports/574975/.

Made in United States
North Haven, CT
15 August 2024